The VICTORY of REASON

How Christianity Led to Freedom, Capitalism, and Western Success

✝

SAVE ON USED BOOKS

Rodney Stark

Praise for
The Victory of Reason

"Rodney Stark is at it again. . . . *The Victory of Reason* is another bold, sharply argued defense of Christian faith's social benefits. It is also an in-your-face challenge to antireligious assumptions of the modern academy." —*Christianity Today*

"All of us can learn much from Mr. Stark's work. Secularists, instead of scorning the past, should learn how Christian understanding led to the most significant intellectual, political, scientific, and economic breakthroughs of the past millennium."
—*World*

"Succinct, highly interesting, and very helpful . . . this book offers arresting facts and passion-arousing arguments, but it also, and most dramatically, alters the horizon within which we wrestle with them." —*The New Criterion*

"Stimulating and provocative . . . [Stark] demonstrates that elements within Christianity actually gave rise not only to visions of reason and progress but also to the evolution of capitalism." —*Publishers Weekly*

"Every once in a while a book comes along that not only provides new answers but also transforms the old questions. *The Victory of Reason* is such a book."
—THE REVEREND RICHARD JOHN NEUHAUS, editor in chief of *First Things*,
and one of the "25 Most Influential Evangelicals in America" (*Time*)

"A bracing antidote to the secularist smog that chokes education today."
—GEORGE WEIGEL, Ethics and Public Policy Center

"Rodney Stark may be the most influential religious researcher of the past hundred years. He has revolutionized contemporary thought about religion and economics, and in this book—his most provocative yet—he makes a compelling case for the claim that we owe our prosperity, freedom, and progress to centuries of faith in one great, loving, and rational God. *The Victory of Reason* is itself a victory of reason in a field long dominated by anti-Western, anticapitalist, and antireligious myth. Stark's extraordinary scholarship has made it possible to again ask, and perhaps finally answer, some of the most enduring questions about faith and spirituality."
—LAURENCE IANNACCONE, Koch Professor of Economics,
George Mason University

The Victory of Reason

The Victory of Reason

HOW CHRISTIANITY LED TO FREEDOM, CAPITALISM, AND WESTERN SUCCESS

Rodney Stark

RANDOM HOUSE TRADE PAPERBACKS

NEW YORK

Contents

Reason and Progress

When Europeans first began to explore the globe, their greatest surprise was not the existence of the Western Hemisphere but the extent of their own technological superiority over the rest of the world. Not only were the proud Mayan, Aztec, and Inca nations helpless in the face of European intruders; so were the fabled civilizations of the East: China, India, and even Islam were backward by comparison with sixteenth-century Europe. How had this happened? Why was it that although many civilizations had pursued alchemy, it led to chemistry only in Europe? Why was it that, for centuries, Europeans were the only ones possessed of eyeglasses, chimneys, reliable clocks, heavy cavalry, or a system of music notation? How had nations that had arisen from barbarism and the rubble of fallen Rome so greatly surpassed the rest of the world?

Several recent authors have discovered the secret to Western success in geography. But that same geography long sustained European cultures that were well behind those of Asia. Others have traced the rise of the West to steel, or to guns and sailing ships, and still others have credited a more productive agriculture. The trouble is that these answers are part of what needs to be explained: *why* did Europeans excel at metallurgy, shipbuilding, or farming? The most convincing answer to these questions attributes Western dominance to the rise of capitalism, which also took place only in Europe. Even the most militant enemies of capitalism credit it with creating previously undreamed of productivity and progress. In *The Communist Manifesto,* Karl Marx and Friedrich Engels proposed that prior to the rise of capitalism, humans engaged "in the most slothful indolence" and that the capitalist system was "the first to show what man's activity can bring about . . . [it] has created more massive and more colossal productive forces than all the preceding generations together." Capitalism achieves this "miracle" through regular reinvestment to increase productivity—through either greater capacity or improved technology—and by motivating both management and labor through ever-rising payoffs.

Supposing that capitalism did produce Europe's great leap forward, it remains to be explained why it developed only in Europe. Some have found the roots of capitalism in the Protestant Reformation; others have traced it back to various political circumstances. But if one digs deeper, it becomes clear that the truly fundamental basis not only for capitalism but for the rise of the West was an extraordinary faith in *reason*.

The Victory of Reason explores a series of developments in which reason won the day, giving unique shape to Western culture and institutions. The most important of these victories occurred within Christianity. While the other world religions emphasized mystery and intuition, Christianity alone embraced reason and logic as the primary guide to religious truth. Christian faith in reason was influenced by Greek philosophy. But the more important fact is that Greek philosophy had little impact on Greek religions. These remained typical mystery cults, in which ambiguity and logical contradictions were taken as hallmarks of sacred origins. Similar assumptions concerning the fundamental inexplicability of the gods and the intellectual superiority of introspection dominated all of the other major world religions. But from early days, the church fathers taught that reason was the supreme gift from God and the means to *progressively increase* their understanding of scripture and revelation. Consequently, Christianity was *oriented to the future*, while the other major religions asserted the superiority of the past. At least in principle, if not always in fact, Christian doctrines could always be modified in the name of progress as demonstrated by reason. Encouraged by the Scholastics and embodied in the great medieval universities founded by the church, faith in the power of reason infused Western culture, stimulating the pursuit of science and the evolution of democratic theory and practice. The rise of capitalism was also a victory for church-inspired reason, since capitalism is in essence the systematic and sustained application of reason to commerce—something that first took place within the great monastic estates.

During the past century, Western intellectuals have been more than willing to trace European imperialism to Christian origins, but they have been entirely unwilling to recognize that Christianity made any contribution (other than intolerance) to the Western capacity to dominate. Rather, the West is said to have surged ahead precisely as it *overcame* religious barriers to progress, especially those impeding science. Nonsense. The success of the West, including the rise of science, rested entirely on religious foundations, and the people who brought it about were devout Christians. Unfortunately, even many of those historians willing to grant Christianity a role in shaping Western progress have tended to limit themselves to tracing beneficial religious effects of the Protestant Reformation. It is as if the previous fifteen hundred years of Christianity either were of little matter or were harmful. Such academic anti-Catholicism inspired the most famous book ever written on the origins of capitalism.

At the start of the twentieth century, the German sociologist Max Weber published what soon became an immensely influential study: *The Protestant Ethic and the Spirit of Capitalism*.[1] In it he proposed that capitalism originated only in Europe because, of all the world's religions, only Protestantism provided a moral vision that led people to restrain their material consumption while vigorously seeking wealth. Weber argued that prior to the Reformation, restraint on consumption was invariably linked to asceticism and hence to condemnations of commerce. Conversely, the pursuit of wealth was linked to profligate consumption. Either cultural pattern was inimical to capitalism. According to Weber, the Protestant ethic shattered these traditional linkages, creating a culture of frugal entrepreneurs content to systematically reinvest profits in order to pursue ever greater wealth, and therein lies the key to capitalism and the ascendancy of the West.

Perhaps because it was such an elegant thesis, it was widely embraced despite the fact that it was so obviously wrong. Even today,

The Protestant Ethic enjoys an almost sacred status among sociologists,[2] although economic historians quickly dismissed Weber's surprisingly undocumented[3] monograph on the irrefutable grounds that the rise of capitalism in Europe *preceded* the Reformation by centuries. As Hugh Trevor-Roper explained, "The idea that large-scale industrial capitalism was ideologically impossible before the Reformation is exploded by the simple fact that it existed."[4] Only a decade after Weber published, the celebrated Henri Pirenne[5] noted a large literature that "established the fact that all of the essential features of capitalism—individual enterprise, advances in credit, commercial profits, speculation, etc.—are to be found from the twelfth century on, in the city republics of Italy—Venice, Genoa, or Florence." A generation later, the equally celebrated Fernand Braudel complained that "all historians have opposed this tenuous theory [the Protestant ethic], although they have not managed to be rid of it once and for all. Yet it is clearly false. The northern countries took over the place that earlier had been so long and brilliantly occupied by the old capitalist centers of the Mediterranean. They invented nothing, either in technology or business management."[6] Moreover, during their critical period of economic development, these northern centers of capitalism were Catholic, not Protestant— the Reformation still lay well into the future.

From another angle, John Gilchrist, a leading historian of the economic activity of the medieval church, pointed out that the first examples of capitalism appeared in the great Christian monasteries.[7] It also is well established that even in the nineteenth century, Protestant regions and nations on the Continent[8] were *not* significantly ahead of many Catholic places—the "backwardness" of Spain notwithstanding.[9]

Even though Weber was wrong, he was correct to suppose that religious ideas played a vital role in the rise of capitalism in Europe. The material conditions needed for capitalism existed in many civilizations in various eras, including China, Islam, India, Byzantium, and probably ancient Rome and Greece as well. But none of these societies broke through and developed capitalism, as none evolved ethical visions compatible with this dynamic economic system. Instead, leading religions outside the West called for asceticism and denounced profits, while wealth was exacted from peasants and merchants by rapacious elites dedicated to display and consumption.[10] Why did things turn out differently in Europe? Because of the Christian commitment to rational theology—something that may have played a major role in causing the Reformation but that surely predated Protestantism by far more than a millennium.

Even so, capitalism developed in only *some places*. Why not in all? Because in some European societies, as in most of the rest of the world, it was prevented from happening by greedy despots: *freedom* was also essential for the development of capitalism. This raises another matter: *why has freedom so seldom existed in most of the world, and how was it nurtured in some medieval European states?* This too was a victory of reason. Before any medieval European state actually attempted rule by an elected council, Christian theologians had long been theorizing about the nature of equality and individual rights—indeed, the later work of such "secular" eighteenth-century political theorists as John Locke explicitly rested on egalitarian axioms derived by church scholars.[11]

To sum up: the rise of the West was based on four primary victories of reason. The first was the development of faith in progress within Christian theology. The second victory was the way that faith in progress translated into technical and organizational innovations, many of them fostered by monastic estates. The third was that, thanks to Christian theology, reason informed both political philosophy and practice to the extent that responsive states, sustaining a substantial degree of personal freedom, appeared in medieval Europe. The final victory involved the application of reason to commerce, resulting in the development of capitalism within the safe havens provided by responsive states. These were the victories by which the West won.

PLAN OF THE BOOK

The Victory of Reason is divided into two parts. The first focuses on *foundations*. It will survey the role of reason in Christianity, in preparing the way for political freedom and for the emergence of both science and capitalism. The second part recounts the remarkable ways in which Europeans *fulfilled* these foundations.

Chapter 1 is devoted to the nature and consequences of the Christian commitment to rational theology. How did this come to pass? And why did it result in the truly revolutionary notion that the application of reason to scripture will result in *theological progress*? It was a basic axiom of Christian theology that greater understanding of God can be gained over time, that even established doctrines can undergo radical revisions. Having developed the rational and progressive aspects of Christian theology, I turn to examples and implications. First, I demonstrate the absolutely essential role of rational theology for the rise of science, showing the religious reasons why science arose in Europe but failed to do so in China, ancient Greece, or in Islam. Then, attention shifts to important moral innovations achieved by the medieval church. For example, Christianity fostered a very strong conception of *individualism* consistent with its doctrines concerning free will and salvation. In addition, medieval monasticism cultivated regard for the virtues of *work* and *plain living* that fully anticipated the Protestant ethic by almost a millennium. This chapter also outlines the role of early and medieval Christianity in fostering new ideas about *human rights*. For capitalism to develop, it was essential that Europe ceased to be a collection of slave societies. As with Rome and all other contemporary civilizations, slavery existed everywhere in early medieval Europe. But among all major faiths, Christianity was unique in evolving moral opposition to slavery, and in about the seventh century, serious religious opposition to it began. By the tenth century slavery had disappeared in most of the West, lingering only at the frontiers.[12] That centuries later slavery was reinstituted in Europe's New World colonies is a separate matter, although here too it was Christianity that produced and sustained the abolition movements.[13]

Chapter 2 examines the material and religious foundations of capitalism that were laid down during the so-called Dark Ages. It begins by demonstrating that rather than being a period of ignorance and backwardness, the era from the fall of Rome through the Middle Ages was a time of spectacular technological and intellectual progress that erupted when innovation was freed from the grip of Roman despotism. Christian commitment to progress played an important role not only by prompting the search for new technology but by encouraging its rapid and widespread adoption. Moreover, the response of church leaders and scholars to all the progress going on around them resulted in some remarkable theological revisions. Just as have the other world religions, for centuries Christianity proclaimed the moral and spiritual superiority of asceticism and expressed antagonism toward commerce and finance. But these teachings were resoundingly rejected in the twelfth and thirteenth centuries by Catholic theologians who stoutly defended private property and the pursuit of profits. How could this have occurred? Because as new commercial activities began in the great monastic estates, their moral status was reassessed by theologians who concluded that previous prohibitions had been based on an inadequate theology.

Chapter 3 begins with a brief sketch of command economies: how despotic regimes squelch innovation and commerce as wealth is hoarded, consumed, or expropriated, but seldom invested. Since the rise of capitalism required that despotic states be overcome, the remainder of the chapter is devoted to explaining the appearance of freedom in Europe—of small, often surprisingly democratic political units. First, the Christian foundations of Western democratic theory are explored—the evolution of doctrines of individual moral equality, of private property rights, and the separation of church and state. Then, the emergence of relatively democratic rule in some Italian city-states and in northern Europe will be described and explained.

Chapter 4 traces the perfection of capitalism in the Italian city-states—how the management and financial techniques needed to sustain large, rational, industrial firms were developed. Chapter 5 traces the spread of "colonial" Italian capitalist firms to northern cities, most of them located in what is today Belgium and the Netherlands, and shows how the locals soon learned to create their own capitalist firms. The chapter concludes with a long section on how the English developed the most powerful capitalist economy in Europe.

Chapter 6 examines the leading *negative* cases because an adequate explanation of why capitalism developed in some parts of Europe must also explain why it failed to appear (or was destroyed) in other parts. Why was it that Spain, the richest and most powerful nation in sixteenth-century Europe, remained a precapitalist, feudal state? Why did Spanish rule destroy the capitalist vitality of the Italian city-states and the Spanish Netherlands? And then, why did Spain so rapidly become a third-rate power, stripped of its empire? As for France, why did capitalism and liberty languish there too? To answer these questions, I turn again to the stifling economic effects of despotism.

Against this background, Chapter 7 shifts to the New World and to the dramatic economic differences that came to distinguish the United States and Canada from Latin America. Telling this story will also serve as an extensive summary of the book, since the factors involved were essentially a reenactment of the economic history of Europe. Here too, Christianity, freedom, and capitalism played the crucial roles. The conclusion briefly considers whether this is still true. Can globalization create fully modern societies that are not Christian, not capitalist, and not even free?

Part I: Foundations

CHAPTER ONE

Blessings of Rational Theology

THEOLOGY IS IN DISREPUTE AMONG MOST WESTERN INTELLECTUALS. The word is taken to mean a passé form of religious thinking that embraces irrationality and dogmatism. So too, Scholasticism. According to any edition of Webster's, "scholastic" means "pedantic and dogmatic," denoting the sterility of medieval church scholarship. John Locke, the eighteenth-century British philosopher, dismissed the Scholastics as "the great mintmasters" of useless terms meant "to cover their ignorance."[1] Not so! The Scholastics were fine scholars who founded Europe's great universities and launched the rise of Western science. As for theology, it has little in common with most religious thinking, being a sophisticated, highly *rational* discipline that is fully developed only in Christianity.

Sometimes described as "the science of faith,"[2] theology consists of *formal reasoning about God*. The emphasis is on *discovering* God's nature, intentions, and demands, and on understanding how these define the relationship between human beings and God. The gods of polytheism cannot sustain theology because they are far too inconsequential. Theology necessitates an image of God as a conscious, rational, supernatural being of unlimited power and scope who cares about humans and imposes moral codes and responsibilities upon them, thereby generating serious intellectual questions such as: Why does God allow us to sin? Does the Sixth Commandment prohibit war? When does an infant acquire a soul?

To fully appreciate the nature of theology, it is useful to explore why there are no theologians in the East. Consider Taoism. The Tao is conceived of as a supernatural essence, an underlying mystical force or principle governing life, but one that is impersonal, remote, lacking consciousness, and definitely not a being. It is the "eternal way," the cosmic force that produces harmony and balance. According to Lao-tzu, the Tao is "always nonexistent" yet "always existent," "unnamable" and the "name that can be named." Both "soundless and formless," it is "always without desires." One might meditate forever on such an essence, but it offers little to reason about. The same applies to Buddhism and Confucianism. Although it is true that the popular versions of these faiths are polytheistic and involve an immense array of small gods (as is true of popular Taoism as well), the "pure" forms of these faiths, as pursued by the intellectual elite, are godless and postulate only a vague divine essence—Buddha specifically denied the existence of a conscious God.[3] The East lacks theologians because those who might otherwise take up such an intellectual pursuit reject its first premise: the existence of a conscious, all-powerful God.

In contrast, Christian theologians have devoted centuries to reasoning about what God may have really meant by various passages in scripture, and over time the interpretations often have evolved in quite dramatic and extensive ways. For example, not only does the Bible not condemn astrology but the story of the Wise Men following the star might seem to suggest that it is valid. However, in the fifth century Saint Augustine *reasoned* that astrology is false because to believe that one's fate is predestined in the stars stands in opposition to God's gift of free will.[4] In similar fashion, although many early Christians, including the apostle Paul, accepted that Jesus had brothers,[5] born of Mary and fathered by Joseph, this view came increasingly into conflict with developing theological views about Mary. The matter was finally resolved in the thirteenth century, when Saint Thomas Aquinas analyzed the doctrine of Christ's virgin birth to deduce that Mary did not bear other children: "So we assert without qualification that the mother of God conceived as a virgin, gave birth as a virgin and remained a virgin after the birth. The brothers of the Lord were not natural brothers, born of the same mother, but blood-relations."[6]

These were not mere amplifications of scripture; each was an example of careful deductive reasoning leading to *new doctrines:* the church did prohibit astrology; the perpetual virginity of Mary remains the official Catholic teaching. As these examples demonstrate, great minds could, and often did, greatly alter or even reverse church doctrines on the basis of nothing more than persuasive reasoning. And no one did this better or with greater influence than Augustine and Aquinas. Of course, thousands of other theologians also tried to make their mark on doctrines. Some succeeded, most were ignored, and some of them were rejected as heretics: the point being that an accurate account of any aspect of Christian theology must be based on major, authoritative figures. It would be easy to assemble a set of quotations to demonstrate all manner of strange positions, if one selectively culled through the work of the thousands of minor Christian theologians who have written during the past two millennia. That approach has been all too common; but it is not mine. I will quote minor figures *only* when they expressed views ratified by the major theologians, keeping in mind that the authoritative church position on many matters often evolved, sometimes to the extent of reversing earlier teachings.

Leading Christian theologians such as Augustine and Aquinas were not what today might be called strict constructionists. Rather, they celebrated reason as the means to gain greater insight into divine intentions. As Quintus Tertullian instructed in the second century: "Reason is a thing of God, inasmuch as there is nothing which God the Maker of all has not provided, disposed, ordained by reason—nothing which He has not willed should be handled and understood by reason."[7] In the same spirit, Clement of Alexandria warned in the third century: "Do not think that we say that these things are only to be received by faith, but also that they are to be asserted by reason. For indeed it is not safe to commit these things to bare faith without reason, since assuredly truth cannot be without reason."[8]

Hence, Augustine merely expressed the prevailing wisdom when he held that reason was indispensable to faith: "Heaven forbid that God should hate in us that by which he made us superior to the animals! Heaven forbid that we should believe in such a way as not to accept or seek reasons, since we could not even believe if we did not possess rational souls." Augustine acknowledged that "faith must precede reason and purify the heart and make it fit to receive and endure the great light of reason." Then he added that although it is necessary "for faith to precede reason in certain matters of great moment that cannot yet be grasped, surely the very small portion of reason that persuades us of this must precede faith."[9] Scholastic theologians placed far greater faith in reason than most philosophers are willing to do today.[10]

Of course, some influential churchmen opposed the primacy given to reason and argued that faith was best served by mysticism and spiritual experiences.[11] Ironically, the most inspiring advocate of this position expressed his views in elegantly reasoned theology.[12] Dissent from the priority of reason was, of course, very popular in some of the religious orders, especially the Franciscans and the Cistercians. But these views did not prevail—if for no other reason than because official church theology enjoyed a secure base in the many and growing universities, where reason ruled.[13]

CHRISTIAN FAITH IN PROGRESS

Judaism and Islam also embrace an image of God sufficient to sustain theology, but their scholars have tended not to pursue such matters. Rather, traditional Jews[14] and Muslims incline toward strict constructionism and approach scripture as *law to be understood and applied,* not as the basis for inquiry about questions of ultimate meaning. For this reason scholars often refer to Judaism and Islam as "orthoprax" religions, concerned with correct (*ortho*) practice (*praxis*) and therefore placing their "fundamental emphasis on law and regulation of community life." In contrast, scholars describe Christianity as an "orthodox" religion because it stresses correct (*ortho*) opinion (*doxa*), placing "greater emphasis on belief and its intellectual structuring of creeds, catechisms, and theologies."[15] Typical intellectual controversies among Jewish and Muslim religious thinkers involve whether some activity or innovation (such as reproducing holy scripture on a printing press) is consistent with established law. Christian controversies typically are doctrinal, over matters such as the Holy Trinity or the perpetual virginity of Mary.

Of course, some leading Christian thinkers have concentrated on law and some Jewish and Muslim scholars have devoted themselves to theological issues. But the primary thrust of the three faiths has differed in this respect and with very significant consequences.

Legal interpretation rests on precedent and therefore is anchored in the past, while efforts to better understand the nature of God assume the possibility of *progress*. And it is the assumption of progress that may be the most critical difference between Christianity and all other religions. With the exception of Judaism, the other great faiths have conceived of history as either an endlessly repeated cycle or inevitable decline—Muhammad is reported to have said, "The best generation is my generation, then the one that follows it, and then the ones that follow that."[16] In contrast, Judaism and Christianity have sustained a directional conception of history, culminating in the Millennium. However, the Jewish idea of history stresses not progress but only procession, while the idea of progress is profoundly manifest in Christianity. As John Macmurray put it, "That we think of progress at all shows the extent of the influence of Christianity upon us."[17]

Things might have been different had Jesus left a written scripture. But unlike Muhammad or Moses, whose texts were accepted as divine transmissions and therefore have encouraged literalism, Jesus wrote nothing, and from the very start the church fathers were forced to reason as to the implications of a collection of his remembered sayings—the New Testament is not a unified scripture but an *anthology*.[18] Consequently, the precedent for a theology of deduction and inference and for the idea of theological progress began with Paul: "For our knowledge is imperfect and our prophesy is imperfect."[19] Contrast this with the second verse of the Qur'an, which proclaims itself to be "the Scripture whereof there is no doubt."[20]

From very early days, Christian theologians have assumed that the application of reason can yield an *increasingly accurate* understanding of God's will. Augustine noted that although there were "certain matters pertaining to the doctrine of salvation that we cannot yet grasp . . . one day we shall be able to do so."[21] Augustine celebrated not only theological progress, but earthly, material progress as well. Writing early in the fifth century, he exclaimed: "Has not the genius of man invented and applied countless astonishing arts, partly the result of necessity, partly the result of exuberant invention, so that this vigour of mind . . . betokens an inexhaustible wealth in the nature which can invent, learn, or employ such arts. What wonderful—one might say stupefying—advances has human industry made in the arts of weaving and building, of agriculture and navigation!" He went on to admire the "skill [that] has been attained in measures and numbers! With what sagacity have the movements and connections of the stars been discovered!" And all of this was due to the "unspeakable boon" that God conferred upon his creation, a "rational nature."[22]

Augustine's optimism was typical; progress beckoned. As Gilbert de Tournai wrote in the thirteenth century, "Never will we find truth if we content ourselves with what is already known. . . . Those things that have been written before us are not laws but guides. The truth is open to all, for it is not yet totally possessed."[23] Especially typical were the words preached by Fra Giordano in Florence in 1306: "Not all the arts have been found; we shall never see an end to finding them. Every day one could discover a new art."[24] Compare this with the prevailing view in China at this same time, well expressed by Li Yen-chang: "If scholars are made to concentrate their attention solely on the classics and are prevented from slipping into study of the vulgar practices of later generations, then the empire will be fortunate indeed!"[25]

The Christian commitment to progress through rationality reached its heights in the *Summa Theologica* of Saint Thomas Aquinas, published in Paris late in the thirteenth century. This monument to the theology of reason consists of logical "proofs" of Christian doctrine and set the standard for all subsequent Christian theologians. Aquinas argued that because humans lack sufficient intellect to see directly into the essence of things, it is necessary for them to reason their way to knowledge, step by step. Thus, although Aquinas regarded theology as the highest of the sciences, since it deals directly with divine revelations, he advocated the use of the tools of philosophy, especially the principles of logic, in seeking to construct theology.[26] Consequently, Aquinas was able to use his powers of reason to find the most profound humanism in God's creation.[27]

Aquinas and his many gifted peers could not have excelled at rational theology had they conceived of Jehovah as an inexplicable essence. They could justify their efforts only because they assumed that God was the absolute epitome of reason.[28] Moreover, their commitment to the progressive reasoning out of God's will required them to accept that the Bible is not only or always to be understood literally. This too was the conventional Christian view, since, as Augustine noted, "divers things may be understood under these words which yet are all true." In fact, Augustine frankly acknowledged that it is possible for a later reader, with God's help, to grasp a scriptural meaning even though the person who first wrote down the scripture "understood not this." Thus, he continued, it is necessary to "enquire . . . what Moses, that excellent minister of Thy faith, would have his reader understand by those words . . . let us approach together unto the words of Thy book, and seek in them Thy meaning, through the meaning of Thy servant, by whose pen Thou hast dispensed them."[29] Moreover, since God is incapable of either error or falsehood, if the Bible seems to contradict knowledge, that is because of a lack of understanding on the part of the "servant" who recorded God's words.

These views were entirely consistent with the fundamental Christian premise that God's revelations are always limited to the current capacity of humans to comprehend. In the fourth century, Saint John Chrysostom noted that even the seraphim do not see God as he is. Instead, they see "a condescension accommodated to their nature. What is this condescension? It is when God appears and makes himself known, not as he is, but in the way one incapable of beholding him is able to look upon him. In this way God reveals himself proportionately to the weakness of those who behold him."[30] Given this long tradition, there was nothing even slightly heretical about John Calvin's assertion that God accommodates his revelations to the limits of human understanding, that the author of Genesis, for example, "was ordained to be a teacher of the unlearned and primitive, as well as the learned; so could not achieve his goal without descending to such crude means of instruction." That is, God "reveals himself to us according to our rudeness and infirmity."[31]

The Christian image of God is that of a rational being who *believes in human progress,* more fully revealing himself as humans *gain* the capacity to better understand. Moreover, because God is a rational being and the universe is his personal creation, it necessarily has a rational, lawful, stable structure, *awaiting increased human comprehension*. This was the key to many intellectual undertakings, among them the rise of science.

THEOLOGY AND SCIENCE

The so-called Scientific Revolution of the sixteenth century has been misinterpreted by those wishing to assert an inherent conflict between religion and science. Some wonderful things were achieved in this era, but they were not produced by an eruption of secular thinking. Rather, these achievements were the culmination of many centuries of systematic progress by medieval Scholastics, sustained by that uniquely Christian twelfth-century invention, the university. Not only were science and religion compatible, they were inseparable—the rise of science was achieved by deeply religious Christian scholars.[32]

It is important to recognize that science is not merely technology. A society does not have science simply because it can build sailing ships, smelt iron, or eat off porcelain dishes. Science is a *method* utilized in *organized* efforts to formulate *explanations of nature,* always subject to modifications and corrections through *systematic observations*.

Put another way, science consists of two components: *theory* and *research*. Theorizing is the explanatory part of science. Scientific theories are *abstract statements* about *why* and *how* some portion of nature (including human social life) fits together and works. However, not all abstract statements, not even all of those offering explanations, qualify as scientific theories, otherwise theology would be a science. Rather, abstract statements are scientific only if it is possible to deduce from them some definite predictions and prohibitions about what will be observed. And that's where research comes in. It consists of making those observations that are relevant to the empirical predictions and prohibitions. Clearly, then, science is limited to statements about natural and material reality—about things that are at least in principle observable. Hence, there are entire realms of discourse that science is unable to address, including such matters as the existence of God.

Note too that science is an organized effort, in that it is not random discovery, nor is it achieved in solitude. Granted, some scientists have worked alone, but not in isolation. From earliest days, scientists have constituted networks and have been very communicative.

Consistent with the views of most contemporary historians as well as philosophers of science, this definition of science excludes all efforts through most of human history to explain and control the material world, even those not involving supernatural means. Most of these efforts can be excluded from the category of science because until recent times "technical progress—sometimes considerable—was mere empiricism," as Marc Bloch put it.[33] That is, progress was the product of observation and of trial and error but was lacking in explanations—in theorizing. Hence, the earlier technical innovations of Greco-Roman times, of Islam, of China, let alone those achieved in prehistorical times, do not constitute science and are better described as lore, skills, wisdom, techniques, crafts, technologies, engineering, learning, or simply knowledge. Even without telescopes the ancients excelled in astronomical observations, but until they were linked to testable theories, these observations remained merely *facts*. Charles Darwin expressed this point vividly: "About thirty years ago there was much talk that geologists ought to observe and not theorize; and I well remember someone saying that at that rate a man might as well go into a gravel-pit and count the pebbles and describe the colours. How odd it is that anyone should not see that all observation must be for or against some view if it is to be of any service!"[34]

As for the intellectual achievements of Greek or Eastern philosophers, their empiricism was quite atheoretical, and their theorizing was nonempirical. Consider Aristotle. Although praised for his empiricism, he didn't let it interfere with his theorizing. For example, he taught that the speed at which objects fall to earth is proportionate to their weight—that a stone twice as heavy as another will fall twice as fast.[35] A trip to any of the nearby cliffs would have allowed him to falsify this proposition.

The same can be said of the rest of the famous Greeks—either their work is entirely empirical or it does not qualify as science for lack of empiricism, being sets of abstract assertions that disregard or do not imply observable consequences. Thus, when Democritus proposed that all matter is composed of atoms, he did not anticipate scientific atomic theory. His "theory" was mere speculation, having no basis in observation or any empirical implications. That it turned out to be correct is no more than a linguistic coincidence that lends no greater significance to his guess than to that of his contemporary Empedocles, who asserted that all matter is composed of fire, air, water, and earth, or Aristotle's version a century later, that matter consists of heat, cold, dryness, moistness, and quintessence. Indeed, for all his brilliance and analytical power, Euclid was not a scientist, because in and of itself, geometry lacks substance, having only the capacity to describe some aspects of reality, not to explain any portion of it.

Real science arose only once: in Europe.[36] China, Islam, India, and ancient Greece and Rome each had a highly developed alchemy. But only in Europe did alchemy develop into chemistry. By the same token, many societies developed elaborate systems of astrology, but only in Europe did astrology lead to astronomy. Why? Again, the answer has to do with images of God.

As the great, if neglected, medieval theologian-scientist Nicole d'Oresme put it, God's creation "is much like that of a man making a clock and letting it run and continue its own motion by itself."[37] In contrast with the dominant religious and philosophical doctrines in the non-Christian world, Christians developed science because they *believed* it *could* be done, and *should* be done. As Alfred North Whitehead put it during one of his Lowell Lectures at Harvard in 1925, science arose in Europe because of the widespread "faith in the possibility of science . . . derivative from medieval theology."[38] Whitehead's pronouncement shocked not only his distinguished audience but Western intellectuals in general once his lectures had been published. How could this great philosopher and mathematician, coauthor with Bertrand Russell of the landmark *Principia Mathematica* (1910–13), make such an outlandish claim? Did he not know that religion is the mortal enemy of scientific inquiry?

Whitehead knew better. He had grasped that Christian theology was essential for the rise of science in the West, just as surely as non-Christian theologies had stifled the scientific quest everywhere else. As he explained: "The greatest contribution of medievalism to the formation of the scientific movement [was] the inexpugnable belief that ... there is a secret, a secret which can be unveiled. How has this conviction been so vividly implanted in the European mind? ... It must come from the medieval insistence on the rationality of God, conceived as with the personal energy of Jehovah and with the rationality of a Greek philosopher. Every detail was supervised and ordered: the search into nature could only result in the vindication of the faith in rationality."[39]

Whitehead ended with the remark that the images of gods found in other religions, especially in Asia, are too impersonal or too irrational to have sustained science. Any particular "occurrence might be due to the fiat of an irrational despot" god, or might be produced by "some impersonal, inscrutable origin of things. There is not the same confidence as in the intelligible rationality of a personal being."[40]

Indeed, most non-Christian religions do not posit a creation at all: the universe is eternal, and while it may pursue cycles, it is without beginning or purpose, and most important of all, having never been created, it has no creator. Consequently, the universe is thought to be a supreme mystery, inconsistent, unpredictable, and arbitrary. For those holding these religious premises, the path to wisdom is through meditation and mystical insights, and there is no occasion to celebrate reason.

The critical point in all of this is methodological. Centuries of meditation will produce no empirical knowledge. But to the extent that religion inspires efforts to comprehend God's handiwork, knowledge will be forthcoming, and because to comprehend something fully it is necessary to explain it, science arises as the "handmaiden" of theology. And that's precisely how those who took part in the great achievements of the sixteenth and seventeenth centuries saw themselves: as pursuing the secrets of the creation. New-ton, Kepler, and Galileo regarded the creation itself as a *book*[41] that was to be read and comprehended. The sixteenth-century French scientific genius René Descartes justified his search for natural "laws" on grounds that such laws must exist because God is perfect and therefore "acts in a manner as constant and immutable as pos-sible," except for the rare exceptions of miracles.[42] In contrast, these critical religious concepts and motivations were lacking in those societies that seem otherwise to have had the potential to develop science but did not: China, Greece, and Islam.

China

Only three years before his coauthor Alfred North Whitehead pro-posed that Christianity provided the basis for the pursuit of science, Bertrand Russell found the lack of Chinese science rather baffling. From the perspective of his militant atheism, China should have had science long before Europe. As he explained: "Although Chinese civilization has hitherto been deficient in science, it never contained anything hostile to science, and therefore the spread of scientific knowledge encounters no such obstacles as the Church put in its way in Europe."[43]

Despite his confidence that China would soon far surpass the West,[44] Russell failed to see that it was precisely religious obstacles that had prevented Chinese science. Although for centuries the common people of China have worshiped an elaborate array of gods, each of small scope and often rather lacking in character, Chi-nese intellectuals prided themselves in following "godless" reli-gions, wherein the supernatural is conceived of as an essence or principle governing life—such as the Tao—that is impersonal, re-mote, and definitely not a being. Just as small gods do not create a universe, neither do impersonal essences or principles—indeed they don't seem able to *do* anything.

As conceived by Chinese philosophers, the universe simply is and always was. There is no reason to suppose that it functions accord-ing to rational laws or that it could be comprehended in physical rather than mystical terms. Consequently, through the millennia

Chinese intellectuals pursued "enlightenment," not explanations. This is precisely the conclusion reached by the very distinguished Joseph Needham, the Oxford historian of science who devoted most of his career and many volumes to the history of Chinese technology. Having spent several decades attempting to discover a materialist explanation, Needham concluded that the failure of the Chinese to develop science was due to their religion, to the inability of Chinese intellectuals to believe in the existence of laws of nature because "the conception of a divine celestial lawgiver imposing ordinances on non-human Nature never developed." Needham continued: "It was not that there was no order in Nature for the Chinese, but rather that it was not an order ordained by a rational personal being, and hence there was no conviction that rational personal beings would be able to spell out in their lesser earthly languages the divine code of laws which he had decreed aforetime. The Taoists, indeed, would have scorned such an idea as being too naïve for the subtlety and complexity of the universe as they intuited it."[45] Exactly.

Several years ago Graeme Lang, the respected anthropologist at Hong Kong City University, dismissed the notion that the influence of Confucianism and Taoism on Chinese intellectuals was the reason science failed to develop in China, on the grounds that all culture is flexible and that "if scholars in China had wanted to do science, philosophy alone would not have been a serious impediment."[46] Perhaps. But Lang missed the more basic question: why didn't Chinese scholars *want* to do science? Because, as Whitehead, Needham, and many others have recognized, it didn't occur to the Chinese that science was *possible*. Fundamental theological and philosophical assumptions determine whether anyone will attempt to do science. Western science was born of the enthusiastic conviction that the human intellect can penetrate nature's secrets.

Greece

For centuries the ancient Greeks seemed on the verge of achieving science. They were interested in explaining the natural world with suitably abstract, general principles. Some were careful, systematic observers of nature—although Socrates considered empiricism such as astronomical observations a "waste of time," and Plato agreed, advising his students to "leave the starry heavens alone."[47] And the Greeks formed coordinated scholarly networks—the famous "schools." But in the end, all they achieved was nonempirical, even antiempirical, speculative philosophies; atheoretical collections of facts; and isolated crafts and technologies—never breaking through to real science.

There were three reasons for this. First, Greek conceptions of the gods were inadequate to allow them to serve as conscious creators. Second, the Greeks conceived of the universe as not only eternal and uncreated but as locked into endless cycles of progress and decay. Third, prompted by defining various heavenly bodies as actual gods, the Greeks transformed inanimate objects into living creatures capable of aims, emotions, and desires—thus short-circuiting the search for physical theories.[48]

As for the gods, none of the numerous divinities in the Greek pantheon was a suitable creator of a lawful universe, not even Zeus. As were humans, so too the gods were subject to the inexorable workings of the natural cycles of all things. Some Greek scholars, including Aristotle, did posit a "God" of infinite scope having charge of the universe, but they conceived of this god as essentially an essence much like the Tao. Such a god lent a certain spiritual aura to a cyclical universe and its ideal, abstract properties, but being an essence, "God" *did* nothing and never had. Plato posited a very inferior god, called the Demiurge, as the creator of the world, the supreme "God" being too remote and spiritual for such an enterprise; this accounts for the "fact" that the world was so poorly made.

Many scholars doubt that Plato really meant for his postulated Demiurge to be taken literally.[49] But whether real creator or metaphor, Plato's Demiurge pales in contrast with an omnipotent God who made the universe out of nothing. Moreover, for Plato the universe had been created not in accord with firm operating principles but in accord with ideals. These consisted primarily of ideal shapes. Thus, the universe must be a sphere because that is the symmetrical and perfect shape, and heavenly bodies must rotate in a circle because that is the motion that is most perfect.[50] As a collection of a priori assumptions, Platonic idealism long served as a severe impediment to discovery—many centuries later, his unshakable belief in ideal shapes prevented Copernicus even from entertaining the thought that planetary orbits *might* be elliptical, not circular.

In many ways it is strange that the Greeks sought knowledge and technology at all, having rejected the idea of progress in favor of a never-ending cycle of being. Plato at least proposed that the universe had been created, but most Greek scholars assumed that the universe was uncreated and eternal. Aristotle condemned the idea "that the universe came into being at some point in time . . . as unthinkable."[51] Although the Greeks saw the universe as eternal and unchanging, they did allow for the obvious fact that history and culture are ever-changing, *but* only within the strict confines of endless repetition. In *On the Heavens,* Aristotle noted that "the same ideas recur to men not once or twice but over and over again," and in his *Politics* he pointed out that everything has "been invented several times over in the course of ages, or rather times without number," and since he was living in a Golden Age, the levels of technology of his time were at the maximum attainable, precluding further progress. As for inventions, so too for individuals—the same persons would be born again and again as the blind cycles of the universe rolled along. According to Chrysippus in his now lost *On the Cosmos,* the Stoics taught that the "difference between former and actual existences of the same people will be only extrinsic and accidental; such differences do not produce another man as contrasted with his counterpart from a previous world-age."[52] As for the universe itself, according to Parmenides, all perceptions of change are illusions, for the universe is in a static state of perfection, "uncreated and indestructible; for it is complete, immovable, and without end."[53] Other influential Greeks, such as the Ionians, taught that although the universe is infinite and eternal, it also is subject to endless cycles of succession. Plato saw things a bit differently, but he too firmly believed in cycles, and that eternal laws caused each Golden Age to be followed by chaos and collapse.

Finally, the Greeks insisted on turning the cosmos, and inanimate objects more generally, into *living things*. Plato taught that the

Demiurge had created the cosmos as "a single visible living creature." Hence, the world has a soul, and although "solitary," it is "able by reason of its excellence to bear itself company, needing no other acquaintance or friend but sufficient to itself."[54]

But if mineral objects are animate, one heads in the wrong direction in attempting to explain natural phenomena—the causes of the motion of objects, for example, will be ascribed to *motives,* not to natural forces. The Stoics, particularly Zeno, may have originated the idea of explaining the operations of the cosmos on the basis of its conscious purposes, but this soon became the universal view. Thus, according to Aristotle, celestial bodies move in circles because of their affection for this action, and objects fall to the ground "because of their innate love for the centre of the world."[55]

Ultimately, Greek learning stagnated of its own inner logic. After Plato and Aristotle, very little happened beyond some extensions of geometry. When Rome absorbed the Greek world, it embraced Greek learning—Greek scholars flourished under the republic as well as during the reign of the Caesars. But possession of Greek learning did not prompt significant intellectual progress in Rome.[56] Nor did it do so in the East. Greek learning was never lost in Byzantium, but here too it failed to prompt innovation.[57] The decline of Rome did not interrupt the expansion of human knowledge any more than the "recovery" of Greek learning enabled this process to resume. Greek learning was a *barrier* to the rise of science! It did not lead to science among the Greeks or the Romans, and it stifled intellectual progress in Islam, where it was carefully preserved and studied.

ISLAM

It would seem that Islam has a conception of God appropriate to underwrite the rise of science. Not so.[58] Allah is not presented as a lawful creator but is conceived of as an extremely active God who intrudes on the world as he deems it appropriate. This prompted the formation of a major theological bloc within Islam that condemns all efforts to formulate natural laws as blasphemy in that they deny Allah's freedom to act. Thus, Islam did not fully embrace the notion that the universe ran along on fundamental principles laid down by God at the creation but assumed that the world was sustained by his will on a continuing basis. This was justified by the statement in the Qur'an that "verily, God will cause to err whom he pleaseth, and will direct whom he pleaseth." Although the line refers to God's determination of the fate of individuals, it was interpreted broadly to apply to all things.

Whenever the subject of Islamic science and learning is raised, most historians emphasize that throughout the centuries when Christian Europe knew virtually nothing of Greek learning, it was alive and deeply appreciated in Islam. That is certainly true, as is the fact that some classical manuscripts reached Christian Europe through contact with Islam. But the possession of all of this enlightenment did not prompt much intellectual progress within Islam, let alone eventuate in Islamic science. Instead, Muslim intellectuals regarded Greek learning, especially the work of Aristotle, as virtual scripture[59] to be *believed* rather than pursued.

Greek learning stifled all possibility of the rise of an Islamic science for the same reasons it stagnated of itself: fundamental assumptions antithetical to science. The *Rasa'il*, the great encyclopedia of knowledge produced by early Muslim scholars, fully embraced the Greek conception of the world as a huge, conscious, living organism having both intellect and soul.[60] Nor were outlooks more conducive to science achieved by the celebrated Muslim philosopher Averroes and his students in the twelfth century, despite their efforts to exclude all Muslim doctrines from their work, in direct conflict with those who sustained the *Rasa'il*. Instead, Averroes and his followers became intransigent and doctrinaire Aristotelians—proclaiming that his physics was complete and infallible and that if an observation were inconsistent with one of Aristotle's views, the observation was certainly incorrect or an illusion.

As a result of all this, Islamic scholars achieved significant progress only in terms of specific knowledge, such as certain aspects of astronomy and medicine, which did not require any general theoretical basis. And as time passed, even this sort of progress ceased.

Clearly, then, and contrary to the received wisdom, the "recovery" of Greek learning did not put Europe back on the track to science. Judging from the impact of this learning on the Greeks, the Romans, and the Muslims, it would seem to have been vital that Greek learning was *not* generally available until after Christian scholars had established an independent intellectual framework of their own. Indeed, when they first encountered the works of Aristotle, Plato, and the rest, medieval scholars were willing and able to dispute them! It was in explicit opposition to Aristotle and other classical writers that the Scholastics advanced toward science. Because medieval scholars outside the sciences (especially those in the arts and in speculative philosophy) had become such ardent admirers of the Greco-Roman classics, many of the great scientists of the sixteenth and seventeenth centuries often paid lip service to their "debts" to Aristotle and others, but their actual work negated almost everything the Greeks had said about how the world works.

This is not to minimize the impact of Greek learning on Christian theology as well as on European intellectual life in general. Augustine was heir to the entire legacy of Greek philosophy, and Aquinas and his peers acknowledged their deep debts to Hellenic scholarship. But the antiscientific elements of Greek thought were withstood by Augustine and by the Scholastics, and long before Greco-Roman learning was confined to classics departments, it was *not* the philosophy of scientists. While it is true (and constantly cited by classicists) that Newton remarked in a letter to Robert Hooke in 1675 that "if I have seen further (than you and Descartes), it is by standing on the shoulders of giants," such high regard for the ancients is not expressed or reflected in his work or in his usual presentations of self. Instead, Newton and his peers achieved their breakthroughs in obvious opposition to the Greek "giants." What the great figures involved in the sixteenth- and seventeenth-century blossoming of science—including Descartes, Galileo, Newton, and Kepler—did confess was their absolute faith in a creator God, whose work incorporated rational rules awaiting discovery.

The rise of science was not an extension of classical learning. It was the natural outgrowth of Christian doctrine: nature exists because it was created by God. In order to love and honor God, it is necessary to fully appreciate the wonders of his handiwork. Because

God is perfect, his handiwork functions in accord with *immutable principles*. By the full use of our God-given powers of reason and observation, it ought to be possible to discover these principles.

These were the crucial ideas that explain why science arose in Christian Europe and nowhere else.

MORAL INNOVATIONS

The blessings of a theology of reason were not confined to the sciences. From its earliest days, Christianity was equally inventive in its conceptions of human nature and in confronting issues of morality. Chief among these were propositions concerning fundamental human rights such as liberty and freedom. And underlying these ideas was something even more basic: the "discovery" of individualism—of the self.

The notion that individualism was *discovered* seems absurd to the modern mind, and to some extent it is. All normal humans know themselves as separate creatures who necessarily look out upon the world from a unique point of vision and whose nerve endings are absolutely singular. Nevertheless, some cultures emphasize feelings of separate individuality while others stress collectivity and suppress the sense of self. In the latter kind of culture, which seem to be in the great majority, a person's real sense of "being" is quite collective: whatever rights individuals possess are accorded not to them but to their *group* and are, in turn, conferred upon them *by their group*. In such circumstances, no one supposes that "I am the master of my fate." Instead, it is the idea of fatalism that rings true: that one's fate is beyond one's control, being fully determined by great external forces.

Even the Greek philosophers had no concept quite equivalent to our notion of the "person."[61] Thus, when Plato was writing the *Republic,* his focus was on the polis, on the city, not on its citizens—indeed, he even denounced private property. In contrast, it is the individual citizen who was the focus of Christian political thought, and this, in turn, explicitly shaped the views of later European political philosophers such as Hobbes and Locke. This was, quite literally, revolutionary stuff, for the Christian stress on individualism is "an eccentricity among cultures."[62] Freedom is another concept that simply doesn't exist in many, perhaps most, human cultures—there isn't even a word for freedom in most non-European languages.[63]

No wonder that all of the more advanced of these cultures embraced slavery and sustained despotic states wherein the phrase "individual human rights" would have been incomprehensible. So long as that was true, the freedom essential to the rise of capitalism was lacking. Therefore, to account for the emergence of freedom and the rise of capitalism in Europe it is necessary first to understand how and when Europeans developed and accepted notions such as individualism, freedom, and human rights.

THE RISE OF INDIVIDUALISM

Compare Shakespeare's tragedies with those of the ancient Greeks. As Colin Morris pointed out, Oedipus did nothing to earn his sad end. His "personal character . . . is really irrelevant to his misfortunes, which were decreed by fate irrespective of his own desires."[64] Not that Oedipus was without faults, but his crime lacked any guilty intent; he simply fell victim to his destiny. In contrast, Othello, Brutus, and the Macbeths were not captives of blind fate. As Cassius pointed out to Brutus, "The fault, dear Brutus, is not in our stars, but in ourselves."[65]

Much has been written about the origins of individualism.[66] All of these books and articles are learned and even excessively literate, but they also are surprisingly vague and allusive, perhaps because of a reluctance to express their fundamental thesis too openly: that the Western sense of individualism was largely a Christian creation.

From the beginning, Christianity has taught that sin is a personal matter—that it does not inhere primarily in the group, but each individual must be concerned with her or his personal salvation. Perhaps nothing is of greater significance to the Christian emphasis on individualism than the doctrine of free will. If, as Shakespeare wrote, the fault is "in ourselves," it is because we believe we have the opportunity to choose, and the responsibility to choose well. Unlike the Greeks and Romans, whose gods were remarkably lacking in virtues and did not concern themselves with human misbehavior (other than failures to propitiate them in an appropriate manner), the Christian God is a judge who rewards "virtue" and punishes "sin." This conception of God is incompatible with fatalism. To suggest otherwise is to blame one's sins upon God: to hold that God not only punishes sins but causes them to occur. Such a view is inconsistent with the entire Christian outlook. The admonition "Go and sin no more" is absurd if we are mere captives of our fate. Rather, Christianity was founded on the doctrine that humans have been given the capacity and, hence, the responsibility to determine their own actions. Saint Augustine wrote again and again that we "possess a will," and that "from this it follows that whoever desires to live righteously and honorably, can accomplish this."[67] Nor is this view inconsistent with the doctrine that God knows ahead of time what choices we will make. Writing in refutation of Greek and Roman philosophers, Augustine asserted "both that God knows all things before they come to pass, and that we do by our free will whatsoever we know and feel to be done by us only because we will it. But that all things come from fate we do not say; nay we affirm that nothing comes to pass by fate."[68] While God knows what we will freely decide to do, he does not interfere! Therefore it remains up to us to choose virtue or sin.

Augustine's views were echoed across generations of Christian thought. Thomas Aquinas reaffirmed Augustine when he taught that the doctrines that humans are free to make moral choices and that God is omnipotent are entirely compatible: "A man can direct and govern his own actions also. Therefore the rational creature participates in the divine providence not only in being governed but also in governing."[69] Indeed, Augustine fully anticipated Descartes' famous "I think, therefore I am" in many passages,[70] including this one: "But, without any delusive representation of images or phantasms, I am most certain that I am, and that I know and delight in this. In respect to these truths, I am not at all afraid of the arguments of the Academicians, who say, What if you are deceived? For if I am deceived, I am. For he who is not cannot be deceived; and if

I am deceived, by this same token I am. . . . And, consequently, neither am I deceived in knowing that I know. For, as I know that I am, so I know this also, that I know."[71]

The idea of free will did not originate with Christians (Cicero expressed views somewhat similar to Augustine's),[72] but for them it was not an obscure philosophical matter. Rather, it was the fundamental principle of their faith. Thus, while ordinary Greek or Roman pagans embraced fatalism, whatever reservations about it some ancient philosophers might have expressed, Jesus taught that each individual must atone for moral lapses precisely because these are *wrong choices*. There could be no more compelling intellectual emphasis on self and individuality than this.

THE ABOLITION OF MEDIEVAL SLAVERY

The rise of individualism not only prompted self-examination but raised questions concerning the boundaries of personal freedom. If we are unique beings, all to be judged by our actions freely taken, what is the duty of Christians with regard to another's freedom to act? As the church fathers pondered the implications of free will, and especially after the fall of Rome, they grew increasingly uncomfortable with the institution of slavery.

Unlike Asian languages, Greek and Latin have words for freedom, and many Greeks and Romans regarded themselves as free. But their freedom stood in contrast to a mass of slaves, for in classical times freedom was a privilege, not a right.

Plato did oppose enslavement of his fellow "Hellenes" (Greeks) but assigned "barbarian" (foreign) slaves a vital role in his ideal republic—they would perform all of the productive labor.[73] In fact, the rules Plato laid out concerning the proper treatment of slaves were unusually brutal,[74] for he believed not that becoming a slave was simply a matter of bad luck but that nature creates a "slavish people" lacking the mental capacity for virtue or culture, and fit only to serve. Plato did suggest that although slaves should be sternly disciplined, in order to prevent needless unrest, they generally should not be subject to excessive cruelty.[75] As enumerated in his will, Plato's estate included five slaves.

As for Aristotle, he rejected the position advanced by the Sophists that all authority rests on force, and therefore is self-justifying, because he sought to condemn political tyranny. But then, how to justify slavery? Without slaves to do the labor, Aristotle argued, enlightened men would lack the time and energy to pursue virtue and wisdom. He also drew upon Plato's biological claims—slavery is justified because slaves are more akin to dumb brutes than to free men: "From the hour of their birth, some are marked out for subjection, others for rule."[76] Upon his death, Aristotle's personal property included fourteen slaves.

Slavery began to decline in the latter days of the Roman empire as a direct result of military weakness. No longer were victorious commanders dispatching throngs of prisoners to the slave markets. Since fertility was very low among Roman slaves, due both to privation and to a lack of women, their numbers rapidly fell, and the shortage of slaves soon caused the conversion of agriculture and industry to reliance on free laborers.

After the fall of Rome, with the successful military expeditions of the new Germanic kingdoms, slavery regained a major role in production. Though no one really knows how many slaves there were in Europe during, say, the sixth century, they seem to have been plentiful, and their treatment was, if anything, harsher than in classical times. In the legal codes of the various Germanic groups that ruled in place of Roman governors, slaves were equated not with other humans but specifically with animal livestock. Nevertheless, several centuries later slavery was on the way out.

Some historians deny that there ever was an end to medieval slavery—that nothing happened other than a linguistic shift in which the word "slave" was replaced by the word "serf."[77] Here it is not history but historians who are playing word games. Serfs were not chattels; they had rights and a substantial degree of discretion. They married whom they wished, and their families were not subject to sale or dispersal. They paid rent and thus controlled their own time and the pace of their work.[78] If, as in some places, serfs owed their lords a number of days of labor each year, the obligation was limited and more similar to hired labor than to slavery. Although serfs were bound to a lord by extensive obligations, so too was their lord bound by obligations to them as well as to a higher authority, and so on up the line, for sets of *mutual* obligations were the fundamental nature of feudalism.[79]

While no one would argue that medieval peasants were free in the modern sense, they were not slaves, and that brutal institution had essentially disappeared from Europe by the end of the tenth century. Although most recent historians agree with that conclusion, it remains fashionable to deny that Christianity had anything to do with it. As Robert Fossier put it, "The progressive elimination of slavery was in no way the work of Christian peoples. The Church preached resignation, promised equality in the hereafter . . . [and] felt no compunction about keeping large herds of animals with human faces."[80] Georges Duby also dismissed any role of the church in ending slavery: "Christianity did not condemn slavery; it dealt it barely a glancing blow."[81] Rather, slavery is said to have disappeared because it became an unprofitable and outdated mode of production.[82] Even Robert Lopez accepted this view, claiming that slavery ended only when technological progress such as the waterwheel "made slaves useless or unproductive."[83] Hence the claim that the end of slavery was not a moral decision but one of pure self-interest on the part of the elite. That same argument has been made concerning the abolition of slavery in the Western Hemisphere. Both claims are consistent, of course, with Marxist doctrine but are quite inconsistent with economic realities. Even as late as the start of the American Civil War, Southern slavery remained a very profitable "mode of production."[84] The same was true in early medieval Europe.

But enough! Slavery ended in medieval Europe *only* because the church extended its sacraments to all slaves and then managed to impose a ban on the enslavement of Christians (and of Jews). Within the context of medieval Europe, that prohibition was effectively a rule of universal abolition.

In the beginning, the church asserted the legitimacy of slavery but did so with a certain ambiguity. Consider the most-cited New

Testament passage on slavery. Writing to the Ephesians (6:5, 8) Paul admonished: "Slaves, be obedient to those who are your earthly masters, in fear and trembling, in singleness of heart, as to Christ . . . knowing that whatever good any one does, he will receive the same again from the Lord, whether he is slave or free." Those who eagerly quote this passage very seldom go on to quote the next verse: "Masters, do the same to them, and forbear threatening, knowing that he who is both their Master and yours is in heaven, and that there is no partiality with him." That God treats all equally is fundamental to the Christian message: all may be saved. It was this that encouraged the early church to convert slaves and when possible to purchase their freedom—Pope Callistus (died 236) had himself been a slave.

So long as the Roman empire stood, the church continued to affirm the legitimacy of slavery. In 324, the Christian Council of Granges condemned anyone who encouraged discontent among slaves,[85] which suggests, of course, that such activities were taking place. However, the tension between support for slavery and emphasis on the equality of all in the eyes of God continued to grow, and with the demise of the empire, the strain grew ever more intense because the church continued to extend its embrace to those in slavery, denying them only ordination into the priesthood. Pierre Bonnassie has expressed the matter as well as anyone: "A slave . . . was baptised [and] had a soul. He was, then, unambiguously a man."[86]

With slaves fully recognized as human and Christian, priests began to urge owners to free their slaves as an "infinitely commendable act" that helped ensure their own salvation.[87] Many manumissions were recorded in surviving wills. The doctrine that slaves were humans and not cattle had another important consequence: intermarriage. Despite their being against the law in most of Europe, there is considerable evidence of mixed unions by the seventh century, usually involving free men and female slaves. The most celebrated of these unions took place in 649, when Clovis II, king of the Franks, married his British slave Bathilda. When Clovis died in 657, Bathilda ruled as regent until her eldest son came of age. Bathilda used her position to mount a campaign to halt the slave trade and to redeem those in slavery. Upon her death, the church acknowledged Bathilda as a saint.

At the end of the eighth century, Charlemagne opposed slavery, while the pope and many other powerful and effective clerical voices echoed Saint Bathilda. As the ninth century dawned, Bishop Agobard of Lyons thundered: "All men are brothers, all invoke one same Father, God: the slave and the master, the poor man and the rich man, the ignorant and the learned, the weak and the strong . . . none has been raised above the other . . . there is no . . . slave or free, but in all things and always there is only Christ."[88] At the same time, Abbot Smaragde of Saint-Mihiel wrote in a work dedicated to Charlemagne: "Most merciful king, forbid that there should be any slave in your kingdom."[89] Soon, no one "doubted that slavery in itself was against divine law."[90] Indeed, during the eleventh century both Saint Wulfstan and Saint Anselm campaigned to remove the last vestiges of slavery in Christendom, and soon it could be said "that no man, no real Christian at any rate, could thereafter legitimately be held as the property of another."[91] But exceptions remained, all of them involving extensive interaction with Islam. In Spain, Christian and Muslim armies continued to enslave each other's captives taken in battle, and slave trading involving northern Italian export firms and Muslim buyers persisted into the fifteenth century, in defiance of the church. The number of slaves involved in this trade was small. They were purchased from Slavic tribes in the Caucasus (the word "slave" is a corruption of the word "Slav"). A few were kept as a form of luxury goods by very wealthy Italians such as the Medici, but most were exported to Islam—white slaves being "more precious than gold in trading with Egypt."[92] This residual slave trade was periodically condemned by local clergy and slowly withered away, only to reappear with a vengeance in the New World. The church responded vigorously, and a series of angry bulls against New World slavery were issued by sixteenth-century popes—but the popes had no serious temporal power in this era, and their vigorous opposition was to no avail.[93]

The theological conclusion that slavery is sinful has been unique to Christianity (although several early Jewish sects also rejected slavery).[94] Here too can be seen the principle of theological progress

at work, making it possible for theologians to propose new interpretations without engendering charges of heresy. As noted, the
other major religions are strongly oriented to the past, and to the
principle that, if anything, history is regressive and later generations are prone to error. Therefore, to say that the sages or saints in
times past may have had an imperfect or limited understanding of
religious truths is rejected out of hand by Buddhists, Confucianists,
Hindus, and even by Muslims. While Christian theologians could
plausibly correct Saint Paul's understanding of God's will concerning slavery, such corrections were (and are) essentially precluded in
the other faiths—except as heresies. A second factor is that, of the
major world faiths, only Christianity has devoted serious and sustained attention to human rights, as opposed to human duties. Put
another way, the other great faiths minimize individualism and
stress collective obligations. They are, as Ruth Benedict so aptly put
it, cultures of shame, rather than cultures of guilt.[95] Keep in mind
that there is not even a word for freedom in the languages in which
their scriptures are written—including Hebrew.[96]

As for Islam, there is a uniquely insuperable barrier to theological condemnations of slavery: Muhammad bought, sold, captured,
and owned slaves.[97] The Prophet did advise that slaves should be
treated well: "Feed them what you eat yourself and clothe them
with what you wear. . . . They are God's people like unto you and be
kind unto them."[98] Muhammad also freed several of his slaves,
adopted one as his son, and married another. In addition, the
Qur'an teaches that it is wrong to "compel your slave girls to pros-
titution" (24.33), and that one can gain forgiveness for killing a fellow believer by freeing a slave (4.92). Muhammad's admonition and
example probably often mitigated the conditions of slaves in Islam,
as contrasted with those in Greece and Rome. But the fundamental
morality of the institution of slavery was not in doubt. While Christian theologians were able to work their way around the biblical ac-
ceptance of slavery, they probably could not have done so had Jesus
kept slaves.[99] That Muhammad owned slaves has presented Muslim
theologians with a fact that no intellectual maneuvering could
overcome, even had they desired to do so.

success rests upon victories of reason, then the rise of Christianity surely was the most important single event in European history. It was the church that gave steadfast testimony to the power of reason and to the possibility of progress—to the guiding principle that "one day we shall." And so, one day we did. Nor was the fulfillment of this promise long delayed by centuries of ignorance and superstition, as claimed by spurious tales about "Dark Ages." Rapid intellectual and material progress began as soon as Europeans escaped from the stultifying grip of Roman repression and mistaken Greek idealism.

CHAPTER TWO

Medieval Progress:
Technical, Cultural, and Religious

CHRISTIAN COMMITMENT TO REASON AND PROGRESS WASN'T ALL talk; soon after the fall of Rome, it encouraged an era of extraordinary invention and innovation. To appreciate this remarkable achievement it is necessary to confront an incredible lie that long disfigured our knowledge of history.

For the past two or three centuries, every educated person has known that from the fall of Rome until about the fifteenth century Europe was submerged in the "Dark Ages"—centuries of ignorance, superstition, and misery—from which it was suddenly, almost miraculously rescued, first by the Renaissance and then by the Enlightenment.[1] But it didn't happen that way. Instead, during the so-called Dark Ages, European technology and science overtook and surpassed the rest of the world![2]

The idea that Europe fell into the Dark Ages is a hoax originated by antireligious, and bitterly anti-Catholic, eighteenth-century intellectuals who were determined to assert the cultural superiority of their own time and who boosted their claim by denigrating previous centuries as—in the words of Voltaire—a time when "barbarism, superstition, [and] ignorance covered the face of the world."[3] Views such as these were repeated so often and so unanimously that, until very recently, even dictionaries and encyclopedias accepted the Dark Ages as an historical fact.[4] Some writers even seemed to suggest that people living in, say, the ninth century described their own time as one of backwardness and superstition.

Fortunately, in the past few years these views have been so completely discredited that even some dictionaries and encyclopedias have begun to refer to the notion of Dark Ages as mythical.[5] Unfortunately, the myth has so deeply penetrated our culture that even most scholars continue to take it for granted that—in the words of Edward Gibbon—after Rome fell came the "triumph of barbarism and religion."[6] In part this is because no one has provided an adequate summary of what really took place.

This chapter aims to fill that gap—to show that when the breakup of the Roman empire "released the tax-paying millions . . . from a paralysing oppression,"[7] many new technologies began to appear, and were rapidly and widely adopted, with the result that ordinary people were able to live far better, and after centuries of decline under Rome, the population began to grow again. No longer were the productive classes bled to sustain the astonishing excesses of the Roman elite, or to erect massive monuments to imperial egos, or to support vast armies to hold Rome's many colonies in thrall. Instead, human effort and ingenuity turned to better ways to farm, to sail, to transport goods, to build churches, to make war, to educate, and even to play music. But because, so many centuries later, examples of classical Greek and Roman public grandeur still stand as remarkable ruins, many intellectuals have been prompted to mourn the loss of these "great civilizations." Many who are fully aware of what this grandeur cost in human suffering have been quite willing even to write off slavery as merely "the sacrifice which had to be paid for this achievement."[8]

In many respects, the fall of Rome involved the collapse of a city, not of a civilization. During the second century, the population of Rome approached 1 million; by the eighth century, Romans numbered fewer than fifty thousand; and by 1377, when the pope moved his court back from its captivity in Avignon, the city contained only about fifteen thousand inhabitants. Although urban populations declined in some other parts of Europe also, in Italy the losses were moderate in most cities and were soon made up[9] (even at the height of imperial power, aside from Rome, these were not very large cities—only Milan and Capua had more than thirty thousand inhabitants).[10] It is, of course, true that, along with the decline of the city of Rome, the empire broke into many pieces. But that was tragic only if one admires profligate rulers, literary Latin, and the pursuits of the idle rich.

To put it plainly, for too long too many historians have been as gullible as tourists, gaping at the monuments, palaces, and conspicuous consumption of Rome (or Athens, or Istanbul) and then drawing invidious comparisons between such "cosmopolitan" places and "provincial" communities such as medieval merchant towns. Somehow, although being themselves of modest means, these scholars always seemed to assume they would have been among the elite, rather than among the sullen, impoverished masses. Far better that they had longed to have been burghers in a dull medieval town.

And maybe not so dull. Freed of the grip of tyrants, the so-called Dark Ages saw an extraordinary outburst of innovation in both technology and culture. Some of this involved original inventions, some of it came from Asia. But what was most remarkable about the Dark Ages was the way in which the full capacities of new technologies were rapidly recognized and widely adopted, as would be expected of a culture dominated by faith in progress—recall Augustine's celebrations of "exuberant invention." Nor was innovation limited to technology; there was remarkable progress in areas of high culture—such as literature, art, and music—as well. Moreover, new technologies inspired new organizational and administrative forms, culminating in the birth of capitalism within the great monastic estates. This, in turn, prompted a complete theological reappraisal of the moral implications of commerce—the leading theologians rejected prior doctrinal objections to profits and interest, thereby legitimating the primary elements of capitalism. For all that these developments were of immense historical importance, they were in many respects a "secret revolution," as R. W. Southern[11] so aptly put it—secret in the sense that we don't know who discovered what or, in most instances, even where or exactly when most of these innovations were accomplished. What we do know is that they soon vaulted the West ahead of the rest of the world.

TECHNICAL PROGRESS

That invention flourished in the aftermath of the fall of Rome demonstrates the principle that despotic states discourage and even prevent progress. Why should farmers seek or adopt new and better agricultural technology if all the increased production will be taken from them? Who will reinvest profits to expand an industry if it is apt to be expropriated by the nobility? Invention and innovation tend to occur only where property is safe from seizure either because the state has become disorganized or because its powers have been curtailed. The remarkable era of innovation that occurred within the political disunity that followed the collapse of Rome was a preview of what lay ahead and also provided the opportunity for rapid innovations and the subsequent appearance of capitalism. Hence, it is pertinent to sketch the magnitude of early medieval technological innovations. These can be separated into three main classes: those that increased productive capacities, those that were of use mainly in war, and those that improved transportation.

Innovations in Production

Perhaps the greatest achievement of the Dark Ages was the creation of the first economies that depended primarily on nonhuman power.

The Romans understood water power but could see no reason to exploit it, because there was no shortage of slaves to do needed tasks. Why would a Roman nobleman spend money to construct a spillway and a waterwheel to grind grain into flour when he had plenty of slaves with the time and energy simply to turn the mill by hand? In contrast, an inventory conducted in the ninth century found that one-third of the estates along the Seine River in the area around Paris had water mills, most of these being on the religious estates.[12] When William the Conqueror had the *Domesday Book* compiled in 1086, this forerunner of the modern census reported that there were at least 5,624 water-powered mills already operating in England, or one for about every fifty families.[13] Across the channel, early in the twelfth century, a company known as the Société du Bazacle was founded in Toulouse to offer shares in a series of water-powered mills along the Garonne River. The shares were freely traded, which led Jean Gimpel to propose that the Société "may well be the oldest capitalistic company in the world."[14] A century later, water mills had become so important that in the center of Paris, along the Seine, there were sixty-eight mills in one section less than a mile long, an average of one mill every seventy feet of river![15]

The mills on the Seine and the Garonne, indeed most of the early water mills, were of the undershot variety—the water passes under the wheel, and the force, or power, is provided entirely by the current of the river or stream. Much greater power can be harnessed by an overshot wheel—the water descends by a spillway to approximate a waterfall striking the top of the wheel, and both the speed and the weight of the water generate power. Hence, except in very rare situations, overshot wheels require dams. No one really knows when overshot wheels came into use. There are many references to them in fourteenth-century materials, but given the fact that dams were built considerably before that time, overshot wheels must have appeared much sooner too. Although dams are sometimes built for flood control, even today their primary purpose is to back up water so as to exploit its weight and pressure to generate power. At least as early as the twelfth century some very large dams were constructed— one at Toulouse was more than thirteen hundred feet across, consisting of thousands of giant oak logs driven into the riverbed to form a front and a rear palisade, then filled with dirt and stone.[16] Various cranks and gear assemblies were attached to waterwheels, both to increase their power and to convert their motion from rotary to reciprocating action. Soon waterpower was also utilized for sawing lumber and stones, for turning lathes, grinding knives and swords, for fulling (pounding) cloth, for hammering metal and drawing wire, and to pulp rags to make paper.[17] As for that last use, Jean Gimpel noted that paper, "which was manufactured by hand and foot for a thousand years or so following its invention by the Chinese and adoption by the Arabs, was manufactured mechanically as soon as it reached medieval Europe in the thirteenth century. . . . Paper had traveled around the world, but no culture or civilization on its route had tried to mechanize its manufacture"[18] until medieval Europeans did so.

But it wasn't only the rapid spread, improvement, and adaptations of waterpower that distinguished the Dark Ages. Medieval Europeans quickly harnessed the wind as well. The great hydraulic empires of the Middle East and Asia benefited from putting water onto their fields; medieval Europe greatly increased its agricultural production by pumping water off potential cropland—large areas of what is now Belgium and the Netherlands were under the sea in Roman times. They were reclaimed by thousands of windmills that pumped day and night throughout most of the Dark Ages.

Windmills proliferated even more rapidly than waterwheels because there was wind everywhere. In order to take full advantage of the wind even when it shifted direction, medieval engineers invented the post mill, which mounted the sails on a massive post, leaving them free to turn with the wind. By late in the twelfth century, Europe was becoming so crowded with windmills that owners began to file lawsuits against one another for blocking their wind.[19]

Not content, medieval Europeans turned their attention to greatly increasing horsepower—literally. Neither the Roman nor other classical civilizations knew how to harness horses effectively. Before Europeans learned better during the Dark Ages, horses were harnessed in the same way as oxen. In order to avoid strangling in such a harness, a horse must keep its head thrown back and can pull only light loads. Fully aware of the problem, Romans responded via legislation. The Theodosian Code decreed severe punishments for anyone who hooked a horse to a load in excess of five hundred kilograms (expressed in a modern metric).[20] In contrast, during the Dark Ages a rigid, well-padded collar was adopted that properly placed the weight on the horse's shoulders instead of its neck, enabling the horse to pull as much as the ox and to pull it much faster. Having adopted the horse collar, European farmers soon switched from oxen to horses, with an immense gain in productivity—a horse could plow more than twice as much per day as an ox.[21]

It was also not until after the fall of Rome that Europeans developed iron shoes nailed to horses' hooves to protect them from the wear and tear that often causes unshod horses to become lame. The Romans had experimented with various kinds of horse sandals (Nero had some made of silver), but these fell off if the horse even trotted. Now, with iron shoes firmly attached, horses were far less subject to going lame and could dig their hooves in more effectively to gain traction.

Having gained a much more efficient substitute for the ox, medieval Europeans promptly invented the heavy, wheeled plow to improve the productivity of their fertile, but very heavy, soil. Until sometime in the sixth century, farming depended on the scratch plow, which was nothing but a multiple set of digging sticks arranged in rows.[22] The scratch plow does not turn the soil but is simply dragged over the surface, leaving undisturbed soil between shallow furrows—often requiring cross-plowing. This may be adequate for thin, dry soils such as those in Italy, but is not very effective with the heavy, often damp, soil of most of northern Europe. What was needed was a very heavy plow, with a heavy share (blade), that would dig a deep furrow. To this was added a second share at an angle to cut off the slice of turf that was being turned over by the first share. Then, a moldboard was added to turn over the sliced-off turf entirely. Finally, wheels were attached to the plow to facilitate moving it from one field to another and to make it possible to set the share to plow at different depths. Presto! Land that the Romans could not farm at all suddenly became very productive, and even on thinner soil, crop yields were nearly doubled by improved plowing alone.[23] These incredible gains in agricultural productivity so reduced the need for farm labor and increased yields that they greatly facilitated the formation and feeding of towns and cities.[24]

Besides growing grain and other crops, farmers in the early Middle Ages also grew fish. The Romans had done a bit of fish farming too, but the industry exploded in the eighth century, when the church prohibited the eating of meat on Fridays and other fast days (which added up to 150 days at the time). Since fish were not classified as meat, all across western Europe artificial lakes and ponds were constructed, many specialized to suit particular kinds of fish or to sustain the life cycle of a specific species. Eventually, even castle moats also were put to use.

Monastic estates, particularly those of the Cistercians, were especially active in fish farming since many monks were not permitted to eat any meat at all. Some monasteries built so many ponds and tanks for farming carp and trout that they sold fresh fish to everyone in the area.[25] The nobility were very active fish farmers too: William the Conqueror had a large and elaborate system of ponds constructed in York about 1086, which supplied the English court for centuries. In time, ingenious farmers discovered that the bottoms of their fishponds became extremely fertile from fish excretions, and so they drained them every few years, planted them with crops, and after a bountiful harvest, restocked them with fish.[26] Farms were the major source of fish in all of Europe until commercial fishing fleets were organized along the North and Baltic Seas in about the twelfth century.

The ability of medieval agriculture to produce surplus was greatly increased also by adoption of the *three-field system,* wherein farmland was divided into three plots—one planted in a winter crop, such as wheat; the second in a spring crop, such as oats (especially important once horses came into use), legumes (such as peas and beans), and vegetables; and the third allowed to lie fallow (un planted). The next year the plot that was fallow was planted in the winter crop, the second in a spring crop, and the plot that had grown a spring crop the previous year was left fallow. (Before the era of chemical fertilizers, land needed to lie fallow frequently so as to recover its growing capacity.)

The three-field system first appeared in the eighth century and was adopted so widely and rapidly that during the nineteenth century many historians erroneously assumed it dated from Roman times. But the Romans knew only a two-field system of agriculture, because they did not know that legumes helped to restore the land, and thus land needed to lie fallow less often. Thus, half of their land lay fallow each year, compared with one-third under the medieval three-field system.[27] Not only did most Europeans eat far better during the Dark Ages than in Roman times but they were healthier, more energetic, and probably more intelligent.

Using the fallow plot for grazing also had dramatic effects on medieval and then on early capitalist economies. "Manure was highly prized, for it was a rare and precious product, none of which must be wasted. The most blessed of all the animals was the sheep."[28] Sheep provided milk, butter, cheese, and meat. Their skins provided the parchment on which scribes copied out books. But most of all, sheep provided wool. Since wool cloth was in very high demand during the Middle Ages, wool fleeces were the major industrial raw material. Woolen cloth industries dominated the early days of capitalism, and cloth manufacturers in Italy and Flanders used "millions of fleeces each year."[29]

That, of course, brings us to another major area of medieval innovation: cloth making. Until medieval Europeans invented treadle-powered looms, water-powered fulling machines, spinning wheels, and metal-toothed carding machines, cloth making was extremely labor intensive and was done on a very small scale, entirely by hand. Only the mechanization of cloth making allowed the growth of major cloth-making centers and industries, and these served as a major engine of commerce and, therefore, of finance.

In addition to technology used directly and specifically in production, medieval Europeans benefited from three inventions of immense indirect importance: chimneys, eyeglasses, and clocks.

Roman buildings were essentially unheated. There were no fireplaces, stoves, or furnaces because no one had figured out an efficient way to ventilate the smoke. In their shacks and hovels, Roman peasants clustered around an open fire while the smoke rose through a large hole left in the roof, which also let in rain, snow, wind, and cold.[30] Urban Romans even lacked holes in their roofs; as they cooked over wood or charcoal braziers, the smoke was simply allowed to concentrate indoors. Asphyxiation was avoided because the buildings were extremely drafty, since they lacked windowpanes and were closed only by hanging drapes made of cloth or skin.[31] But if the Caesars huddled against the cold and endured the smoke coming from their kitchens, medieval Europeans—peasants as well as the nobility—soon learned to live much better. They invented the chimney and the fireplace, whereupon even roaring blazes did not smoke up the room. Nor was it any longer necessary to have drafty homes. With the smoke rising harmlessly up their chimneys, folks in the Dark Ages ate better-prepared food, breathed far better air, and were a lot warmer in winter.

It is a fact of human biology that many people have defective eyesight from childhood and that, for most of the rest, sight begins to decline by middle age. Before the invention of eyeglasses, a very large proportion of working adults, especially those engaged in crafts, were greatly hindered in what tasks they could perform. Thus, the invention of eyeglasses, in about 1284 in northern Italy, had dramatic effects on productivity. Without glasses, large numbers of medieval craft workers were washed up at forty. With glasses, not only could most of these people continue but because of their experience, their most productive years still lay ahead.[32] Not only that but many tasks are greatly facilitated by use of magnifiers, even by persons with fine eyesight. These tasks were often beyond ancient craftspeople. No wonder glasses spread with amazing speed. Within a century after their invention, the mass production of eyeglasses occupied plants in both Florence and Venice, turning out tens of thousands of eyeglasses a year. Even so, in 1492, when Columbus set sail, eyeglasses still were known only in Europe.[33]

Sometime during the thirteenth century, someone somewhere in Europe invented a dependable mechanical clock. Soon, Europe was the only society where people really knew what time it was. As Lewis Mumford remarked, "the clock, not the steam engine, is the key machine of the industrial age,"[34] because it made possible precise scheduling and coordination of activities. Early mechanical clocks were very large, so a town or a neighborhood often had only one (on a church or a public clock tower), and systems of bell ringing were adopted to signal the accurate time to an entire community.

Like eyeglasses, for centuries mechanical clocks existed only in the West. Apparently several mechanical clocks were built in China at the start of the twelfth century, but the hostility of the Mandarins toward mechanical contrivances was so great that they soon ordered them destroyed, and no clocks existed in China again until modern times.[35] In 1560 it was reported that public clocks were rejected by the Ottoman empire (as well as by other Islamic cultures) because they would secularize time.[36] Islam was not alone in resisting the clock: the Eastern Orthodox hierarchy refused to permit any mechanical clocks in their churches until the twentieth century.[37] Fortunately for western Europe, the Roman Catholic hierarchy had no reservations about knowing the time of day and installed large mechanical clocks on the towers of thousands of church buildings.

These are only some of the innovations and inventions by which Europeans living in the alleged Dark Ages prepared the productive foundations for capitalism. Many others could be listed, including improvements to cranes and hoists, advances in mining, smelting, and metalworking technology, remarkable improvements in seeds, even the invention of the wheelbarrow. However, the success of Europe involved far more than improved methods of production and a higher standard of living. Europeans also advanced beyond the rest of the world in the means for making war.

Innovations in War

Prior to the Dark Ages, there was no heavy cavalry. Mounted troops did not charge headlong at a gallop, putting the full weight of horse and rider behind a long lance.[38] The reason was the lack of stirrups and a proper saddle. Without stirrups to brace against, a rider attempting to drive home a lance will be thrown off his horse. The ability of a rider to withstand sudden shocks is also greatly increased by a saddle with a very high pommel and cantle—the latter being curved to partly enclose the rider's hips.[39] It was not Rome or any other warlike empire that produced heavy cavalry: their mounted troops all rode on light, almost flat, pad saddles, or even bareback, and they had no stirrups. It was the "barbarous" Franks who, in 732, fielded the first heavy cavalry: armored knights astride massive horses, who charged behind long lances, secure in their high-backed Norman saddles and braced in their stirrups.

Charging knights in armor were a major factor in war until well after the introduction of artillery. The Chinese were the first to use an explosive powder, but they were content to use it only for fireworks and as an incendiary. Eventually, the Chinese did develop a crude cannon,[40] probably at about the same time as knowledge of this Chinese explosive arrived in Europe, sometime between 1300 and 1310. But while the Chinese were very slow to develop cannons and then made little use of them, and also failed to apply this technology to individual firearms, in Europe the application to gunnery was immediate—cannons probably were first used in battle during a siege of Metz in 1324.[41] What is certain is that by 1325 cannons were in use all over western Europe.[42] And in European hands, the cannon revolutionized warfare. The nobility no longer could retire to their castles, safe from any enemy not willing to undertake a long siege, while on the battlefield even expensive suits of armor gave no protection against artillery fire. Cannons could spread so rapidly because the capacity to cast them already existed all over Europe in the church bell industry.

Medieval Europe also made major breakthroughs in terms of sea power. In the long run the commercial value of these innovations probably outweighed their military significance, but without the latter, the former may not have mattered—it was only because their warships controlled the world's sea-lanes that Europeans were able to monopolize long-distance trade and to build overseas empires.[43]

One of the first naval innovations was the sternpost rudder. The Greeks and Romans controlled their vessels with steering oars, usually a pair with one on each side of the stern. By early in the eleventh century, Europeans were attaching a rudder to the sternpost, which made ships far more maneuverable. To facilitate use of this rudder on larger vessels, mechanical linkages were developed to make it possible for a single helmsman to steer the ship even in heavy seas—an early form of power steering.[44] A second innovation was in shipbuilding. Roman and Greek shipbuilders constructed their hulls by attaching one plank to another by mortise and tenon and inserted a supporting skeleton (or framework) afterward. Medieval Europeans built the frame first and then attached the hull planks in overlapping fashion, pegged them in place, and caulked the seams rather than using elaborate joints. This technique resulted in a hull that was not as strong, but the immense savings in skilled labor meant many more boats for the same cost.[45] A third innovation was to recognize the superiority of firepower in sea battles. From its earliest days, galley warfare consisted of infantry battles fought from deck to deck. Hence, battle galleys were stuffed to nearly the sinking point with soldiers. Having developed the cannon into a highly accurate weapon, Europeans realized, sensibly, that it was far better to sink enemy boats at a distance. This approach produced the astonishingly complete victory over the Turks at Lepanto in 1571, which effectively ended Muslim sea power. The European galleys not only had far more and far better cannons than did the Turks but they no longer had their forward fire zone blocked by a high ramming beak—since they meant to blow the Turks out of the water, not ram into them. Firing powerful forward volleys, the Europeans annihilated Ottoman galleys while still rowing toward them; the Turks had to stop and turn sideways to fire, presenting much larger targets.[46]

But perhaps the most important medieval naval innovation was the round ship (galleys were relatively flat-bottomed), a tall vessel with castles both fore and aft, multiple masts, and a complex set of sails, some of them square, some of them lateen (triangular). The earliest round ships were called "cogs," and first appeared in the thirteenth century.[47] The cog had no oars but was a true sailing ship, capable of long voyages with large cargoes. Rigged as a fighting ship, the round ship and its descendents could support large numbers of big guns—eventually having as many as three gun decks, one above the other. Thus did the Dark Ages gain access to the open seas, ships no longer having to hug the shore or remain within protected waters such as the Mediterranean. Indeed, these big ships ventured out during the winter, something galley captains had been loath to do, and winter sailing greatly increased the profits earned from each vessel.

If the round ships no longer needed to hug the shore for safety, they still needed to be guided by landmarks. Then came the compass. The claim that the magnetic compass reached Europe from China through the Muslim world is false. It was invented independently in both China and Europe, probably in about the eleventh century. The Chinese were satisfied with a very crude compass, involving a magnetized needle floating in a liquid, that enabled them to determine the north-south axis, which was primarily of interest for performing magical rites—the Chinese may not, in fact, have used this device aboard ships until long after Europeans were doing so. In contrast, soon after discovering the floating needle compass, medieval Europeans added the compass card and then the sight, which allowed mariners not only to know which way was north but to determine their precise heading. They could now set accurate courses in any direction. The temporal clustering of written reports of this new invention demonstrates that it spread among sailors from Italy to Norway in only a few years.[48] Once they had the compass, European navigators began creating charts showing compass headings between ports. This allowed them to travel safely even when the sky was too overcast to permit use of the stars to fix their position.[49] Without a compass Columbus could not have sailed, nor could others have retraced his route.

All of these remarkable developments can be traced to the unique Christian conviction that progress was a God-given obligation, entailed in the gift of reason. That new technologies and techniques would always be forthcoming was a fundamental article of Christian faith. Hence, no bishops or theologians denounced clocks or sailing ships—although both were condemned on religious grounds in various non-Western societies. Rather, many major technical innovations probably were made by monks and were eagerly adopted by the great monastic estates. Innovations spread very rapidly from one place to another because, contrary to the Dark Age tales concerning an insular and immobile Europe, the means of medieval transportation soon surpassed those of Roman times.

Innovations in Land Transportation

One of the most misleading claims about the decline of Europe into the Dark Ages concerns the neglect of the Roman roads—in many places the paving stones were taken up and reused in local construction. As the roads decayed, the story goes, so did long-distance trade, and Europe became an archipelago of isolated and inward-looking communities. Overlooked in this account is that, aside from bringing grain to feed the city of Rome's swollen and idle population, long-distance Roman trade mainly dealt in luxuries and was unproductive—trade played little role in the economic life of Roman cities, since the wealth of the urban elites came mainly from their rural estates,[50] supplemented by political graft and the loot of conquest. In part, the decline in long-distance trade reflected the lack of demand for many luxuries caused by the demise of fabulous personal wealth. But more significant, most of what has been called long-distance Roman trade wasn't really trade at all, but extraction. It was "a traffic in rent and tribute" that did not generate income as real trade does but "simply impoverished those from whom it was extorted."[51] Also overlooked has been the fact that the trading activities that survived were of substantial value to exporters as well as to importers.[52] As for the neglect of the Roman roads, this occurred because they were largely useless.

The claim that medieval Europeans lacked the judgment or means to sustain the "magnificent" Roman road system originated with classicists who either never actually inspected one of the many surviving examples or were so lacking in practical experience that they failed to notice such obvious shortcomings as the fact that the Roman roads were too narrow for large wagons[53] and in many places were far too steep for anything but foot traffic. In addition, the Romans often did not build bridges, relying on fords that could be crossed on foot but often were too deep and steep for carts and wagons [54] These inadequacies existed because the sole purpose of Roman roads was to permit soldiers to march quickly from one part of the empire to another. Of course, civilian pedestrians used them too, as did animal and human pack trains. But even the soldiers preferred to walk along the sides of the roads whenever possible, and that's where nearly all civilian travelers walked or led their beasts. Why? Because the Roman roads were often paved with stone and therefore were hard on legs and feet when dry, and very slippery when wet. Such roads were hard enough on an unshod horse's hooves; they were very unsuitable for horses wearing iron shoes.

Recall that until the Dark Ages no one knew how to harness horses so that they could pull heavy loads. Not only did the introduction of the horse collar revolutionize agriculture but in combination with crucial innovations in the construction of wagons, the horse collar revolutionized transportation as well. The Romans were limited to using slow oxen to pull heavy loads. Worse yet, their carts and wagons were so primitive that seldom was anything of substantial weight moved very far overland. Consider that because Roman carts and wagons had no brakes they were extremely unsafe except on flat surfaces! Worse yet, the front axles on their four-wheeled wagons did not pivot, so they couldn't turn these vehicles but could only drag them around corners.[55] Here again classicists long misled us, perhaps no one more so than the early-nineteenth-century German scholar Johann Ginzrot, whose "illustrations" have appeared in countless books, classical dictionaries, and encyclo-pedias.[56] In his celebrated work *Die Wagen and Fahrwerke* (1817), Ginzrot published superbly detailed drawings of Greek and Roman wagons and their undercarriages, depicting a surprisingly modern swivel to allow the front axle to turn, as well as an excellent braking system. Unfortunately, Ginzrot's scholarly readers ignored his ad-mission that these were drawings "as I imagine it, because I have nowhere found a picture on ancient monuments which would be suitable for this."[57] Indeed, the overwhelming majority of ancient artists lacked any mechanical sense whatever, and their pictures often show wheels without axles or any attachment to the cart body, wheels of different sizes, oxen and horses pulling a wagon without any harnesses, and other obvious errors. These illustrations are not useful. It has taken careful textual analysis and archeological find ings to discover the truth about Roman carts and wagons.

What is apparent, however, is that it was not until the Dark Ages that Europeans developed the means for long-distance overland transportation of heavy and bulky goods. Not only rulers and mu-nicipal councils built roads and bridges; so too did religious houses, merchant guilds, and literally hundreds of private benefactors.[58] It was anonymous medieval innovators who designed wagons with brakes and with front axles that could swivel, and created harnesses that allowed large teams of horses to pull big wagons. With their large round ships, Europeans could also now cope with the At-lantic, opening new and cheaper trade routes from the Italian city-states to England and the Low Countries.

Finally, it was medieval Europeans who invented harnesses and reins that permitted large teams of horses or oxen to be lined up in columns of pairs. Previously, teams of horses or oxen were arranged abreast, which severely limits the number of animals that can be employed. For example, to harness fifty-two oxen abreast is incon-ceivable, but in the eleventh century "ignorant" medieval Europe-ans used a fifty-two-oxen team, harnessed in a column of twenty-six pairs, to move large pieces of marble during the construction of the soaring cathedral in the French village of Conques.[59]

PROGRESS IN HIGH CULTURE

Even if Voltaire, Gibbon, and other proponents of the Enlightenment could be excused for being oblivious to engineering achievements and to innovations in agriculture or commerce, surely they must be judged severely for ignoring or dismissing the remarkable achievements in high culture accomplished by medieval Europeans.

Music. The Romans and Greeks sang and played monophonic music: a single musical line sounded by all voices or instruments. It was medieval musicians who invented polyphony, the simultaneous sounding of two or more musical lines, hence harmonies. Just when this occurred is uncertain, but it was already well known when described in a manual published around 900.[60] Moreover, it was during the Dark Ages that the instruments needed to fully exploit harmonies were perfected: the pipe organ, the clavichord and harpsichord, the violin and bass fiddle among others. And in about the tenth century, an adequate system of musical notation was invented and popularized so that music could be accurately performed by musicians who had never heard it.

Art. Unfortunately, the remarkable artistic era that emerged in eleventh-century Europe is known as Romanesque, despite the fact that it was quite different from anything done by the Romans. This name was imposed by nineteenth-century professors who taught that Europe only recovered from the Dark Ages by *going back* to Roman culture. Hence, this could only have been an era of poor imitations of things Roman. But art historians now acknowledge that Romanesque architecture, sculpture, and painting were original and powerful in ways having nothing in common with Roman art.[61] Then, in the twelfth century, the Romanesque period was followed by the even more original and striking Gothic era. It seems astonishing, but Gothic architecture and painting were scorned by critics during the Enlightenment for not conforming to "the standards of classical Greece and Rome: 'May he who invented it be cursed.' "[62] These same critics mistakenly thought the style originated with the "barbarous" Goths, hence the name, and as anyone who has seen one of Europe's great Gothic cathedrals knows, the artistic judgment of these critics was no better than their history, to say nothing of their disregard for the architectural inventions, including the flying buttress, that made it possible for the first time to build very tall buildings with thin walls and large windows, thus prompting major achievements in stained glass. Finally, artists in northern Europe in the thirteenth century were the first to use oil paint and to put their work on stretched canvas rather than on wood or plaster. This "allowed the painter to take his time, to use brushes of amazing delicacy, to achieve effects . . . which seemed close to miracles."[63] Anyone who thinks that great painting began with the Italian Renaissance should examine the work of the Van Eycks. So much, then, for notions that the millennium following the collapse of Rome was an artistic blank or worse.

Literature. Gibbon wrote *The Decline and Fall of the Roman Empire* in English, not Latin. Voltaire wrote exclusively in French, Cervantes in Spanish, and Machiavelli and da Vinci wrote in Italian. This was possible only because these languages had been given literary form by medieval giants such as Dante, Chaucer, the nameless authors of the chansons de geste, and the monks who, beginning in the ninth century, devoted themselves to writing lives of saints in French.[64] Thus was vernacular prose formulated and popularized. So much for Dark Age illiteracy and ignorance.

Education. When founded by the church early in the twelfth century, the university was something new under the sun—an institution devoted exclusively to higher learning. This Christian invention was quite unlike Chinese academies for training Mandarins or a Zen master's school. The new universities were not primarily concerned with imparting the received wisdom. Rather, just as is the case today, faculty gained fame through innovation. Consequently, medieval university professors gave their primary attention to the pursuit of knowledge. They did not settle for repeating the received wisdom of the Greeks but were fully prepared to criticize and correct the ancients.[65]

The first two universities appeared in Paris and Bologna, in the middle of the twelfth century. Then, Oxford and Cambridge were founded about 1200, followed by a flood of new institutions during the remainder of the thirteenth century: Toulouse, Orléans, Naples, Salamanca, Seville, Lisbon, Grenoble, Padua, Rome, Perugia, Pisa, Modena, Florence, Prague, Cracow, Vienna, Heidelberg, Cologne, Ofen, Erfurt, Leipzig, and Rostock. There is a widespread misconception that these were not really universities but consisted of only three or four teachers and a few dozen students. To the contrary, early in the thirteenth century Paris, Bologna, Oxford, and Toulouse probably enrolled a thousand to fifteen hundred students each—approximately five hundred new students enrolled in the University of Paris every year. As to quality, it was in these same early universities that science was born. Keep in mind that these were deeply Christian institutions: all of the faculty were in holy orders and, consequently, so too were most of the famous early scientists.

Science. For generations, historians claimed that a Scientific Revolution began in the sixteenth century when Nicolaus Copernicus proposed a heliocentric model of the solar system. But what occurred was an evolution, not a revolution.[66] Just as Copernicus simply took the next implicit step in the cosmology of his day, so too the flowering of science in that era was the culmination of the gradual progress that had been made over the previous several centuries. To briefly recapitulate this progression to the heliocentric solar system, it is best to start with the Greeks, who assumed that vacuums were impossible and therefore that space was filled with transparent matter. That being the case, heavenly bodies had to overcome friction in order to keep moving, which in turn required the continuous application of force. Some located this force by conceiving of the heavenly bodies as gods, speeding on their way. Others posited the existence of supernatural beings assigned to push each sphere along.

The need for pushers ended when Jean Buriden (1300–58), rector of the University of Paris, anticipated Newton's First Law of Motion by proposing that space is a vacuum, and that once God had put the heavenly bodies in motion ("impressed an impetus on each"), their motion was "not decreased or corrupted afterwards because there was not inclination of the celestial bodies for other movements. Nor was there resistance which could be corruptive or repressive of that impetus."[67] Buriden also suggested a next step leading to Copernicus's model: that the earth turns on its axis. But it was left for a subsequent rector of the University of Paris to clinch that proposition: Nicole d'Oresme (1325-82), the most brilliant of the Scholastic scientists. His work was remarkably mathematical, thereby setting a high standard for subsequent work in mechanics and astronomy. The idea that the earth turns, rather than that the sun circles the earth, had occurred to many people over the centuries. But two objections had always stood in the way. First, why wasn't there a constant and powerful wind from the east, caused by the rotation of the earth in that direction? Second, why did an arrow shot straight up into the sky not fall well behind (or in front of) the shooter? Since this does not happen, since the arrow comes straight back down, the earth must not turn. Oresme overcame both objections. There is no wind from the east because the motion of the earth is imparted to all objects on the earth or close by, including the atmosphere. That also answers the second objection: arrows shot into the air not only have vertical impetus imposed on them by the bow but also have horizontal impetus conferred on them by the turning earth.

Then came Bishop Nicholas of Cusa (1401-64), who argued that "whether a man is on earth, or the sun, or some other star, it will always seem to him that the position he occupies is the motionless center, and that all other things are in motion." It followed that humans need not trust their perceptions that the earth is stationary; perhaps it isn't. From here it required no leap in the dark to propose that the earth circles the sun.

All of this Dark Age theorizing was well known to Copernicus, who was not an isolated church canon in a remote part of Poland, as he is so often depicted, but one of the best-educated men of his generation, having trained at the Universities of Cracow, Bologna (possibly the best university in Europe), Padua, and Ferrara.

So much progress took place during the so-called Dark Ages that by no later than the thirteenth century, Europe had forged far ahead of Rome and Greece, and ahead of the rest of the world as well.[68] Why? Primarily because Christianity taught that progress was "normal" and that "new inventions would always be forthcoming."[69] This was the revolutionary idea. Nor was faith in progress limited to technology or to high culture. Medieval Europeans were equally attuned to developing *better ways to get things done*.

INVENTING CAPITALISM

Capitalism was not invented in a Venetian countinghouse, let alone in a Protestant bank in Holland. It was evolved, beginning early in the ninth century, by Catholic monks who, despite having put aside worldly things, were seeking to ensure the economic security of their monastic estates. Even more remarkable is the fact that as they developed capitalism, these devout Christians found it necessary to reformulate fundamental doctrines to make their faith compatible with their economic progress. Before taking up these matters, however, it is necessary to turn aside and define precisely what capitalism is.

On Capitalism

Several thousand books have been written about capitalism, but very few authors explain what they mean by that term. This is not because no definition is needed;[70] it is because capitalism is very difficult to define, having originated not as an economic concept but as a pejorative term first used by nineteenth-century leftists to condemn wealth and privilege. Adapting the term for serious analysis is a bit like trying to make a social scientific concept out of "reactionary pig."[71] Even so, no one has dealt with the development of the concept of capitalism and its elusive meanings so well as Fernand Braudel.[72] The term "capital" came into use in the fourteenth century to identify *funds having the capacity to return income,* rather than simply being of consumable value. Thus, in early usage, "capital*ism*" referred to the *use* of wealth (or money) to *earn* wealth (or money). Put another way, the word "capitalism" implied using wealth to provide income with the intention that the initial value of the wealth not be reduced, as with money lent at interest. It is *investment*, the systematic risking of wealth in pursuit of gain, that distinguishes the capitalist from those who merely exact their wealth through rents, taxes, conquest, or banditry. But in addition to being investors, capitalists usually take a more active role in their enterprises as compared with a pure investor such as a moneylender. That is, capitalists tend to invest in *productive activities* whereby new wealth is created. Moreover, capital (or wealth) is not merely money—which is why some prefer the term "capital goods." Factories, land, ships, mines, and warehouses all are obvious capital goods. But it is equally true that for a peasant a cleared plot of ground, tools, and an ox are capital goods in that they can be used to create additional wealth (such as foodstuffs). The same could be said of the spear or club of the Stone Age hunter or the basket carried by his wife when she went gathering. So if we don't want to equate capitalism with any and all human economic activity, the definition must be narrowed. The term "capitalism" implies some degree of *management*, of *supervising* activities (as opposed simply to performing them); and these activities involve *commercial complexity, duration,* and *planning,* as well as a certain degree of *autonomy* in selecting opportunities and directing activities. But even after sketching these many aspects involved in capitalism, Braudel chose not to commit himself to an explicit definition.

Although I am fully aware that it might be good strategy to let readers supply their own meaning of "capitalism," it seems irresponsible to base extended analysis on an undefined term. Therefore: *Capitalism is an economic system wherein privately owned, relatively well organized, and stable firms pursue complex commercial activities within a relatively free (unregulated) market, taking a systematic, long-term approach to investing and reinvesting wealth (directly or indirectly) in productive activities involving a hired workforce, and guided by anticipated and actual returns.*

The phrase "complex commercial activities" implies the use of credit, some degree of diversification, and little reliance on direct producer-to-consumer transactions. The term "systematic" implies adequate accounting practices. "Indirect" investment in productive activities extends the definition to include bankers and passive stockholders. The definition excludes profit-seeking ventures assembled for short-term activities, such as an elite-backed voyage by privateers or a one-shot trade caravan. It also excludes commerce conducted directly by the state or under extensive state control (or exclusive license), such as foreign trade in ancient China or tax farming in medieval Europe. Undertakings based on coerced labor such as Roman slave-based industries are excluded too. Most of all, this definition excludes simple commercial transactions—the buying and selling that has gone on among merchants, traders, and the producers of commodities through the centuries and around the world.

Consistent with this definition, everyone writing on capitalism (whether or not they actually define the term) accepts that it rests upon free markets, secure property rights, and free (uncoerced) labor.[73] Free markets are needed in order for firms to enter areas of opportunity, which is precluded when markets are closed or highly regulated by the state. Only if property rights are secure will people invest in pursuit of greater gains, rather than hide, hoard, or consume their wealth. Uncoerced labor is needed so firms can attract *motivated* workers or dismiss them in response to market conditions. Coerced labor not only lacks motivation but may be difficult to obtain and hard to get rid of. It is the capacity to motivate work and the systematic reinvestment of profits that account for the immense productivity of capitalism, just as both Weber and Marx pointed out more than a century ago.

The Rise of Religious Capitalism

The Bible often condemns greed and wealth—"For the love of money is the root of all evil"[74]—but it does not directly condemn commerce or merchants. However, many of the very early church fathers shared the views prevalent in the Greco-Roman world that commerce is a degrading activity and, at best, involves great moral risk—that it is very difficult to avoid sin in the course of buying and selling.[75] However, soon after the conversion of Constantine (312 C.E.), the church ceased to be dominated by ascetics, and attitudes toward commerce began to mellow, leading Augustine to teach that wickedness was not inherent in commerce but that, as with any occupation, it was up to the individual to live righteously.[76]

Augustine also ruled that price was a function not simply of the seller's costs, but also of the buyer's desire for the item sold. In this way, Augustine gave legitimacy not merely to merchants but to the eventual deep involvement of the church in the birth of capitalism[77] when its earliest forms began to appear in about the ninth century on the great estates belonging to monastic orders. Because of the immense increases in agricultural productivity that resulted from such significant innovations as the switch to horses, the heavy moldboard plow, and the three-field system, the monastic estates were no longer limited to mere subsistence agriculture. Instead, they began to specialize in particular crops or products and to sell these at a profit that allowed them to purchase their other needs, which led them to initiate a cash economy. They also began to reinvest their profits to increase their productive capacity, and as their incomes continued to mount, this led many monasteries to become banks, lending to the nobility. As Randall Collins noted, this was not merely a sort of proto-capitalism involving only the "institutional preconditions for capitalism . . . but a version of the developed characteristics of capitalism itself."[78] Collins referred to this as "religious capitalism,"[79] adding that the "dynamism of the medieval economy was primarily that of the Church."[80]

Throughout the medieval era, the church was by far the largest landowner in Europe, and its liquid assets and annual income far surpassed not only those of the wealthiest king, but probably those of all of Europe's nobility added together.[81] A substantial portion of this wealth flowed into the coffers of the religious orders, much of it in payments and endowments in return for liturgical services— Henry VII of England paid to have ten thousand masses said for his soul.[82] In addition to receiving many gifts of land, most orders reinvested wealth in buying or reclaiming more land, thus initiating an era of rapid growth, which often resulted in extensive property holdings scattered over a large area. Although dwarfed by the huge monastic center at Cluny, which may have had a thousand priories by the eleventh century, many monasteries had established fifty or more outposts.[83] In the twelfth century, under the leadership of Saint Bernard of Clairvaux, the Cistercians protested against the extravagance of Cluny, but being well organized and frugal, they quickly amassed some of the largest estates in Europe—many Cistercian houses farmed 100,000 acres, and one in Hungary had fields totaling 250,000 acres.[84] In addition to gifts, much of this growth was achieved by incorporating previously untilled tracts as well as by clearing forests and draining submerged areas. For example, monks at the monastery of Les Dunes recovered about 25,000 acres of fertile fields from the marshes along the Flanders coast.[85]

This period of great expansion was motivated in part by population growth,[86] and in even greater part by increases in productivity. Until this era the estates were largely self-sufficient—they produced their own food, drink, and fuel; they made their own cloth and tanned their own leather; they maintained a smithy and often even a pottery. But with the great gains in productivity came *specialization* and *trade*. Some estates only produced wine, others only grew several grains, some only raised cattle or sheep—the Cistercians at Fossanova specialized in raising fine horses.[87] Meanwhile, the rapid increase in agricultural surpluses encouraged the founding and growth of towns and cities—indeed, many of the monastic centers themselves became cities. Writing about the great monastery of Saint Gall in Switzerland in 820, Christopher Dawson noted that it was "no longer the simple religious community envisaged by the old monastic rules, but a vast complex of buildings, churches, workshops, store-houses, offices, schools and alms-houses, housing a whole population of dependents, workers and servants like the temple cities of antiquity."[88]

When estates grew into small cities and sustained many scattered outposts, and as they became specialized and dependent on trade, three very important developments occurred. First, they evolved a more sophisticated and farseeing *management*. This was facilitated in the monastic estates by virtue of the fact that, unlike the nobility's, their affairs were not subject to the vagaries of inherited leadership. The essential meritocracy built into the orders could ensure a succession of talented and dedicated administrators having the capacity to pursue plans of long duration. As Georges Duby put it, the new era forced monastic "administrators to turn their attention to the domestic economy, to reckon up, to handle figures, to calculate profits and losses, to think about ways and means of expanding production."[89]

Attendant to specialization was a second development, a shift from a barter to a *cash economy*. It was simply too complicated and unwieldy for a wine-making estate, say, to barter for its other needs, transporting goods hither and yon. It proved far more efficient to sell its wine for cash and then buy whatever was needed from the most convenient and economical sources. Beginning late in the ninth century, the reliance on cash spread rapidly. Perhaps the monks in Lucca (near Florence) were the first to adopt a cash economy, but it was well established across Europe when, in 1247, a Franciscan chronicler wrote of his order's estate in Burgundy that the friars "do not sow or reap, nor do they store anything in barns, but they send wine to Paris, because they have a river right at hand that goes to Paris, and they sell for a good price, from which they get all their food and all of the clothes they wear."[90] In contrast, although the estates of Greco-Roman times (as elsewhere in the world) were expected to produce rents in the form of agricultural surpluses for their rich landlords, they were entirely, or primarily, self-sufficient, subsistence operations. Moreover, they were so unproductive that a wealthy family required huge estates in order to live in style. But even in its earliest stages, capitalism brought immense wealth to orders having only modest fields and flocks.

The third development was *credit*. Barter does not lend itself to credit—to conclude a trade by agreeing to a future payment of three hundred chickens can easily lead to dispute as to the value of the owed poultry: are these to be old hens, roosters, or pullets? But the precise meaning of owing someone two ounces of gold is not in doubt. Not only did the great church estates begin to extend one another monetary credit; as they became increasingly rich they also began to *lend money at interest*, and so did some bishops. During the eleventh and twelfth centuries Cluny lent large sums at interest to various Burgundian nobles,[91] while in 1071 the Bishop of Liège lent the incredible sum of 100 pounds of gold and 175 marks of silver to the Countess of Flanders and subsequently lent 1,300 marks of silver and 3 marks of gold to the Duke of Lower Lorraine. In 1044 the Bishop of Worms lent 20 pounds of gold and a large (unspecified) amount of silver to Emperor Henry III. There were many similar instances—according to surviving records, in this era bishops and monasteries were the usual sources of loans to the nobility.[92] By the thirteenth century, monastic lending often took the form of a *mortgage* (literally, "dead pledge"), wherein the borrower pledged land as security and the lender collected all income from that land during the term of the loan and did not deduct this income from the amount owed. This practice often resulted in additions to the monastery's lands because the monks were not hesitant to foreclose.[93]

But the monks did more than invest in land or lend from their bursting treasuries. They began to leave their fields, vines, and barns and retire into liturgical "work," conducting endless paid masses for souls in purgatory and for living benefactors who wished to improve their fates in the next world. Monks now enjoyed leisure and luxury. The monks at Cluny "were given plentiful and choice foods. Their wardrobe was renewed annually. The manual labor prescribed by the rule [of Saint Benedict] was reduced to entirely symbolic tasks about the kitchen. The monks lived like lords."[94] It was the same in the other great houses. And all of this was possible because the great monasteries began to utilize a *hired labor force,* who were not only more productive than the monks had been[95] but also more productive than tenants required to provide periods of compulsory labor. Indeed, these tenants had long since been satisfying their labor obligations by money payments.[96] Thus, as religious capitalism unfolded, monks still faithfully performed their duties, but aside from those engaged in liturgy, the rest now worked as executives and foremen. In this way, the medieval monasteries came to resemble remarkably modern firms—well administered and quick to adopt the latest technological advances.[97]

The Virtues of Work and Frugality

Traditional societies celebrate consumption while holding work in contempt. This is true not only of the privileged elite but even of those whose days are spent in toil. Notions such as the dignity of labor or the idea that work is a virtuous activity were incomprehensible in ancient Rome or in any other precapitalist society. Rather, just as spending is the purpose of wealth, the preferred approach to work is to have someone else do it and, failing that, to do as little as possible. In China the Mandarins grew their fingernails as long as they could (even wearing silver sheaths to protect them from breaking) in order to make it evident that they did no labor. Conversely, capitalism seems to require and to encourage a remarkably different attitude toward work—to see it as intrinsically virtuous and also to recognize the virtue of restricting one's consumption. Of course, Max Weber identified this as the Protestant ethic, so-called because he believed it to be absent from Catholic culture. But Weber was wrong.

Belief in the virtues of work and of simple living did accompany the rise of capitalism, but this was centuries before Martin Luther was born.[98] Despite the fact that many, perhaps even most, monks and nuns were from the nobility and wealthiest families,[99] they honored work not only in theological terms but by actually doing it. In Randall Collins's words, they "had the Protestant ethic without Protestantism."[100]

The virtue of work was made evident in the sixth century by Saint Benedict, who wrote in his famous rule: "Idleness is the enemy of the soul. Therefore the brothers should have specified periods for manual labor as well as prayerful reading. . . . When they live by the labor of their hands, as our fathers and the apostles did, then they are really monks."[101] Or as Walter Hilton, the English Augustinian, put it in the fourteenth century, "By the discipline of the physical life we are enabled for spiritual effort."[102] It is this commitment to manual labor that so distinguishes Christian asceticism from that found in the other great religious cultures, where piety is associated with rejection of the world and its activities. In contrast with Eastern holy men, for example, who specialize in meditation and live by charity, medieval Christian monastics lived by their own labor, sustaining highly productive estates. This not only prevented "ascetic zeal from becoming petrified in world flight"[103] but sustained a healthy concern with economic affairs. Although the Protestant ethic thesis is wrong, it is entirely legitimate to link capitalism to a Christian ethic.

Thus it was that, beginning in about the ninth century, the growing monastic estates came to resemble "well-organized and stable firms" that "pursued complex commercial activities within a relatively free market," "investing in productive activities involving a hired workforce," "guided by anticipated and actual returns." If this was not capitalism in all its glory, it was certainly close enough. Moreover, these economic activities of the great religious orders made Christian theologians think anew about their doctrines concerning profits and interest. Granted, Augustine had approved profits. But are there no moral limits to profit margins? As for usury, the Bible condemns it; but if interest is forbidden, how can one buy on credit or borrow needed funds?

CAPITALISM AND THEOLOGICAL PROGRESS

Christian theology has never crystallized. If God intends that scripture will be more adequately grasped as humans gain greater knowledge and experience, this warrants continuing reappraisal of doctrines and interpretations. And so it was.

Initial Christian Opposition to Interest and Profits

During the twelfth and thirteenth centuries, Catholic theologians, including Thomas Aquinas, declared that profits were morally legitimate, and while giving lip service to the long tradition of opposition to usury, these same theologians justified interest charges. In this way, the Catholic Church made its peace with early capitalism many centuries before there even were any Protestants.

Christianity inherited opposition to interest (usury) from the Jews. Deuteronomy 23:19–20 admonishes: "You shall not charge interest on loans to another Israelite, interest on money, interest on provisions, interest on anything that is lent. On loans to a foreigner you may charge interest, but on loans to another Israelite you may not charge interest."

That interest could be charged to foreigners explains the role of Jews as moneylenders in Christian societies, a role sometimes imposed on them by Christians in need of funds. (It also had the consequence, usually ignored by historians, that medieval Christians with money to lend often masqueraded as Jews.)[104]

Of course, the prohibition in Deuteronomy did not necessarily bar Christians from charging interest, since they were not Israelites. But the words of Jesus in Luke 6:34–35 were taken to prohibit interest: "If you lend to those from whom you hope to receive, what credit is that to you? Even sinners lend to sinners, to receive as much again. But love your enemies, do good, and lend, expecting nothing in return."

Interest on loans was thus defined as the sin of usury, and widely condemned in principle while pretty much ignored in actual practice. In fact, as already noted, by late in the ninth century some of the great religious houses ventured into banking, and bishops were second only to the nobility in their reliance on borrowed money. In addition to borrowing from monastic orders, many bishops secured loans from private Italian banks that enjoyed the full approval of the Vatican. Hence, in 1229, when the Bishop of Limerick failed to fully repay a loan to a Roman bank, he was excommunicated by the pope until he had negotiated a new agreement under which he ended up paying 50 percent interest over the course of eight years.[105] The need for loans often was so great and so widespread that Italian banks opened branches all across the Continent. In 1231 there were sixty-nine Italian banking houses operating branches in England, and nearly as many in Ireland. Although many bishops, monastic orders, and even the Roman hierarchy ignored the ban on usury, opposition to interest lingered. As late as the Second Lateran Council, in 1139, the church "declared the unrepentant usurer condemned by the Old and New Testaments alike and, therefore, unworthy of ecclesiastical consolations and Christian burial."[106] Nevertheless, documents prove "that in 1215 there were usurers at the Papal Court from which a needy prelate could obtain a loan."[107]

As many of the great Christian monastic orders continued to maximize profits and to lend money at whatever rate of interest the market would bear, they were increasingly subjected to a barrage of condemnations from more traditional clergy, who accused them of the sin of avarice. What was to be done?

Theology of the Just Price and of Legitimate Interest

Obviously, people can't be expected simply to give away the products of their labor. But is there no limit to what they should charge? How can we be sure that an asking price is not sinfully high?

Writing in the thirteenth century, Saint Albertus Magnus proposed that the "just price" is simply what "goods are worth according to the estimation of the market at the time of sale."[108] That is, a price is just if that's what uncoerced buyers are willing to pay. Adam Smith could not have found fault with this definition. Echoing his teacher, but using many more words, Saint Thomas Aquinas began his analysis of just prices by posing the question "Whether a man may lawfully sell a thing for more than it is worth?"[109] He answered by first quoting Augustine that it is natural and lawful for "you wish to buy cheap, and sell dear." Next, Aquinas excluded fraud from legitimate transactions. Finally, he recognized that worth is not really an objective value—"the just price of things is not absolutely definite"—but is a function of the buyer's desire for the thing purchased and the seller's willingness or reluctance to sell, so long as the buyer was not misled, or under duress. To be just, a price had to be the same for all potential buyers at a given moment, thus barring price discrimination. Aquinas's respect for market forces is best revealed by his story about a merchant who brings grain to a country suffering a famine and who knows that other merchants soon will bring much more grain to this area. Is it sinful for him to sell at the prevailing, high market price, or should he inform the buyers that soon more grain will arrive, thus causing the price to decline? Aquinas concluded that this merchant can, in good conscience, keep quiet and sell at the current high price.

As to interest on loans, Aquinas was unusually confusing. In some writings he condemned all interest as the sin of usury; in other passages he accepted that lenders deserve compensation, although he was fuzzy as to how much and why.[110] However, prompted by the realities of a rapidly expanding commercial economy, many of Aquinas's contemporaries, especially the canonists, were not so cautious but began discovering many exceptions wherein interest charges were not usurious.[111] For example, if a productive property such as an estate is given as security for a loan, the lender may take all of the production during the period of the loan and not deduct it from the amount owed.[112] Many other exclusions involved the costs to the lender of not having the money available for other commercial opportunities, such as buying goods for resale or acquiring new fields. Since these alternative opportunities for profit are entirely licit, it is licit to compensate a lender for having to forgo them.[113] In this same spirit it was deemed proper to charge interest for goods bought on credit.[114] As for banks, aside from the exemptions just noted, they did not make straight loans at a fixed rate of interest since these would have been deemed usurious on grounds that there was no "adventure of the principal." The notion was that interest was legitimate only if the amount yielded was uncertain in advance, being subject to "adventure." But it took very little finesse for bankers to evade this prohibition by trading notes, bills of exchange, or even currencies in ways that seemed adventuresome but that in fact had entirely predictable returns and thus constituted loans and produced the equivalent of interest.[115] Thus, while the sin of usury remained on the books, so to speak, "usury" had become essentially an empty term.

So by no later than the thirteenth century, the leading Christian theologians had fully debated the primary aspects of emerging capitalism—profits, property rights, credit, lending, and the like. As Lester K. Little summed up: "In each case they came up with generally favorable, approving views, in sharp contrast to the attitudes that had prevailed for six or seven centuries right up to the previous generation."[116] Capitalism was fully and finally freed from all fetters of faith.[117]

It was a remarkable shift. These were, after all, theologians who had separated themselves from the world. Most of them had taken vows of poverty. Most of their predecessors had held merchants and commercial activities in contempt. Had asceticism truly prevailed in the religious orders, it seems most unlikely that Christian disdain for and opposition to commerce would have mellowed, let alone have been radically transformed. This theological revolution was the result of direct experience with worldly imperatives. For all their genuine acts of charity, monastic administrators were not about to give all their wealth to the poor or to sell their products at cost. It was the active participation of the great houses in free markets that caused monastic theologians to reconsider the morality of commerce, which was abetted by the marked worldliness of the church hierarchy.

Unlike those in the religious orders, few holding higher church positions had taken vows of poverty and many displayed a decided taste for profligate living. Bishops and cardinals were among the very best clients of usurers. That is not surprising since nearly everyone holding an elite church position had purchased his office as an investment, anticipating a substantial return from church revenues. Indeed, men often were able to buy appointments as bishops or even cardinals without having held any prior church positions, sometimes before they were ordained, or even baptized![118] This aspect of the medieval church was an endless source of scandal and conflict, spawning many heretical mass sect movements and culminating in the Reformation. But these worldly aspects of the church paid serious dividends in the development of capitalism. The church didn't stand in the way—rather it both justified and took an active role in the Commercial Revolution of the twelfth and thirteenth centuries.[119] Had this not occurred, the West may have ended up much like the nations of Islam.

ISLAM AND INTEREST

The Qur'an condemns all interest (*riba*) on borrowed money. Profit on exchanges of goods and services is licit, but exchanges of money as in lending and repaying loans are legal only when the sums lent and repaid are the same. As the Qur'an advises (2:275): "God has permitted trade and forbidden *riba*."

As in Christendom, medieval Muslims often ignored prohibitions on lending money at interest, but almost exclusively to fund consumption, not as investments.[120] That may explain why lending activities did not lead to theological reinterpretation and *riba* remained officially sinful. Maxime Rodinson suggests that Islam did not reconsider its economic rules because the elite held commerce in contempt and because state interference so limited and distorted the economy that nothing like the pressure for theological change that built up in Europe ever developed in Islam. Indeed, the elite no doubt favored keeping their creditors in potential religious jeopardy and having a legitimate basis for settling their debts by usurpation. In any event, even today banks exist in Islamic societies only by means of extremely cumbersome work-arounds[121] of the absolute prohibition of usury, which remains defined as any compensation given in return for a loan. A frequent modern solution to the prohibition of interest involves banks going into business partnership with those to whom they advance commercial loans. This allows loans to be repaid for no more than the sum borrowed, while the reward for lending (the interest) comes from shared profits. Another ploy is to charge extensive fees for servicing loans. Even so, the huge fortunes produced by petroleum have mostly taken refuge in Western investments, rather than financed domestic economic development. Religious opposition to interest, combined with the avarice of repressive regimes, prevented capitalism from arising in Islam, and still does. Victories of reason have yet to be won.

The path to modern times did not suddenly open during the Renaissance any more than it sprang from the forehead of Zeus. Western civilization arose progressively over many centuries subsequent to the fall of Rome: the so-called Dark Ages were a period of profound enlightenment in both the material and the intellectual spheres, which when combined with Christian doctrines of moral equality, created a whole new world based on political, economic, and personal freedom.

CHAPTER THREE

Tyranny and the "Rebirth" of Freedom

THE SUCCESS OF THE WEST DEPENDED ON THE DEVELOPMENT OF free societies able to provide secure havens for early capitalism. Here too, Christianity played the key role, providing a moral basis for democracy far beyond anything envisioned by classical philosophers.

This chapter begins by exploring how tyrannies stifle economic development. Next, it examines basic Christian doctrines that assert human moral equality while denouncing despots. These doctrines take life as the chapter explores the appearance of relatively independent communities in various parts of Europe and demonstrates how an initial degree of freedom allowed emerging merchant, commercial, labor, and religious groups to gain a substantial voice in governance.

COMMAND ECONOMIES

Despotic states produce universal avarice. When rulers concentrate on exacting the maximum amount from those they control, their subjects become notably avaricious too, and respond by consuming, hoarding, and hiding the fruits of their labor, and by failing to produce nearly as much as they might. And even when some people do manage to be productive, chances are that in the end their efforts will merely enrich their rulers. The result is a standard of living far below the society's potential productive capacities.

Late in the tenth century, an iron industry began to develop in parts of northern China.[1] By 1018, it has been estimated, the smelters were producing more than thirty-five thousand tons a year, an incredible achievement for the time, and sixty years later they may have been producing more than a hundred thousand tons. This was not a government operation. Private individuals had seized the opportunity presented by a strong demand for iron and the supplies of easily mined ore and coal. With the smelters and foundries located along a network of canals and navigable rivers, the iron could be easily brought to distant markets. Soon these new Chinese iron industrialists were reaping huge profits and reinvesting heavily in the expansion of their smelters and foundries. Production continued to rise rapidly. The availability of large supplies of iron soon led to the introduction of iron agricultural tools, which in turn rapidly increased food production. In short, China began to develop capitalism and enter an industrial revolution. But then it all stopped, as suddenly as it had begun. By the end of the eleventh century, only tiny amounts of iron were produced, and soon after that the smelters and foundries were abandoned ruins. What had happened?

Eventually, Mandarins at the imperial court had noticed that some commoners were getting rich by manufacturing and were hiring peasant laborers at high wages. They deemed such activities to be threats to Confucian values and social tranquillity. Commoners must know their place; only the elite should be wealthy. So, they declared a state monopoly on iron and seized everything. And that was that. As Winwood Reade summed up, the reason for China's many centuries of economic and social stagnation is plain: *"Property is insecure. In this one phrase the whole history of Asia is contained."*[2]

An equally astonishing example was revealed in the aftermath of the battle of Lepanto (1571), wherein Europeans smashed an Ottoman fleet.[3] Victorious Christian sailors looting the Turkish vessels still afloat or gone aground discovered an enormous fortune in gold coins in the *Sultana,* the captured flagship of Ali Pasha, the Ottoman commander. Fortunes nearly as huge were found in the galleys of several other Muslim admirals. As Victor David Hanson explained, "Without a system of banking, fearful of confiscation should he displease the sultan, and always careful to keep his assets hidden from the tax collectors, Ali Pasha toted his huge personal fortune to Lepanto."[4] Ali Pasha was not a peasant hiding harvest surplus but a member of the upper elite, married to the sultan's sister. If such a person could find no safe investments and dared not even leave his money at home, how could anyone else hope to do better?

No wonder that progress is slow and uneven within despotic states. For it is not only portable wealth such as Ali Pasha's that is in danger of being confiscated by the state; anything of value—land, crops, livestock, buildings, even children—can be arbitrarily seized, and as the Chinese iron magnates learned, it often is. Worse yet, the tyrannical state invests very little of the wealth it extracts to increase production but consumes it instead—often in various forms of display. The Egyptian pyramids, the Tuileries, and the Taj Mahal were all built as beautiful monuments to repressive rule; they were without productive value, and were paid for by misery and want. This is why the economic system of despotic states has come to be known as the "command economy"[5]—both markets and labor are commanded and coerced rather than allowed to function freely, and the exaction and consumption of wealth is the primary goal of the state.

Command economies began with the earliest states and have lasted in many parts of the modern world—indeed, command economies still attract ardent advocates.[6] But command economies neglect the most basic economic fact of life: *all wealth derives from production*. It must be grown, dug up, cut down, hunted, herded, fabricated, or otherwise created. The amount of wealth produced within any society depends not only on the number of people involved in production but on their motivation and the effectiveness of their productive technology. When wealth is subject to devastating taxes and the constant threat of usurpation, the challenge is to *keep* one's wealth, not to make it productive. This principle applies not merely to the wealthy but with even greater force to those with very little—which accounts for the substantial underproduction of command economies. Faced with exorbitant taxes to enrich the few, even free peasants become far more concerned to hide portions of their crops than to increase their yields, while those engaged in forced labor—be they slaves or peasants required to provide an annual period of free labor—can benefit only to the extent that they manage to do as little as possible. As for the rich and powerful, they typically sneer at those who, despite the hazards and handicaps involved, manage to keep the economy afloat.

In 829 Emperor Theophilus of Byzantium watched a beautiful merchant ship sail into the harbor of Constantinople. When he asked who owned the ship, he was enraged to learn it belonged to his wife. He snarled at her, "God made me an emperor, you would make me a ship captain!" and ordered that the ship be burned at once. For centuries, Byzantine historians praised Theophilus for this act.[7] The classical philosophers would have done so too.

Aristotle condemned commercial trade as unnatural, unnecessary, and inconsistent with "human virtue."[8] Thus, he proposed that the agora be merely a meeting place, not a market—that it "should be clear of all merchandise, and neither a workingman nor a farmer nor any other such person should be permitted to enter unless summoned by the magistrates."[9] Aristotle also held that exchanges should occur only among people who have a binding social relationship and should always eventuate in reciprocal value—as though values were as intrinsic to goods as their color or weight.

Aristotle's was not a voice in the wilderness; this was the conventional view in Greece. Labor was for slaves and commerce was for noncitizens. Even when citizens invested in land, they were, according to M. I. Finley, motivated by "considerations of status, not maximization of profits." Finley reported that there is absolutely no mention in any of the original Greek sources of any investment (including loans) for improvements in land or for manufacturing, in contrast with the "considerable evidence of relatively large-scale borrowing for conspicuous consumption and for expensive political obligations."[10]

Although the Roman elite often dabbled in commerce and lent one another money at interest,[11] their attitudes were much like Aristotle's. A law proclaimed by Constantius noted, "Let no one aspire to enjoy any standing or rank who is of the lowest merchants, the money-changers, lowly officers or foul agents of some service, all offscourings of offices and supported on assorted disgraceful profits."[12] For Plutarch, the issue was not the moral standing of commerce but that *all* activities devoted to needs and practical matters are "ignoble and vulgar."[13] And Cicero wrote with contempt that "there is nothing noble about a workshop."[14]

Consequently, the fall of Rome was not a tragic setback; had the empire prevailed, there would be nothing to call Western Civilization. If Rome still ruled, Europe would be mired in a brutal command economy, there would have been very little innovation of any kind, and the rest of the world probably would be much as Europeans found it in the fifteenth and sixteenth centuries. Empires are the enemies of progress!

F. A. Hayek explained: "Nothing is more misleading . . . than the conventional formulae of historians who represent the achievement of a powerful state as the culmination of cultural evolution: it often marked its end." He specifically noted that "the expansion of capitalism—and European civilization—owes its origins and *raison d'être* to political anarchy."[15] Where no repressive imperial structures prevailed in Europe, small political units emerged that often tended to be quite responsive to various internal interest groups, including merchants, manufacturers, and the workers' guilds. Geography played a major role in the disunity of Europe, but of course, it had no direct effects on the evolution of political theories or on the establishment of democratic regimes. As with so many other aspects of medieval history, Christian theology provided the intellectual basis for experiments with political freedom.

THEOLOGICAL FOUNDATIONS OF MORAL EQUALITY

An immense amount is being written nowadays about equality, but almost without exception it is concerned entirely with equality of outcomes. Is affirmative action desirable? Should tax policies embrace distributive justice? It has been a long time since much was written about whether there is any basis for saying that in some sense human beings *are* or *deserve to be* equals.[16] "This proposition is for the most part assumed to be self-evident. Where proof is attempted, it adds nothing of substance."[17] Yet through most of human history and in many parts of the world even now, this is not assumed! To the contrary, in most times and places, any expression of belief in equality would provoke scorn. Even in the West, no sensible person argues that everyone is equal in terms of abilities, diligence, or character; the assumption is that there exists a *moral equality* that takes precedence. It is belief in moral equality that has informed Western political and legal practices guaranteeing equality before the law and many other forms of equal rights.

To the extent that participants in controversies over equality of outcomes take any interest in the origins of the assumption of moral equality, they mostly trace it to "secular" political theorists who wrote during the eighteenth-century Enlightenment or even later—many are content simply to attribute it to "liberalism."[18] Many also express admiration for John Locke's seventeenth-century works as a major source for modern democratic theory, seemingly without the slightest awareness that Locke explicitly based his entire thesis on Christian doctrines concerning moral equality.[19] Most textbook accounts of the birth of our nation now carefully ignore the religious aspect, as if a bunch of skeptics had written these famous lines from the Declaration of Independence: "We hold these truths to be self-evident, that all men are created equal, that they are endowed by their Creator with certain unalienable Rights, that among these are Life, Liberty, and the pursuit of Happiness."

Nor will it do to attribute the "rebirth" of democracy in some medieval European states to the influence of newly recovered Greek philosophy. While the classical world did provide examples of democracy, these were not rooted in any general assumptions concerning equality beyond an equality of the elite. Even when they were ruled by elected bodies, the various Greek city-states and Rome were sustained by huge numbers of slaves. And just as it was Christianity that eliminated the institution of slavery inherited from Greece and Rome, so too does Western democracy owe its essential intellectual origins and legitimacy to Christian ideals, not to any Greco-Roman legacy. It all began with the New Testament.

Jesus asserted a revolutionary conception of moral equality, not only in words but in deeds. Over and over again he ignored major status boundaries and associated with stigmatized people, including Samaritans, publicans, immoral women, beggars, and various other outcasts, thereby giving divine sanction to spiritual inclusiveness. And it was precisely in this spirit that Paul admonished: "There is neither Jew nor Greek, there is neither bond nor free, there is neither male nor female: for ye are all one in Christ Jesus."[20] How could this be? Paul hardly meant that there were no Christian slaves or that women had the same rights as men. What he meant was that, regardless of worldly inequalities, there is no inequality in the most important sense: in the eyes of God and in the life to come. Indeed, Paul warned slave masters of this very point when he admonished them to treat their slaves well, since "he who is both their Master and yours is in heaven, and there is no partiality with him."[21] In that statement, as in many others in the New Testament, Paul makes it clear that equality in the eyes of God has implications for how people ought to be treated in this world, as Jesus demonstrated.

Thus was the pattern set. In an extremely status-conscious Roman world, early Christians strove to embrace a universalistic conception of humanity. This was fully elaborated by the third-century Christian theologian L. Caecilius Firmianus Lactantius in his remarkable *Divine Institutes:*

The second constituent of Justice is *equality*. I mean this . . . in the sense of treating others as one's equals. . . . For God who gives being and life to men wished us all to be equal. . . . But someone will say, "Don't you have poor and rich, slaves and masters in your community?" "Aren't there distinctions between one member and another?" Not at all! This is precisely the reason that we address one another as "Brother," since we believe we are one another's equals. Since human worth is measured in spiritual not in physical terms, we ignore our various physical situations: slaves are not slaves to us, but we treat them and address them as brothers in the spirit, fellow slaves in devotion to God. Wealth, too, is no ground for distinction, except insofar as it provides the opportunity for preeminence in good works. To be rich is not a matter of *having,* but of *using* riches for the tasks of justice. . . . Yet although our attitude of humility makes us one another's equals, free and slave, rich and poor, there are, in fact, distinctions which God makes, distinctions in virtue, that is: the juster the higher. For if justice means behaving as the equal of inferiors, then, although it is *equality* that one excels in, yet by conducting oneself not merely as the equal of one's inferiors, but as their subordinate, one will attain a far *higher* rank of dignity in God's sight . . . if we are all given a life of soul and spirit by one God, what are we but brothers—closer, indeed, as soul brothers than as physical brothers?[22]

From here it was but a very short step to suggest that each individual has rights that must not be infringed upon without due cause: doctrines of equality before the law and the security of one's home and property. Such doctrines were, of course, anathema to despots.

PROPERTY RIGHTS

The Bible takes private property rights for granted, often condemning infringements such as theft or fraud. Even so, some of the early church fathers, including Saint Ambrose, only grudgingly accepted private property rights, claiming that God had originally intended that all things be held in common and that private property came into existence only because of the fall from grace, thereby being a product of sin. However, Saint Augustine regarded private property as a natural condition. And over the next several centuries, this became the prevalent view. By late in the eleventh century, the writer known only as Norman Anonymous wrote in one of his thirty-four influential tracts that private property is a human *right*: "God has made poor and rich from the one and the same clay; poor and rich are supported on one and the same earth. It is by human right that we say 'My estate, my house, my servant.' "[23] A century later, Giles of Rome charged rulers with the duty to defend private property: "It will be the duty of the earthly power to do justice in these respects, so that no one may injure another in his own body or in his own property, but every citizen and every faithful man may enjoy his goods."[24] Giles's contemporary John of Paris argued that private property is necessary for the maintenance of civil order: "For if things were held unreservedly in common, it would not be easy to

keep peace among men. It was for this reason that private possession of property was instituted."[25]

At about the same time Saint Albertus Magnus said private property existed for "the convenience and utility of man."[26] Thomas
Aquinas added his immense authority to that position, asserting
that "private ownership is both legitimate and necessary." Aquinas
justified this statement by noting that private property contributes
to the common good. "Firstly, because everyone takes more care of
things for which he is privately responsible than of things held
in common, the responsibility for which is left to the next man.
Secondly, because human affairs are more efficiently organized
when each person has his own distinct responsibility to discharge.
Thirdly, because there is a greater chance of keeping the peace when
everyone is content with his own matters."[27] Finally, Aquinas noted
that although private property is not ordained by divine law, it is in
accord with natural law—that is, inherent in human nature as derived through reason.

Of course, given the celebration of poverty in some of the religious orders, not even Aquinas could extinguish all support for the
idea that there should be no private property. However, in 1323 Pope
John XXII condemned as heretical the Franciscan claim that Jesus
advocated that all things be owned in common and that only by
embracing poverty could one truly imitate Christ.[28] And that was
that, so far as official Catholicism was concerned—although the
communal ideal lives on in radical doctrines, both secular and religious.

Christian theologians were not content merely to legitimate private property. Pursuing the logical implications of the right of
private property led William of Ockham and other theologians to
conclude that since it is a *right* that *precedes* the laws imposed by any
sovereign, rulers cannot usurp or arbitrarily seize the property of
those over whom they rule. A sovereign can infringe on private
property only when "he shall see that the common welfare takes
preference over private interest." But "he cannot do this at his own
arbitrary discretion."[29]

Ockham wrote this shortly after the Magna Charta was imposed in 1215 on King John by a coalition of British nobles and church officials, including all of the bishops and the master of the Knights Templar. In fact, the first article "confirmed . . . for ever that the English church shall be free, and shall have its rights undiminished and its liberties unimpaired." The next several articles consist of a long and detailed list of property rights and prohibit all forms of royal usurpation. Then, Article 13 guarantees that "the city of London shall have all its ancient liberties and free customs . . . [and] that all other cities, boroughs, towns, and ports shall have all their liberties and free customs." Here "customs" does not refer to social conventions but to import duties and taxes. Article 40 affirms: "All merchants shall be able to go out of and come into England safely and securely and stay and travel throughout England . . . free from evil tolls, except in time of war." In Article 61 the king agrees that the barons "shall choose any twenty-five barons of the kingdom they wish, who must with all their might observe, hold and cause to be observed, the peace and liberties which we have granted and confirmed them by this present charter." The House of Lords was thereby created. Finally, in Article 62 the king pardons everyone, "clergy and laity," who had been involved in imposing these concessions upon him. Thus did cross and sword combine to begin taming the state and to give the English individual freedoms and secure property rights far beyond anything known on the continent of Europe at that time.

LIMITING STATES AND KINGS

Muhammad was not only the Prophet, he was head of state. Consequently, Islam has always idealized the fusion of religion and political rule, and sultans usually have also held the title of caliph. As Bernard Lewis put it, "At no time did [Muhammad and his successors] create any institution corresponding to, or even remotely resembling, the church in Christendom"[30]—an Islam separate from the state. Lewis is also right to assert that the idea of a separation of church and state "is, in a profound sense, Christian."[31] In most other civilizations religion was so much an aspect of the state that rulers often were regarded as divine—many Roman emperors claimed to be gods, as did the pharaohs, without whose daily intercession, it was thought, the sun would not rise.

Separation of church and state was stipulated by Jesus: "Render therefore unto Caesar the things which are Caesar's; and unto God the things that are God's."[32] Perhaps if Christianity had begun as a faith of the Roman senatorial class, it might have taken a different tack. But having suffered for several centuries as a group of sometimes persecuted outsiders, the church never fully embraced the state. Granted that some church fathers gladly enjoyed monopoly status based on state repression of all religious competitors, and uniformly proclaimed the superior authority of church to state, but they were generally content to leave political power to secular rulers—although when a city grew up around a bishop's palace, he sometimes took the role of prince-bishop.

However, although Paul had argued that Christians must always obey secular rulers, no matter how evil, unless they were ordered to violate a commandment, once the threat of persecution no longer hung over them, Christian theologians became increasingly critical of the moral authority of the state. In *The City of God*, Augustine revealed that while the state was essential for an orderly society, it still was lacking in fundamental legitimacy:

What are kingdoms but great robberies? For what are robberies themselves, but little kingdoms? The band itself is made up of men; it is ruled by the authority of a prince, it is knit together by the pact of the confederacy; the booty is divided by the law agreed on. If, by the admittance of abandoned men, this evil increases to such a degree that it holds places, fixes abodes, takes possession of cities, and subdues people, it assumes more plainly the name of a kingdom, because reality is now manifestly conferred on it, not by the removal of covetousness, but by the addition of impunity. Indeed, that was the apt and true reply which was given to Alexander the Great by a pirate who had been seized. For when the king had asked the man what he meant by keeping hostile possession of the sea, he answered with bold pride, "What thou meanest by seizing the whole earth; but because I do it in a petty ship, I am called a robber, whilst thou who dost it with a great fleet art styled emperor."[33]

This "shocking realism"[34] has often surprised and even upset Augustine's readers. But given the immense authority of the writer, this view shaped Christian political sensibilities ever after: Christian writers could not condemn suggestions for improving the state, or even for dispensing with monarchies. An extremely important step in that direction involved the vigorous rejection of the notion of the "divine right" of kings—silly textbooks to the contrary, although such claims were sometimes asserted by kings, they were *not* ratified by the church.[35] Moreover, by affirming the secularity of kingship, the church made it possible to examine the basis of worldly power and the interplay of rights and rule. Late in the fourteenth century, John Wycliffe pointed out that if kings were chosen by God and ruled with divine rights, then God must assist and approve the sins of tyrants—"a blasphemous conclusion!"[36] Hence, it was not a sin to depose tyrants.

This had already been admitted a century earlier by Aquinas, if rather grudgingly. Having warned of the many perils of acting to remove a tyrant, including the fact that all too often an even worse tyranny results, Aquinas wrote in *On Kingship*: "If to provide itself with a king belongs to the right of a given multitude, it is not unjust that the king be deposed or have his power restricted by that same multitude if, becoming a tyrant, he abuses his royal power." However, Aquinas counseled that "a scheme should be carefully worked out which would prevent the multitude ruled by a king from falling into the hands of a tyrant."[37] And that's precisely what the multitudes in various small European states began to work out: schemes to prevent tyranny. In addition to theological justifications for resisting tyrants, Europeans also benefited from inherent disunity.

EUROPEAN DISUNITY

Rome was essentially a waterfront empire encircling the Mediterranean. True, Caesar did cross the channel and colonize Britain. But even there, Hadrian had to build a wall to isolate the fierce tribes of the north. Much the same happened on the Continent. Romans seldom crossed the Rhine, nor did they venture often or far across the Danube. It is uncertain that Spain or the Levant would have been part of the empire had the legions been required to invade and sustain their rule entirely by land. In any event, most of western Europe never was ruled by Rome. Geographical and cultural impediments limited the scope of the empire.

Much has been written about the political disunity of Europe, but rarely is geography as such taken into account, even though one could sit down with a relief map of Europe and do quite well at drawing in the areas sustaining a self-conscious "nationalism." Indeed, the map of medieval European "states" looks remarkably like a map of hunting-and-gathering cultures in Europe about five thousand years ago.[38] The reason is that, unlike China or India, for example, Europe is not one large plain but a multitude of fertile valleys surrounded by mountains and dense forests, each often serving as the core area of an independent state.[39] Wherever geographic barriers limit communications, cultural diversity always arises. European cultural diversity was also increased by many different waves of "barbarian" migration. In this sense, then, the disunity of Europe is both cultural and natural.

Europe's diversity resulted in many very *small* political units: "statelets" might be the appropriate term. Only the few large plains, such as those surrounding Paris and London, sustained somewhat larger political entities; most of the rest varied between small and tiny. During the fourteenth century there were about a thousand independent statelets in Europe.[40] This proliferation had several very important consequences. First, it tended to make for weak rulers. Second, it provided for creative competition. Third, it offered people some opportunity to depart for a setting more suitable in terms of liberty or opportunity.[41] Consequently, some of these statelets began to develop highly responsive governments. This story begins in about the ninth century in northern Italy.

COMMERCE AND THE CREATION OF RESPONSIVE ITALIAN REGIMES

No despots ruled Rome in the days of the republic. It is thus fitting that when responsive governments first reappeared in Europe, they did so in Italy. Although Christian theology provided the moral basis for the establishment of responsive regimes, these ideals were achieved in only some parts of Christendom. Why were these particular medieval Italian city-states the first to achieve them? There were two major factors. First was their ability to play off imperial, papal, and Byzantine ambitions, and so to establish and maintain their *independence*. Second was their leadership in a rapidly expanding foreign trade that resulted in the *dispersion of political power* among a set of well-matched interest groups: not only the aristocracy, the military, and the clergy but also merchants, bankers, manufacturers, and the workers' guilds. The most revealing and interesting way to examine these developments is by case studies of the big four city-states of northern Italy: Venice, Genoa, Florence, and Milan (see Map 3-1).[42] Similar developments took place in dozens of other, smaller city-states in this region.

What follows is an account not of the rise of capitalism in Italy but of how these city-states achieved relatively democratic regimes, since that was a necessary precondition for the development of capitalism. Some mention of industrial and commercial affairs also must be included because they were vital to the achievement of political freedom.

Venice

Venice began as an offshore village of seafarers, situated on a marshy maze of dozens of islands—an easily defended spot. In 568 the Lombard invasion of Italy produced a rapid migration from the mainland, as "men of wealth moved their residence to the lagoons taking with them their dependents and as much as they could of their property."[43] There, shielded by remarkable natural barriers and with an unimpeded access to the sea, the growing city was able to forestall all Lombard efforts to subordinate it. Indeed, having access to the sea, the Venetians were able to claim to be a province of the Eastern Roman, or Byzantine, empire. This gave them many commercial advantages, such as being free from Byzantine tolls or customs in their trade with the East. But distance, and growing Venetian sea power, made Byzantium's sovereignty over Venice

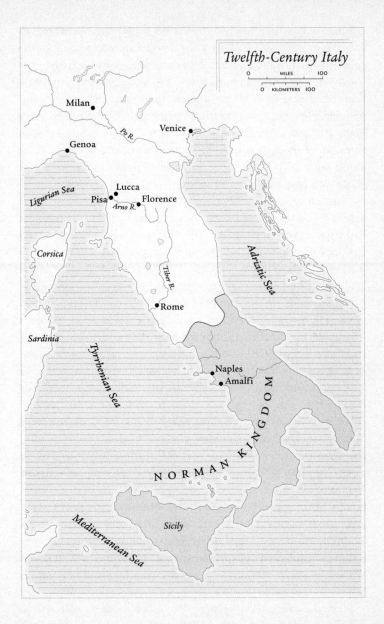

Twelfth-Century Italy

Milan

Po R.

Venice

Genoa

Ligurian Sea

Lucca

Pisa

Florence

Arno R.

Corsica

Tiber R.

Rome

Sardinia

Tyrrhenian Sea

Adriatic Sea

Naples

Amalfi

NORMAN KINGDOM

Sicily

Mediterranean Sea

MAP 3-1

nominal at best. In 810, when the Franks replaced the Lombards as the rulers over much of Italy, they too attempted to conquer the coastal area including Venice. But the marshes and lagoons were too much for them, and in addition, the Byzantine emperor sent a fleet to the support of his province. By now, Venice had become immensely important to Byzantium as its main outlet in the West, made ever more significant as Islam developed a trading network throughout the region, including Spain, Sicily, and the toe of Italy, along with North Africa. Nevertheless, Byzantium's rule over Venice was only a convenient fiction, soon to be discarded.

What emerged was a city populated with an abundance of families who had legitimate claims to noble status but who no longer had rural estates to support them with rents, and who had seized the opportunity to engage in commerce, probably making Venice the first society to live by trade alone.[44] And in the beginning, it was trade, pure and simple, since Venice did not produce any of the principal goods and commodities involved but transported cargoes of salt, grain, woolen cloth, and metals gathered elsewhere to North Africa and the Near East, bringing back silks and spices, most of which were reexported to other Italian cities and to northern Europe. Eventually, however, as Venetian traders considered their business opportunities, it became obvious that more money was to be made if they were not only the middlemen but the actual producers of their exports. For example, why sell only woolen cloth from northern Europe? Why not import fleeces and make their own woolens? And why only wool? With remarkable speed Venice assembled a large and very profitable textile industry, producing woolen, cotton, and silk cloth. Once it had begun along this path, Venice rapidly became a major manufacturer, producing eyeglasses, dyes, glass panes, blown glass, crystal, dishes, iron, brass, jewelry, shoes, weapons, hemp ropes, and leather goods. Industrialization had profound political effects by greatly expanding the independent power centers in a community that already enjoyed substantial democracy.

Since the days of Charlemagne, Venice had been recognized as a dukedom and was administered by a duke, known as the doge. But Venice was unlike most other dukedoms in several ways. For one thing, the doge was not sustained by taxes or rents but owed his wealth to his active participation in commerce. The earliest known medieval reference to a monetary investment was in the will of Doge Giustiniano Partecipazio. When he died in 829, his estate included twelve hundred pounds of "working *solidi,* if they come back safely from sea."[45] Second, unlike in other dukedoms, the position of doge was not hereditary (although sons sometimes followed their fathers). According to Venetian tradition, even the very first doge was chosen by the "people," and Venetians had enjoyed substantial political freedom from earliest days. Whether or not this was true, as far back as reliable records go, the doge was elected. And even if the people did not include all inhabitants of Venice, they did make up a substantial number of them—all those having wealth, military responsibilities, or business establishments, or who were members of the clergy. And as time passed, the people became an increasingly inclusive group, incorporating representatives of the various craft and trade guilds, grown increasingly large and powerful due to the city's rapid industrial growth. Meanwhile, the power of the doge was gradually reduced as elected councils took greater authority, leading to what came to be known as the "commune"— made up of the body of citizens with voting rights and the executives and legislators elected by them.

Venice was not the first Italian city-state to develop a commune; that honor may belong to Pisa.[46] But by the middle of the twelfth century, Venice's commune was in full operation, with five layers of government.[47] At the apex of this pyramid was the doge—a chief executive elected for life but without regal pretensions, his powers being carefully limited by his oath of office. Below the doge was the Ducal Council, made up of six members, each representing a geographical area of Venice. Councillors were elected to serve a one-year term and could not be reelected until they had been out of office for two years. The councillors worked in constant and close consultation with the doge, who was required to gain their assent for major decisions. Beneath the Council were the Forty and the Senate. The Forty were akin to a court of appeals, while the Senate consisted of sixty men who were particularly concerned with issues of commerce and foreign policy. The Forty and the Senate were selected from the Great Council (sometimes by election, sometimes by drawing lots), which also elected fleet commanders. Members of the Great Council, which often numbered more than a thousand, were selected from the General Assembly, which consisted of all the thousands of voting Venetians. The General Assembly met irregularly, being summoned to ratify basic legislation and the choice of a new doge. When a doge died in 1071, "countless boats bringing Venetians from all over the lagoons gathered,"[48] and a new doge was agreed upon without any member setting foot on land.

In early days, participation in Venetian politics was limited to various elites, but as time passed, and especially as Venice became a major manufacturing center as well as a major trading port, the franchise was extended. The principal mechanism by which this was accomplished was by the organization of *guilds*—associations or unions of persons engaged in a specific craft or trade. Guilds appeared all over medieval Europe and often served to impose standard fees or wages and to control entry into a particular line of work. Some guilds were made up of lawyers or physicians—prostitutes sometimes had their own guild too. In Venice, as in much of western Europe, many of the guilds represented very highly skilled craftspeople, such as glassblowers, apothecaries, jewelers, tailors, furriers, and organ makers, but even more mundane trades had their guilds too, including butchers, bakers, barbers, and sailmakers. Guilds also united various groups of shopkeepers. Being well organized and possessed of financial resources, the guilds became such a significant political force that they were assigned representation in the councils; thus the masses were given a significant voice in government. To this was added the influence of religious *confraternities,* lay fellowships that featured religious devotions but that also provided for mutual aid, rather like modern fraternal lodges. Some of these confraternities were restricted to persons of various occupations, but others seem to have been open to anyone of good reputation, both rich and poor. In any event, guilds and confraternities effectively mobilized large segments of an urban population, and within the contexts of democratic states, they achieved substantial political influence.

Venice and the other leading medieval Italian city-states were by modern standards medium-sized towns—in the year 1000, Venice had a population of about thirty thousand, and the other three of the big four were considerably smaller.[49] Everyone knew everyone else, current public opinion was quite transparent, and consensus often was easily achieved. This, combined with relatively open political institutions, allowed Venice to sustain a substantial degree of freedom and responsive governance. The secret to it all was a rapidly expanding economy that not only resulted in a few great fortunes but created large numbers of families having considerable means, and brought previously undreamed of affluence to nearly everyone.

Genoa

Situated on the western side of Italy at the head of the Ligurian Sea, Genoa challenged Venice as the major European sea power. Like Venice it was not an old Roman city, and it owed its existence to its very fine harbor, located on a very narrow strip of coast, isolated to the north and east by rugged mountains but easily approached by land from the west or south, as well as from the sea. Consequently, while geography made Venice essentially independent from the start, Genoa was dominated by the Lombards and then was sacked by Muslim raiders in 934–35.[50] Because the best land route from Rome to France and on to Spain passes along this narrow coastal strip, Genoa's central location played a role in making it the dominant port in the western Mediterranean (see Map 3-1). As important a factor was that potential competitor cities along the French and Spanish coasts were handicapped by local despots, "a feudal lord or a king, who collected heavy tributes and embroiled them in his own quarrels,"[51] a state of affairs that soon applied to the ports in southern Italy and Sicily as well. In contrast, like Venice, Genoa was governed by its own commune. But unlike Venice, Genoa received no direct support from Byzantium, and sometimes Genoans had to fight off efforts by various Holy Roman Emperors to impose German rule upon them. Consequently, Genoa often allied itself with Rome, effectively playing the emperor off against the pope. Finally, Genoa rose to unchallenged power in the western Mediterranean by defeating Pisa in a huge sea battle after more than a century of conflict and competition.

Initially, Genoa was ruled by a council of nobles in the tradition of the Roman Senate. And as happened in Rome, the council was taken over by an autocratic coalition. This resulted in two civil wars, from 1164 to 1169 and again from 1189 to 1194. Neither war produced a winner as each side held nearly impregnable castles. But the immense costs of these conflicts, especially as they disrupted commerce and led to the loss of overseas colonies, made it evident to all that both sides would benefit by finding a lasting political solution.[52] Although the political system Genoa adopted seems bizarre, it was fully in accord with modern game theory, and it worked!

Called the *podesteria,* it was a sort of city-manager setup. Each year the city-state hired a non-Genoese *podestà* to be its military commander, chief judge, and political administrator.[53] Although an elected council of nobles selected the *podestà* and set policies and goals, during his term the *podestà* had supreme authority and brought with him a company of soldiers and a set of judges. During his year as ruler of Genoa, neither the *podestà* nor his troops or judges were permitted to marry Genoans, to buy local property, or to engage in any commercial transactions, and at the end of the year they were required to leave and not return for several years. The system worked because the *podestà* had enough troops of his own so that, combined with either Genoan faction, they could defeat the other faction; a dictatorship was prevented because the *podestà* lacked sufficient troops to defeat either faction alone. This system worked so well that it was adopted by many other Italian communes.[54]

With an honest government, unencumbered by local interests or obligations, Genoa entered a golden age. From 1191 to 1214 Genoa's trade increased at a rate of 6 percent a year, and by the end of the century it was the richest of the northern city-states, followed by Milan and Venice.[55] In 1293, sea trade alone produced an income of nearly 4 million Genoese pounds. This amount was ten times the total annual income of the French royal treasury![56]

The Genoan system of government was modified in 1257, when a rebellion by guilds and confraternities resulted in greater democracy. The council was expanded to thirty-two members, four elected from each of the city's wards, each set of four being divided equally between the nobility and the "people." In place of an outside *podestà* serving for a year, henceforth the commune was administered by a "captain," elected for a ten-year term by the council. In this way Genoa evolved into an even more responsive state, giving greater political influence to commoners, as demonstrated by the fact that the first man elected captain was Guglielmo Boccanegra, a rich commoner. His selection suggests that the real basis for the creation of a more democratic regime was Genoa's booming commercial economy. A tiny town having perhaps ten thousand residents at the start of the twelfth century, by 1250 Genoa had a population of about fifty thousand and was one of the largest cities in Europe.[57] And as with Venice, it wasn't simply trade that produced the wealth and growth; Genoa also industrialized until it too was making most of the goods it exported.[58]

Florence

An enormous amount of snobbish nonsense has been written about Florence. Not content to praise the city for having produced Leonardo da Vinci and Michelangelo, many have advanced the spurious claim that Florence led the way out of the Dark Ages. Jakob Burckhardt's work has long been celebrated precisely for popularizing that view. In *The Civilization of the Renaissance in Italy,* Burckhardt went so far as to praise Florence for having produced the "most elevated political thought" and a government that "deserves the name of the first modern state" in the world.[59] As to thinkers, Burckhardt could, of course, invoke such remarkable names as Dante, Machiavelli, Petrarch, and Boccaccio. But just as he mistook art for civilization, Burkhardt wrote a chapter, "The State as a Work of Art," in which he suggested that political philosophy is more authentic than is political reality. And the reality, as Burckhardt well knew, often involved bitter and bloody political turmoil. Nevertheless, Florence became a monument to the productive capacities of capitalism, becoming a major center for manufacturing woolens and silks, and by the thirteenth century, Florence's banks had established branches all across western Europe.

In principle, Florence was a republic. The commune was based on a *parlamento* made up of as many as a thousand members, who met yearly to set policy, levy taxes, and (usually) appoint a *podestà* for the next year. The process was frequently disrupted or distorted by the seizure of power by Guelfs (supporters of the pope) or Ghibellines (supporters of the Holy Roman Emperor). In 1282 a new constitution was adopted in cooperation with the Cardinal of Florence that added a substantial number of representatives of the guilds.[60] Eight years later this expansion of power paid dividends for commoners with the passage of ordinances protecting citizens from abuses by the nobility, actually depriving several hundred noblemen and their relatives of the right to hold public office. To enforce these regulations a new government office was created, backed by a militia of a thousand men.[61] Rioting erupted, the *podestà*'s residence was looted, and the principal author of the ordinances was condemned to death but fled to France. Once again civil strife was the political reality of life in Florence, not only between the Guelf and Ghibelline factions of the nobility but between both of these factions and the commoners. In his *Florentine Histories*, Machiavelli proposed that "the grave and natural enmities that exist between the men of the people and the nobles, caused by the wish of the latter to command and the former not to obey, are the cause of all evils that arise in cities."[62] One must wonder if Machiavelli would have been able to write his remarkable political works had he lived in a city lacking the turmoil and the constant political conspiracies of Florence.

Regardless of which faction was in control, the right of the guilds to a major voice in government was acknowledged. In fact, at the end of the fourteenth century, the guilds took power and created a ruling body of nine men, called the Signoria—six of them representing major guilds, two from minor guilds, and the *gonfaloniere*, the city's standard-bearer, who acted as chairman. Members of the Signoria were elected by a body of citizens known as the Priori, who were selected by a random drawing. And through it all, even the most bitterly divided factions were united in their concern not to kill the goose that was laying so many golden eggs: commerce was encouraged, only lightly taxed, and given free rein, including the importation of needed workers from elsewhere.

By the fifteenth century, the true rulers of Florence were members of the Medici family, although they carefully kept a very low political profile and observed all of the democratic formalities.[63] Even so, they faced several rebellions and attempted coups from which they narrowly escaped. Keep in mind, too, that the Medici were not heirs of landed estates but owed their fortunes to commerce, having founded and managed one of the premier banks of medieval Europe, with many branches in Italy and abroad.[64] As rulers of Florence, they were very protective of private property and of commercial and industrial freedoms, and were sympathetic to commoner interests as well. Of course, this could not continue indefinitely, and by the sixteenth century the Medici had become tyrants who presided over the economic decline of Florence.

Milan

Milan is situated midway in the large plain that crosses northern Italy and nestles against the mountains. Far from the sea, since Roman times Milan had been a key communication center because the primary passes through the Alps converged here. This location was the major reason that Milan became the Roman empire's second city. But the city's rise to medieval greatness was not a given. The Roman city of Milan was devastated in 452 by Attila the Hun and razed by the Goths nearly a century later. In the eighth century, Milan was included in the domain of Charlemagne, and this led to many centuries of effort by the Holy Roman Emperor (as the supposed heir to the Carolingians) to assert and reassert German rule.

Even so, the city proved remarkably resilient and intensely Christian. Within the walls were dozens of churches, and the city's marketplace was "inside the cathedral precinct, in front of the church."[65] Sunday sales were prohibited, but otherwise the church was favorable to commerce. Moreover, by the end of the tenth century, political power was consolidated under the office of the archbishop, who was second only to the pope, the most powerful churchman in Italy. Eventually, this resulted in the same two bitter factions, Guelfs and Ghibellines, that so fractured political life in much of northern Italy, and as did Florence, Milan suffered from chronic bloody civil disputes.

The archbishop's political power rested upon captains, "who held castles in fief of the bishop and were in his court."[66] But in 1045 conflict broke out and a leading captain led the people in support of more democratic rule, whereupon Milan organized as a commune and rapidly evolved into a republic. Then, beginning in 1186, Milan was administered by a *podestà*—although the archbishop retained substantial authority, often using it on behalf of democratic proposals. In 1225 the franchise was greatly expanded to share power with the lesser merchants and the larger guilds.[67] Nevertheless, several times the city had to fight for its life against imperial forces. Moreover, external threats, combined with internal factions among a nobility based on large rural estates rather than commerce, made Milan vulnerable to autocrats able to impose civil order—especially members of the Sforza family, who rose to fame as mercenary soldiers (*sforza* is Italian for "force"). Fortunately for Milan's economic affairs, the Sforzas were realists who understood finance, and during their rule they encouraged investments in manufacturing capacity and were friendly to commercial interests.

It needs to be emphasized that the church often played a vigorous role in advocating and defending democracy in northern Italy. Not only did the church often and unequivocally assert moral equality but it often ventured into the political arena on behalf of expanding the franchise. As mentioned earlier, both the Archbishop of Milan and the Cardinal of Florence made common cause with the guilds. Neither was some kind of strange liberal; both their religious and their political views were quite representative.

To sum up: the modern libertarian slogan concerning free minds and free markets rings true for these Italian city-states. Their commercial revolution required freedom and their political revolution rested on commerce. The negative case of southern Italy gives even greater support to this conclusion.

REPRESSION IN SOUTHERN ITALY: THE CASE OF AMALFI

The absence of booming commercial centers in southern Italy was due to one thing: repression. Unlike the northern big four and their many satellites, the cities in southern Italy were unable to preserve their independence and consequently succumbed to rule by external despots who exploited them ruthlessly. The case of Amalfi is especially poignant and revealing.

In the year 1000, Amalfi may have been the largest city in Italy, with an estimated population of thirty-five thousand.[68] Located on the shores of the Mediterranean, well south of Rome, it was by then a major center of overseas trade. From its founding, probably in the middle of the eighth century, the city combined seafaring and commerce in a triangular pattern involving Muslim North Africa and Byzantium. First came the assembly of local cargoes: grain, wine, fruits, and timber.[69] These were traded for various products and gold in Tunisian ports and for spices and gold in Egypt. Then on to Byzantium, where the gold was used to obtain various Eastern luxury products and especially religious goods such as vestments, altar cloths, and incense.[70] Returning to Amalfi, traders sold these goods in order to buy more local products and to launch new voyages. There was nothing haphazard about this trading system. From the start it showed "organization and a routine of exchanges supported by steadfast political and diplomatic action."[71]

The question must be raised: why not Naples? Situated just north of Amalfi, possessed of a much better harbor and a substantial navy, why did this celebrated old Roman city not overshadow the upstart city to the south? After all, both Cicero and Virgil sojourned here, it was here that Nero made his stage debut, and even in the ninth century Naples probably was significantly larger than Amalfi. The answer to "Why not Naples?" is quite straightforward. Naples sat at the edge of a very large, fertile hinterland, supporting many noble estates. The result was a highly stratified society that allowed very little freedom for commercial ventures.[72] In contrast, Amalfi had no hinterland and no interfering nobles. From earliest days it had been a republic dominated by commerce. As late as the start of the twelfth century, the merchants of Amalfi were major players in Italian foreign trade. And then it ended.

All histories of medieval Europe give much attention to Viking raiders, but beyond incidental admissions that William the Conqueror was a Norman, very little attention is paid to the impact on European society of those Vikings who came south and stayed. Among them was Roger Guiscard, who, with a tiny band of Normans, invaded Sicily in 1060, defeated Muslim opposition, and assumed power. Later he established a foothold on the toe of Italy, a mere fifty miles across the Strait of Messina from Sicily. Roger's son styled himself Roger II, King of the Norman Kingdom of Sicily. As clever and as formidable as his father, in 1131, having built up his forces across the straits, Roger mounted an invasion of southern Italy. Soon the Normans ruled the entire territory from the tip of the Italian boot to well north of Naples (see Map 3-1).

Roger II seems to have been a very enlightened ruler for the times. He encouraged commercial development and even initiated a silk industry in Sicily. However, his son earned the name of William the Bad. He pursued a life of profligate luxury and paid for it in the manner long perfected by despots: usurpation and taxation, which ended the commercial significance of Amalfi.

Some modern historians have defended the Norman Kingdom's suppression of southern Italy on grounds that it brought peace to fractious communities: "Had the kingdom fallen apart into its constituent elements it would not have promoted a golden age of free communities, but would have generated incessant local conflicts."[73] Possibly. But the chronic conflicts among the independent northern Italian city-states did not prevent their commercial golden age. In fact, the commercial mentality became so highly developed in these free and independent northern communities that they soon resorted to hired armies to do all of their fighting, while it was business as usual for everyone else.

NORTHERN FREEDOM

Although capitalism first came into full flower in the Italian city-states, it soon spread northward—but only to places where there was sufficient freedom. With the exception of England, these were not even statelets but merely small cities that had managed to escape from the domination of local lords and to evolve responsive governments. Since these cities eventually replaced the Italian city-states as the major centers of developing European capitalism, it is important to see how they gained their freedom.

There really was no provision for cities within the feudal system, which was a set of mutual obligations that organized rural life into a pyramid of estates, from the small fiefs of individual knights on up to mammoth estates of dukes, kings, and emperors. In earliest medieval times, most urban places (villages, towns, and cities in the making) were "owned" by a local lord, by a bishop (the community having arisen around his palace), or by a monastic order, and inhabitants paid a ground rent on the land upon which their community rested. Consequently, ownership of buildings was ambiguous. Moreover, ownership of the land beneath an urban place always was shared between the local lord and a distant prince or king within whose realm the community stood. This dualism was the opening through which cities gained their independence.[74]

Since trade is an urban activity, as towns grew, communities of well-to-do merchants always emerged, and inevitably they came to resent being taxed and commanded by an outsider who contributed little or nothing to the welfare of their community. In response, they formed strong merchant guilds able to resist their local ruler. Moreover, many of these merchants were not of common origins but were members of the lower nobility who had quickly adapted to the new opportunities and played a leading role in the rise of commerce.[75] That the merchants were not merely a bunch of commoners may help explain the astute tactics by which towns often successfully appealed over their local ruler's head to his more distant superior lord, offering attractive inducements in return for substantial independence.

First to go were the ground rents. In some cities this was achieved by negotiation with the local lord; in many instances the urban land was purchased by affluent citizens. In many other cases towns actually raised or hired troops to support the distant lord against his opponents, especially against subordinate local lords, many of whom were prince-bishops. Because so many towns had grown up around a center that began as the headquarters of a bishop (often founded on the ruins of a Roman garrison), temporal rule had devolved into his hands as well. Early on, German kings had established many bishoprics as princedoms, hoping thereby to more fully control urban challengers. But the contradictions built into the role of prince-bishop soon put church and monarchy at odds, and a natural affinity emerged between the distant monarch and urban leaders.[76] In 1073, for example, when some of the bishops along the Rhine challenged Henry IV, the Holy Roman Emperor, the citizens of Worms turned against their bishop, drove him out of town, and supported Henry. To show his gratitude, Henry granted local authority to a town council, thus making Worms an independent city owing its allegiance exclusively to the crown. Worms was only the first of what came to be known as Free and Imperial Cities as similar deals with the emperor were struck by northern towns— eventually there were eighty-five such cities.[77] Because these cities were so in control of their own affairs, the expression "Town air brings freedom" became a *legal* maxim, not just a popular slogan.[78]

Freedom was actualized in these northern cities by elected councils and subsequently by the progressive expansion of the franchise, all of which was explicitly justified on religious grounds—the very notion of community had sacred aspects to urban residents in this era. Thus, early in the fifteenth century, the Basil city council explained "that the government of every city is established primarily to augment and support the honor of God and to prohibit all injustice."[79] In this spirit the town councils did not limit their attention to secular affairs, such as schools or streets, but often became involved in religious matters, including the reform of local monasteries or the establishment of shrines for holy relics.

The idea that towns and cities should be governed by elected councils probably was imported from Italy, as was the word itself (*concilium*). However, democracy in the northern cities never led to the elaborate structures typical of Italy. First came democracy for the upper classes, in that they selected a group of their members to act as a government. Soon, other significant social groups gained representation until a truly popular government was achieved. Since it was vital to the independence of a city that no claims against inhabitants by outside lords could be sustained, it became established law that any serf who came into a town was free of all feudal obligations to his or her lord after residing in the town for a year and a day—thus emphasizing the fact that feudalism no longer existed within the free, commercial northern towns and cities. Moreover, it wasn't merely that the commercial cities *escaped* from the grasp of local rulers; many of them were *founded* as free communities by merchant traders who secured charters from distant kings and princes who were superior to local aristocrats.

For towns to owe their loyalty to a distant monarch was desirable to both sides. The towns were valuable allies against any schemes involving the monarch's subordinates, and the monarch provided security from local interference. Local lords could not tax or usurp the wealth of these towns, nor could they erect customs barriers to long-distance trade (recall the Magna Charta). In return for their autonomy, the towns paid a modest fixed fee to the monarch, who in no way interfered with the tax system imposed by the townspeople upon themselves. These local taxes were spent primarily on security (building and maintaining city walls, for example) and to facilitate trade and commerce by providing public marketplaces, improving roads and docks, and in some places by annually staging great trade fairs.

The "rebirth" of freedom in some parts of Europe was the result of three necessary elements: Christian ideals, small political units, and within them, the appearance of a diversity of well-matched interest groups. There were no societies like these anywhere else in the world.

Now, with the last of the necessary conditions in place, it is time to observe the rise of capitalism and the success of the West.

Part II: Fulfillment

CHAPTER FOUR

Perfecting Italian Capitalism

Faith in reason is the most significant feature of Western Civilization. In that simple statement lies the key to understanding the evolution of medieval business practices into what came to be known as capitalism.

It all began in the great monastic estates as the monks replaced their subsistence economies and became highly productive, specialized participants in rapidly expanding trading networks, thereby giving birth to capitalism. Even so, the early form of religious capitalism that developed in the monasteries was based primarily on agricultural production and some moneylending; the monks did not go on to create firms devoted entirely to trade or to finance, nor did they found manufacturing firms. What they did do was provide the business model that led to the rise of private capitalist enterprises that pursued these obvious next steps, and it was in the relatively free and well-located city-states of northern Italy that these developments occurred. Soon, Italian firms monopolized trade, banking, and, to a lesser degree, manufacturing in all of western Europe. At its peak in the late thirteenth and fourteenth centuries, Italian commercial power "stretched as far as England, South Russia, the oases of the Sahara Desert, India and China. It was the greatest economic empire that the world had ever known."[1] Consequently, this chapter explores how the Italians perfected capitalism and, in doing so, built this vast financial and industrial empire.

Although capitalism was carefully defined in Chapter 2, more needs to be said about why it is able to so transform the wealth of nations. Obviously, since all wealth must be produced, a society will be wealthier if its people are more productive. A capitalist economy maximizes productivity in the following ways. Since private property is secure and work is not coerced, people benefit directly from their productive efforts, which motivates them to produce more.

Because owners (or investors) benefit from increased production, they will discipline their consumption in order to plow back profits to increase future production, reinvesting in greater capacity, better technology, or a better-motivated or more qualified labor force. Competition among employers will result in rising wages and benefits, which motivates workers by allowing them to increase their consumption. This, in turn, helps to expand the market as those who manufacture, say, cars or television sets also purchase them. Given relatively unregulated markets, new commercial opportunities will attract new producers, creating competition among firms, with the result of raising quality and lowering prices. Hence, the "miracle" of capitalism is simply this: *as time goes by, everyone has more.*

The proximate cause of the rise of Italian capitalism was freedom from the rapacious rulers who repressed and consumed economic progress in most of the world, including most of Europe. Although their political life often was turbulent, these city-states were true republics able to sustain the freedom required by capitalism. Second, centuries of technological progress had laid the necessary foundations for the rise of capitalism, especially the agricultural surpluses needed to sustain cities and to permit specialization. In addition, Christian theology encouraged extremely optimistic views about the future that justified long-term investment strategies, and by this time theology also provided moral justifications for the business practices fundamental to capitalism. But to actually achieve the great "commercial revolution of the middle ages"[2] it was necessary to perfect a new kind of business firm and new ways to do business.

RATIONAL FIRMS

Trade was not invented in medieval Europe—there were traders in the Stone Age and probably even earlier. What Europeans invented was a special approach to trade wherein commerce "ceased to be an adventure"[3] and became routine, repetitive, and as risk-free as possible. This was accomplished by a special kind of organization: the *rational firm*—an organization that is created and managed according to calculable rules.[4] The formation and application of such rules is facilitated by limiting a firm to regular, sustained, carefully defined activities subject to constant monitoring, from which results can be calculated and used to adjust future actions. This requires that written records be kept of all significant actions and a complete set of accounts be maintained. The calculation of results and the supervision and coordination of activities requires clearly defined lines and levels of authority.[5] Those holding higher positions will have received a substantial amount of specialized training in such things as accounting, and their performance will be assessed periodically. Consequently, managers will be hired and promoted primarily on the basis of merit and will not be part-time amateurs but will devote themselves so fully to their positions that they may be held accountable even for aspects of their private lives. Thus, within the context of the rational firm, the perfection of capitalism involved an "objective" approach to personnel as well as to management and financial practices.

Personnel

To grasp the truth about the rise of private capitalism, the place to start is with people. How did capitalist firms in northern Italy train, select, promote, and supervise their personnel? One statistic reveals much: in Florence, in 1338, nearly half of the school-age population was attending school,[6] this in an age when there were no schools in most of Europe, and even many kings were illiterate. Similar levels of schooling were sustained in Venice, Genoa, Milan, and other northern Italian commercial cities. Consequently, it is obvious that not only was "the whole business class . . . thoroughly literate and numerate" but so too were most of the artisans and craftsmen.[7] An impressive measure of the effectiveness of the schools lies in the fact that the many account books, diaries, letters, and other documents from this era display great similarity in terms of penmanship—a tribute to standardized instruction.

Even so, the commercial firms were not satisfied. In most instances, they hired boys who had continued their educations by attending an "abacus school," where they increased their computational skills by use of counting boards, learned to calculate compound interest, and mastered the principles of basic accounting. These schools probably first appeared during the thirteenth century, stimulated by the publication and widespread distribution of a textbook by Leonardo Fibonacci. Also known as Leonardo of Pisa, he was one of the greatest number theorists in the history of mathematics. But he had even greater impact on early capitalism. When his *Liber Abaci* (Book of the Abacus) appeared in 1202, it made Hindu-Arabic numerals and the concept of zero available for the first time outside the circle of professional mathematicians. It was seized upon eagerly all across northern Italy as it provided new, efficient techniques for multiplication and division, tasks that are extraordinarily complicated when using Roman numerals—even addition and subtraction were daunting chores for Romans. Perhaps indicative of his true genius, Fibonacci did not simply present arithmetic in abstract form but carefully made it accessible and relevant by applying basic arithmetic techniques to primary business concerns, such as computing profit margins and interest, converting weights and measures, dividing profits or costs among partners, and the like.[8] As for the effectiveness of instruction, the great economic historian Armando Sapori took the trouble to check all of the computations made in the surviving ledgers of many medieval bookkeepers and found not a single error. Moreover, unlike their modern counterparts, medieval bookkeepers "avoided rounding off figures even in transactions bearing on thousands and hundreds of thousands of pounds."[9] For example, the Bardi Company of Florence once reported an immense current balance as totaling 1,266,775 pounds and 11 shillings.[10]

Abacus schools spread rapidly across northern Italy, and soon nearly half of all boys enrolled in them after completing grammar school. By the 1340s there were at least six abacus schools in Florence alone, and similar schools flourished in all of the major Italian capitalist centers. Keep in mind that these schools were not training mere clerks and bookkeepers.[11] Their graduates dominated the ranks of senior executives, and even those having more modest success could anticipate quite high salaries—in 1335 half of the men employed by the Peruzzi Company in Florence "earned at least seventy gold florins a year, a very handsome income."[12] By about 1400, clerks in the Medici Bank typically earned a hundred gold florins, sufficient to live in a fine house and employ servants.[13] Companies placed such value on abacus school training that they not only sought their graduates but often sent new employees to be trained in such a school. Records of two abacus schools, one in Pisa and one in Florence, reveal that the students were boys between the ages of eleven and fourteen who attended classes both morning and afternoon, six days a week, for two years.[14] Writing in memory of a son who died at age twenty-two, an Italian businessman offered this insight into the making of a merchant:

Since he had a good mind and remarkable ingenuity, he quickly learned how to read and write, and he impressed everybody with his ability. Thus he made such rapid progress that he finished his grammar course in a very short time. Then he started on the abacus, and very soon he became skilled at that also. [At age fourteen] I then took him out of school and put him in the wool businesses. . . . When he was promoted to bookkeeper, he kept the ledger as well as if he had been forty years old . . . he would have become one of the most successful and substantial merchants of the city.[15]

Even as late as the fifteenth century, when a German merchant asked a distinguished university professor of mathematics where to send his son for instruction, he was told that he could learn to add and subtract in Germany, but that to learn to divide and multiply he should go to Italy. Shortly thereafter, abacus schools sprang up in all of the developing capitalist centers in the Low Countries and southern Germany, where they were referred to as Italian schools—Nuremberg soon had forty-eight such schools.[16]

The opportunities available to graduates of the abacus schools clearly suggest that in northern Italy the firms were large and were mainly staffed, at all levels, by employees, not by relatives. The staffs "were drawn from the best and the brightest . . . and surprisingly few were from the shareholders' own families." For example, of 133 factors (employees stationed in a branch office) serving the Peruzzi

Company in the middle 1300s, "only 23 . . . were related to the company's owners . . . the paucity of family scions in the family firm suggests a refreshing lack of nepotism; commerce was too important to place in the hands of the incompetent, however near and dear."[17] Moreover, many of these early rational firms were far-flung enterprises having numerous branches. By no later than about 1250, the Riccardi Bank of Lucca had eleven branches, one as far away as Dublin. Fifty years later the Peruzzi Company of Florence had fifteen branches, including one in London and another in Tunis.

Keep in mind that in these days "banks" were not simply financial institutions; they were as deeply involved in trade and manufacturing as they were in finance. If Bank of America merged with General Motors, the result would be a modern firm comparable to the Riccardi Bank in terms of functions and relative influence.

Many of the branch banks originated as responses to the famous northern trade fairs held in the Champagne region, a cycle of six fairs (each lasting about six weeks). Initially it was here that northern European and Italian merchants met to buy and sell various wares, especially woolens. The Champagne fairs dominated north-south European trade for most of the thirteenth century and then declined when the volume of trade became so large that the Italians decided that rather than sending representatives to travel from fair to fair, it was more efficient to establish permanent branches in the area and to buy directly from the northern European producers on a regular basis.[18] The success of the branches in Flanders, along with those established in Rome in pursuit of church business, led to a proliferation of branches by the major firms.

Although many of these firms could be described as partnerships, in truth they far more closely resembled stock companies than is conveyed to the modern ear by the term "partnership." The typical medieval commercial firm was a partnership in the sense that a group of owners were liable for all debts of the firm, should bankruptcy occur. But most of these firms, and all of the larger ones, were based on "share ownership, with each owner contributing a specific amount of money and sharing in profit or loss" in proportion to his or her (women often took part) investment. Such firms "had corporate by-laws, a company seal, and a set of accounts."[19]

In addition there was a clear distinction made between ownership and management. Especially by the second generation, many owners were only passive stockholders and the firm was managed by a person thought to be the most qualified—often this was someone unrelated to the owners who had risen through the ranks or who, in typical modern style, was recruited from another company.[20] Medieval executives did not draw tables of organization, but most of them easily could have done so. Firms were hierarchically organized, and lines of authority and responsibility were quite clearly understood.

Finally, medieval capitalists often were concerned about the personal morality of those whom they employed, especially those holding more senior positions. The written partnership agreement Cosimo de' Medici had drawn up to establish the Medici Bank's branch in Bruges specifically stated that Angelo Tani, the junior partner who was to manage the firm, could not entertain women in his quarters, or gamble, or accept any gift worth more than one pound.[21]

Management and Financial Practices

As their basic tool of management, early Italian firms maintained very careful and very detailed records and accounts. By the end of the thirteenth century, double-entry bookkeeping had been invented and was rapidly adopted. This facilitated the involvement of multiple bookkeepers and provided easy and constant access to the up-to-date financial situation of the firm and accurate assessments of specific undertakings. However, firms were almost as well documented with single-entry systems and by observing the plethora of adages to put everything in writing, such as

> Never spare the pen and ink.
> The lazy man who is remiss in writing down his dealings cannot live long without damage or mistakes.[22]

But of course, there is far more to capitalism than record keeping; many other major financial innovations were necessary.

When trade no longer is based on barter, the question of payment arises. This became an especially acute problem for long-distance exchanges. The problem was not money, as such, but the fact that in medieval times all money consisted of precious metal, most of it having been minted into coins. As the volume of trade rose, there often was a shortage of coins. Another problem was that coins constantly were being debased by those who minted them—invariably silver coins progressively lost value "as the dark hue of copper and lead shrouded the glitter of fine metal."[23] But even when Florence and Genoa produced a pure, twenty-four-karat gold coin weighing 3.5 grams (which soon was known as the florin) to substitute for the many debased silver coins, the problem was not solved, because of the inherent difficulties of transporting coins from buyers to sellers over long distances. For one thing, coins are very heavy and pose a serious transportation problem when substantial amounts are involved. In addition, a coin has no provenance and belongs to whoever possesses it, which is why it remains extremely risky to transport cash. As a case in point: in the summer of 1328, Pope John XXII needed to pay his mercenary army on duty in Lombardy. So he had sixty thousand gold florins bagged up and loaded on pack animals, and sent 150 cavalrymen to guard the convoy from Avignon over the Alps into Italy. Near Pavia the pope's convoy was ambushed by robbers, who seized more than half of the gold and took many of the cavalrymen captive. In addition to losing much of his treasure, the pope was forced to ransom the captives, and he still owed his army most of their pay.[24] Well aware of these shortcomings of cash, merchants had long before developed a method for transferring funds on paper, even at a distance. And the firms that made these transfers possible came to be known as banks. Banks first appeared in Italy, and for centuries hundreds of Italian banks and their branches formed the core of capitalism, both at home and abroad. *The Cambridge Economic History of Europe* lists 173 major Italian banks in operation during the fourteenth century, not counting branches. Of these, 38 were in Florence, 34 in

Pisa, 27 in Genoa, 21 in Lucca, 18 in Venice, and 10 in Milan. Keep in mind that these were very small communities.

The medieval bank evolved from money changing—the word "bank" itself initially referred to a money changer's table. For centuries, the great variety of coins in circulation and the variations in the extent to which any given coin had been trimmed or debased required specialized knowledge when it came to equating funds for the settlement of debts. Money changers served as middlemen who determined the relative worth of coins: "Do these twenty shillings equal one gold florin, or does a fair exchange require twenty-three of these shillings?" Money changers charged a fee for their services, and this long caused them to be condemned as usurers, but their services could not be done away with. In time the money changers began to maintain accounts of deposit for their clients and to lend as well as change money, thereby becoming banks of deposit. From there it was but a short step to settling a bill between two clients by crediting the correct amount to one account and subtracting it from another.

Next, local bankers began to credit and debit from the accounts of one another's depositors—as with modern checking accounts. In this way, even huge amounts of money could be transferred without involving coins. When such a transfer was made over a considerable distance, it involved a *bill of exchange*—a notarized document authorizing payment to a specific individual or firm. To settle payment for wool cloth shipped from Bruges to Genoa, for example, a bill of exchange was sent to a bank in Bruges from a bank in Genoa, whereupon the Bruges bank credited the account of the woolen firm and entered this in its books as a credit held against the Genoese bank. Being merely a sheet of paper and of no value except to the bank in Bruges, the bill of exchange could be rapidly and safely transported. This lesson was not lost on the church. Rather than repeat Pope John's blunder, bishops began to purchase bills of exchange in order to remit funds to Rome. In 1410, already resentful of the annual flow of wealth to the Vatican, the English House of Commons condemned the sale of bills of exchange to the clergy by Italian bankers operating in London, and in 1449 the Commons imposed a substantial tax on foreign banks.[25]

The constant transmission of payments allowed banks to balance their debits and credits, but this process was greatly simplified and accelerated when the bank in Bruges and the bank in Genoa were branches of the same bank. That's why Italian banks spread everywhere that Italian merchants did business. In similar fashion, of course, banks often lent money as purely paper transactions by crediting and debiting accounts—in fact, bills of exchange frequently were based on bank loans to the payer. It is uncertain just when bills of exchange were invented—contrary to some claims, they were not copied from Islam. The earliest surviving example of a bill of exchange comes from Genoa in the twelfth century,[26] but it is likely that they had been in use previously. Banks of deposit probably appeared slightly earlier.[27]

Long-distance medieval trade involved many risks, especially those resulting from shipwreck or piracy. Early capitalists quickly learned the approximate percentage of cargoes that were lost and used this expectation to minimize risks by spreading their exposure accordingly.[28] For example, a merchant would split his cargo among a number of different ships on the principle that a single loss or two would be offset by the profits of the many shipments that arrived safely. As Antonio explained in Shakespeare's *Merchant of Venice*: "I thank my fortune for it / My ventures are not in one bottom trusted."[29] Eventually someone found a better solution: rather than split the cargo among many ships, the value of a shipment would be guaranteed for a certain fee or premium by a group of investors, each of whom risked a small amount on many different ships: *insurance* had been invented. Once again no one is certain when this took place, but account books from both Florence and Venice contain entries for what seem to be payments of insurance premiums early in the 1300s. And before the end of that century there are many records of the formation of syndicates of "underwriters."[30] For example, in 1396 fourteen investors assumed a risk of 1,250 florins should a cargo of wool fleeces being shipped from Majorca to Venice fail to arrive. The individual underwriter's share of the risk varied from 50 to 200 florins—participants in underwriting syndicates seldom accepted responsibility for more than 200 florins.[31] In addition, some of the largest firms became underwriters without spreading the risk among a syndicate, since they had the resources to spread the risks simultaneously over so many shipments that they could rely on the law of averages. Thus, as early as 1319 the Bardi Company added an 8.75 percent insurance fee to a shipment of cloth purchased at the fairs in Champagne and to be delivered to Pisa, on consignment to a firm in Florence.[32]

As should be clear, the primary institution of medieval capitalism was not only the bank but the *international* bank. Three factors made international banks necessary. First was the fact that medieval trade was international. The woolen trade is a strategic example. Early on, wool was grown in England, shipped to Flanders, woven into cloth, sold to Italian traders at the fair in Champagne, transported to Italy, and shipped from there to Mediterranean markets, particularly in the Middle East and on the north coast of Africa. Second was the fact that the church was by far the largest financial enterprise of the era, it too being an international body that required the frequent and regular transfer of very large sums. Third, the geopolitical affairs of Europe were international. As kingdoms grew larger and especially as their wars became more expensive, the nobility frequently needed large loans and could offer many business privileges and monopolies to lenders having the financial resources to provide these funds.

Consequently, circumstances favored the formation of big banks having the resources to transfer fortunes and to finance kingdoms. These banks became international by establishing branches in the important political and economic centers, since that way they could minimize the risk involved in transferring funds by dealing with their own branches. In this regard Italian banks had an overwhelming advantage because theirs seem to have been the earliest full-service banks, and the Italian domination of international trading led their banks to establish branches early on, and then to use their established market positions to exclude non-Italian competitors. That the pope lived in Italy during much of this time helped too. Given the international networks of branches sustained by the larger Italian banks, and the fact that an Italian bank often had a secure basis for trusting another Italian bank (given the complex connections of family and finance among the stockholders), it became feasible for Italian banks to conduct international finance by correspondence. As discussed earlier, bills of exchange directing that a particular seller be credited from the account of a particular buyer were the lifeblood of medieval commerce and the basis of the Italian banking monopoly. Although sometimes prominent locals were allowed to become minor stockholders in an Italian branch bank, non-Italians were never employed as anything but servants. Even the most distant branches were staffed entirely by people hired and trained in Italy, and all business was conducted in Italian. Consequently, as far as is known, until well into the fifteenth century, even all of the very small banks in western Europe were Italian banks, and certainly there were no non-Italian international banks. It is known that in this era all the banks in England and Ireland were branches of Italian banks, as were all of those in Flanders, and only Italian banks are known to have existed in medieval France and Spain.[33]

But by becoming international, Italian banks faced many of the risks that prevented the rise of capitalism in most times and places. At home in their relatively democratic city-states, they were usually safe from tyrants and in no danger of usurpation. But that was not true of many places in which they established branches. Consequently, international Italian banks often faced a very dangerous dilemma. On the one hand, local rulers could do them irreparable harm if the bankers refused to lend to them and could reward them with extraordinary opportunities for profit should they choose to do so. On the other hand, everyone knew that the immense disparities in power between rulers and bankers made such loans very risky. As a manager of an Italian bank in Bruges wrote to his colleague at a branch in Barcelona, "No one ever becomes embroiled with great lords without losing his feathers in the end."[34] Sometimes banks lost their feathers because great lords decided not to pay up. The most famous example involves the failures of the Peruzzi Bank in 1343 and the Bardi Bank in 1346. These were by far the two largest banks of the era, and they had lent enormous sums to King Edward III of England to help him fund the early days of the Hundred Years War. Although they managed to hold on for several years, these powerful Italian banks were effectively wiped out when

Edward renounced his huge debts—600,000 florins to the Peruzzi Bank and 900,000 florins to the Bardi Bank. The later bankruptcy of the Medici Bank showed the danger of lending to royal losers in the chronic wars of the era. But banks could even be destroyed by becoming too deeply involved with a king who was a winner, and who was entirely honest and honorable, as the managers of the Riccardi Bank were to discover. A profile of this bank, which is considered the first of the three Italian "supercompanies"[35] to be founded during the thirteenth century, will help to convey just how modern and sophisticated medieval banking had become.

THE RISE AND FALL OF THE FIRST ITALIAN SUPERCOMPANY

The Riccardi Company was founded sometime during the 1230s in Lucca, the prosperous commercial city near Florence that its larger neighbor always coveted. Little is known about the bank's earliest days, but by about midcentury it had established branches in Rome, Nîmes, Bordeaux, Paris, Flanders, London, York, and Dublin, as well as in the four towns in Champagne where the great trade fairs were held. In his remarkable reconstruction of the company, Richard Kaeuper wrote that "it was no small feat to coordinate rational business activity across more than a thousand miles of bad roads, swift streams, mountain passes, and competing political jurisdictions." The Riccardi did so through "a constant stream of letters" conveyed by "their own couriers: we read of Stephan, Rubino, and Bocco carrying letters. . . . We can picture these men carrying bulky pouches stuffed with rolls of account, letters of exchange, copies of epistles to important clients, and the company letters themselves."[36]

In one of these letters, the home office in Lucca reported that the branch in Champagne had lent "a great amount of money" to the Paris branch of the Bonsignori Bank of Siena, and that bank had promised to pay it back either to the Riccardi branch in London or to the one in Dublin. When asked about it, various representatives of the Bonsignori Bank "make excuses and say that they do not know if that money has been paid there [London] or in Ireland, nor how much has been paid." The letter went on: "Therefore we ask you to let us know both how much you have received, and when, both you and the men in Ireland." Lucca, Champagne, Paris, Siena, London, and Dublin! How much more international could banking get?

The Riccardi Bank was large not only in the geographic sense but also financially. In an early letter, the office in Lucca estimated that they had a line of credit up to the astonishing amount of 320,000 florins at the Champagne fairs. This was in keeping with the scale of their other operations, as will be seen.

In 1272 the London branch achieved an immense coup, becoming the royal bankers to King Edward I. What they offered the king was a very sophisticated solution to a chronic fiscal problem. As with most governments, Edward's income came in a regular and quite constant stream of rents, taxes, and tariffs. However, in addition to the normal costs of running his government and household, he often faced very sudden and very large financial needs, most of them precipitated by wars: with Wales and Scotland, and to defend his holdings in France. The Riccardi agreed to provide loans to meet these sudden financial needs, and they rationalized the king's finances by taking over some of his regular flows of income. For example, they were assigned all of the customs collected in Bordeaux and Marmande, and eventually they gathered in the tariff on all wool and hides exported from England and Ireland, as well as taxes on all "movable property." These either were used by the Riccardi to retire the king's current indebtedness or were accumulated against a sudden future need.

During their days as the king's bankers (1272–94) the Riccardi lent Edward an average of 112,000 florins a year. It is not clear how much, or in just what fashion, the Riccardi profited directly from this arrangement, although some historians estimate that they charged the king about 17 percent per year on his debt, withholding it from the flow of present income. But it is entirely clear that their indirect profits from their royal connection were immense. The government exerted itself to collect unpaid debts from Edward's subjects. In 1277 Edward directed the barons of the exchequer "to summon all Riccardi debtors before them and give aid and counsel in the recovery of the sums due."[37] Later the king's sheriffs were assigned to collect debts owed the Riccardi Bank. Being the king's bankers also gave the Riccardi great credibility within Edward's realm, and they used it to become the major lenders and to arrange business deals such as long-term contracts to buy English wool directly from the growers.

In addition to being the king's bankers, the Riccardi enjoyed a special relationship with the pope, often collecting funds due him and transferring them to Rome. This took on a three-way aspect in connection with a special tax the pope had imposed in order to support the Crusades. This money was earmarked for kings and other great lords who led a company of Crusaders. Edward had in fact joined the Ninth Crusade in 1270, returning in 1274, upon the death of his father, to be crowned king. For a variety of reasons the pope disagreed that this qualified Edward to receive the Crusade tax, and years passed while king and pope disputed the matter. All the while these funds piled up in the Riccardi Bank, eventually amounting to more than 500,000 florins.

In 1291 the King of France arrested the Italians in his realm, and the Riccardi were forced to pay very large fines. At the same time, the pope changed his mind and awarded Edward the crusading funds. Of course, being good businessmen, the Riccardi had not simply put the pope's money in a vault but had it invested far and wide. Taken entirely by surprise, they had to scramble to come up with the cash, and this put them in a very vulnerable position. Then, in 1294 Edward I and Philip the Fair of France went to war over title to Gascony, "a dress rehearsal for the Hundred Years War fought by their descendants."[38] The war also caught the Riccardi by surprise, and having so extended themselves to give Edward the pope's funds, they were unable to provide the massive new loans Edward needed to sustain an army across the channel. An enraged king had all of the Riccardi bankers in London arrested, seized all of their possessions and all assets of the bank, and then sent them packing. Many another king would have taken their heads.

Adding to their woes, the King of France again arrested the resident Riccardi bankers, this time charging that they were foreign agents in that they were Edward's bankers. This provoked a run on the Paris and Bordeaux branches. Finally, in 1301 the bank closed, a lasting financial disaster for all involved.

It would be inappropriate to conclude discussion of the financial affairs of Italian capitalist firms without noting their commitment to charity. "Each time they drew up or revised a budget, a fund for the poor was created with some of the capital of the company. These funds were entered in the books in the name of 'our Good Lord God' as representing the poor, who in this way, were made partners in the company. When dividends were paid, a proportional part went to the poor."[39] In fact, when a company was liquidated, the poor were always included among the creditors in proportion to their share of the capital. Most companies also maintained a petty cash box from which the apprentices were assigned to distribute money to any beggars who showed up asking for alms. All of this was in keeping with the frequent asides offering thanks to God made in the ledgers and account books of these companies.[40] Of course, not all of these could be described as charitable: "Let us hope in God and in the Virgin that shortly we will be in a position to give to everyone in the same way as they have dealt with us. For the time being it is more suitable if we keep our mouths shut."[41] This was written around 1291 by a bookkeeper for the Riccardi Bank in London.

ITALIAN CAPITALISM, "PURITANISM," AND FRUGALITY

Obviously, capitalism was not born of the Protestant ethic, having appeared in full flower in Italian city-states centuries before the Reformation. In fact, many economic historians have argued the reverse, that the Protestant ethic was born of capitalism.[42] Unfortunately, these historians let their attention remain fixed on the sixteenth century as they attempted to demonstrate that the Reformation occurred because the rapidly rising commercial classes (the bourgeoisie) favored a more individualistic, less institutionalized religious option—the idea being that Christianity made capitalism possible, but capitalism in turn shaped religious preferences and sensibilities. If capitalism has religious implications, the better place to look for them perhaps is not in the chaos of the sixteenth century but in the first capitalist societies. Did something akin to Puritanism and a Protestant ethic appear in the northern Italian city-states? Yes. The rise of industrial capitalism in northern Italy was accompanied by the spread of an intensely ascetic, proto-Puritan religious movement, of the Humiliati—Latin for "the humbled ones." In addition, norms of frugality became so popular in these city-states that they were repeatedly enacted into law.

Italian Puritans

Although the Humiliati were devout Roman Catholics, theirs was not another religious order. Like the later Puritans, they were primarily a lay movement, composed of people who pursued ascetic religious standards while remaining within secular life.[43] Eventually, three levels of membership emerged. The first level consisted of clergy, who sustained a typical monastic community. The second level was made up by men and women who chose to unite in communal living groups and observe rules like those of regular religious houses, but without taking formal vows. These two levels grew out of the third level, which not only was how the Humiliati began but which remained by far the largest and most influential element of the movement: laypeople, most of them married, who practiced "a limited form of voluntary poverty."[44] Eventually there were thousands, perhaps tens of thousands, of Humiliati in northern Italy.

As their name suggests, members of the Humiliati aspired to a life of humility, pledging that they would not eat more than twice a day or wear fine clothing, committing themselves instead to "austerity, prayer, fellowship and manual labour, while living with their families."[45] To fulfill the commitment to manual labor, many Humiliati became weavers. Others worked at a variety of crafts, and some seem to have continued as merchants. But all of them pledged to give all of their "excess income" to the poor.[46]

The Humiliati began in or around Milan sometime in the twelfth century and spread from there to other northern capitalist cities, including Genoa, although Lombardy remained their center.

It seems likely that the unparalleled affluence of these cities was essential to the birth of this movement, since the appeal of the Humiliati movement was a reaction not to poverty but to privilege. Several generations of Marxist scholars got things backward when they identified the rise of the Humiliati as a proletarian protest against exploitation by bourgeois capitalists.[47] Later, less dogmatic scholars confirmed that capitalism *did* play a central role in generating the Humiliati but that theirs was a reaction by wealthy people against materialism. Records show the involvement of "rich burghers, nobles, clerics," and other privileged people in the Humiliati, but "of the participation of 'proletarians' there is not a trace."[48]

The Humiliati did not accept austerity, they *chose* it. Most of them were "literate . . . including many from the nobility . . . [who] bound themselves 'to be poor and live with the poor,' adopting this rule which was no less real to them [just] because it would have seemed ridiculous to those they wished to emulate."[49] All this was typical of medieval ascetics. People who have gone hungry do not seem to take up fasting—austere faiths appeal primarily to those who have failed to find satisfaction in (usually inherited) affluence and materialism.[50] But rather than withdraw into monastic sanctuaries, the Humiliati attempted to establish a new lifestyle for all Christians, as did the Puritans centuries later.

Of course, the overwhelming majority of Italian capitalists did not join the Humiliati, nor did their heirs. Nevertheless, the example set by the Humiliati played a significant part in establishing new, more restrictive standards for everyday living in the capitalist cities of Italy—standards that fully anticipated somber Puritanism and the Protestant ethic.

Frugality

Consider this maxim: "Money . . . lies dead [when] converted into vanities."[51] Consider too that it was not merely a popular saying; it is taken from the preamble of a law prohibiting many kinds of luxury expenditures in Venice. Laws such as this were known as *sumptuary laws*. They originated as a means to prevent commoners from dressing like their betters—in many places scarlet clothing or sable trim on sleeves and hems could be worn only by the upper nobility. The intention of such statutes was to limit the status threat stemming from affluent commoners. But it was *frugality*, not caste, that shaped the sumptuary laws in capitalist Italy.

Beginning in about 1300, many sumptuary laws prohibiting conspicuous consumption and luxurious lifestyles were adopted throughout the northern Italian city-states. Between 1299 and 1499, forty-two different sumptuary statutes were adopted in Venice, sixty-one in Florence (between 1281 and 1497), nineteen in Genoa (1157 to 1484), and five in Milan (1343 to 1498). The intent of the laws is clearly revealed by these excerpts from their preambles:[52]

To revoke the grave and onerous expenses which have uselessly been made by all the men of the city . . . for clothing and other various ornaments for men and women. (1334)

To avoid the useless expenses which are continually made by the citizens. (1342)

In order to curb the vain ambition of women and to stop the useless and costly ornaments of their clothing, we decree with this most holy law. (1333)

As is explicit in this last quotation, there were many admissions that a major factor in the adoption of these laws was the desire by wealthy men to reinvest income rather than to let their wives spend it frivolously. Where it was illegal to wear finery, frugal husbands could not be accused of being cheap or unappreciative. When the laws were extended to home furnishings, husbands were further enabled to save and reinvest. Moreover, law not only may reflect popular notions of propriety; it often shapes them as well. In this instance, frugality may have earned a person public respect. Writing of the homes of wealthy Florentines, Christopher Hibbert reported that "even those of the richest families had been furnished with plain wooden tables and the most uninviting beds. The walls were generally whitewashed . . . floors were of bare stone, rarely covered with anything other than reed matting; the shuttered windows were usually made of oiled cotton," not glass.[53]

As time passed the gender conflict involved in sumptuary laws became increasingly strident. The preamble of a statute adopted in Lucca in 1380 expressed only concern that such laws were needed because so few marriages were taking place because the young men couldn't, or wouldn't, spend the large amounts needed to provide a wife with the "inordinate multitude of furs, ornaments, pearls, garlands, belts and other expenses that are required by custom." Two centuries later the city fathers in Padua were less diplomatic: "The nature and condition of the female sex, full of vanity through sloth . . . and the harmful expenses made for new fashions and superfluous ornaments, lead this poor city of Padua to great misery." They went on to condemn "these lascivious and excessive luxuries, which are displeasing to God and to the world and are a bad example."

However, the very fact that these Italian city-states passed sumptuary laws again and again indicates that the laws were not entirely successful—why keep outlawing what few people are doing? Clearly, a lot of people, especially in Venice and Florence, continued to pursue luxuries, and probably weren't even very circumspect in public. Surely Medici women did not dress in rags or in drab, voluminous dresses. There was nothing all that odd about the relative ineffectiveness of sumptuary laws in the Italian city-states. Historically, a substantial amount of noncompliance has been rather typical in places aspiring to Puritan standards. As will be seen, most men in Puritan Amsterdam did not dress in somber black, despite Rembrandt's paintings and the city's Puritan leadership. As for Puritan Boston, in 1740 George Whitefield noted in his journal that even among the avowed Puritans, "jewels, patches, and gay apparel are commonly worn by the female sex."

That sumptuary laws were so often adopted must mean that they reflected the common culture. That the laws were poorly observed suggests that many people who favored frugal living by others exempted themselves. This is often true of an "ethic." Americans strongly favor safe driving and require substantial driver's education in high schools. Yet most drivers break traffic laws. In similar fashion, for all of his emphasis on saving and frugality, Ben Franklin was no cheapskate—except with his wife.

In any event, it would be wrong to suppose that a culture of frugality caused, or even helped to cause, the rise of capitalism in these Italian cities. At the very least, to make that claim requires that the culture precede the commerce, and that simply isn't so. Capitalism was well along before the appearance of the Humiliati or the adoption of any sumptuary laws. If these phenomena are linked, it can only be that early capitalism stimulated a form of Puritanism and an ethic of frugality. But perhaps more important is that even if these were responses to capitalism, they were *not favorable* responses: they were reactions *against* capitalist affluence. As will be seen, even as Amsterdam became the center of continental capitalism, its Puritan preachers railed against covetousness and materialism. No, it was not through Puritan or Protestant doctrines that Christianity contributed to the rise of capitalism. It did so directly by declaring in favor of commerce and indirectly by encouraging individualism and freedom.

At this point it is appropriate to consider a great human tragedy that struck Europe in the fourteenth century and its impact on the rise of capitalism.

THE BLACK DEATH

In 1347, galleys returning from the Near East brought bubonic plague to the major Italian port cities. When Genoa was alerted to the peril, the first infected galleys to arrive "were driven from the port by burning arrows and divers engines of war."[54] But it was too late. Within a year the Black Death had spread along the trade routes all across Europe.[55] By the time it ended in 1350, a third of the population—about 30 million people—had died. This was a terrible human tragedy, but ironically, its economic and political impact was largely positive, and the survivors and their children lived better because of it.[56]

The initial result of the plague was a labor shortage. Predictably, wages rose rapidly, prompting ineffective efforts by various kings and councils to impose wage limits. Thus, the English Parliament passed a Statute of Laborers in 1349 that fixed wages at the levels of 1346. But landlords still had to compete for workers and easily evaded the law by adding many noncash inducements to their offers. Among these, and far more important than higher wages, were issues of freedom and choice, with the result that large numbers of serfs became free tenants. And perhaps because tenants have far greater motivation, agricultural production declined far less than did demand (given a much smaller population), and for a time substantial surpluses depressed food prices. This, in turn, spurred urban growth, and by the end of the fourteenth century western Europe was substantially more urban than before the plague—despite the fact that the death rates from plague had been far higher in the cities than in the countryside. Of primary significance for early capitalism was a substantial increase in the purchasing power of the average European: there were far fewer people, but they were a far better market for goods. Statistics on English woolens offer insight into this remarkable fact. In the wake of the plague, the number of English cloths exported to the Continent declined by almost two-thirds in 1349 and 1350, and lingered at that level through 1353. But in 1354, the preplague export level was achieved once again, "and during the next four years [the woolen export business] was to become more prosperous than before the pestilence . . . [and] had doubled within a decade."[57] So, shortly after the plague the factories all across Europe became busier than ever, the transportation system ran at full capacity, the banking ledgers showed remarkable incomes, and in many places ordinary people enjoyed a standard of living beyond their parents' wildest dreams. Capitalism was growing and spreading.

The economic miracles produced by Italian capitalism were too obvious to go unnoticed. Travelers from northern Europe to Italy brought back tales of incredible wealth and productivity. And soon residents of Flanders, England, and various cities along the Rhine had only to look around to see these miracles for themselves as Italian "colonial" firms took over and reorganized their local industries and commerce, creating very lucrative and efficient firms. Soon the locals formed their own capitalist firms, and widespread affluence was no longer confined to Italy or to the Italian enclaves in northern Europe. Then, for many centuries, capitalism remained the West's most valuable secret.

CHAPTER FIVE

Capitalism Moves North

It was woolen cloth that first brought capitalism to northern Europe. Even in Roman times, the towns of Flanders were famous for making the finest woolens in the world, and by the tenth century their woolens probably produced more income than any other product manufactured in Europe. Cloth from Flanders was the chief item at the great trade fairs held in the Champagne region beginning in the eleventh century, where the primary buyers were Italian merchants seeking goods to resell all around the Mediterranean. Eventually the Italians established northern branch banks, and rather than continue to depend upon the fairs, they arranged to make regular purchases of woolens directly from the local producers. As they gained familiarity with the local scene, the bankers soon recognized the remarkable opportunity offered by the fact that the Flanders woolen "industry" consisted of a disorganized maze of tiny weaving shops and home-based piece workers. Immense gains in productivity and efficiency were soon realized as the Italians submerged hundreds of these small producers as subcontractors to a few large firms capable of efficient management, planning, and marketing.

Having brought capitalism to Flanders, the Italians soon took it north to Holland, expanding their scope from woolen manufacturing to many other products and industries. Meanwhile, Italian banks had also worked their capitalist magic in England, here too starting with the woolen industry. The rapid spread of capitalism in England initiated many centuries of remarkable industrial growth that laid the economic and military basis for what became a global empire. Of course, none of this could have occurred had these areas not already enjoyed a considerable degree of freedom.

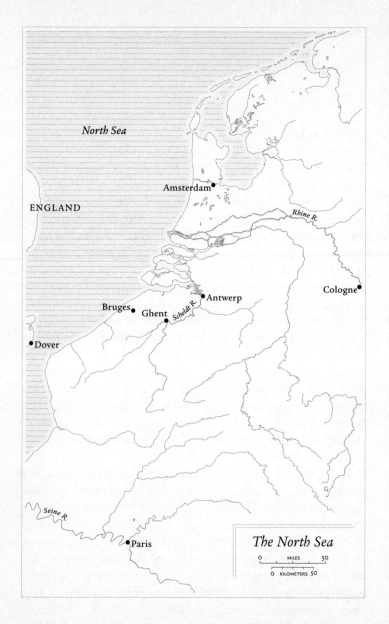

North Sea

ENGLAND

Amsterdam

Rhine R.

Cologne

Bruges

Ghent

Scheldt R.

Antwerp

Dover

Seine R.

Paris

The North Sea

0   MILES   50

0   KILOMETERS   50

MAP 5-1

THE WOOLEN CITIES OF FLANDERS

Medieval Flanders (the name means "flooded land") was a powerful principality in the southwestern section of the Low Countries, roughly equivalent to modern Belgium and part of southern Holland (see Map 5-1). Prior to the arrival of Italian banks, cloth-making "firms" consisted mainly of small shops with only three or four looms and owned by a master weaver.[1] There were no stockholders; profits were mostly consumed, not reinvested; and firms remained very small. Partnerships were formed only for a specific, short-term venture. Nor were these firms engaged in trade. They sold nothing but their own cloth and usually did so at the nearest town hall to buyers who resold it at one of the regional trade fairs. To the degree that the activities of the weaving firms were at all coordinated and organized, it was through the local merchant weavers' guild, to which all owner-operators belonged. And that was the problem. For generations, capitalism could not develop in the woolen industry for the lack of freedom.

With the full backing of the local ruler in return for regular permission fees, the merchant weavers' guilds in the various towns and cities operated as repressive cartels, narrowly restricting the entire industry and able to impose truly severe punishment on nonconformists. For example, anyone found to have varied the formula for a popular scarlet dye could be "condemned to the crushing fine of £105 or, failing payment, to the loss of his right hand."[2] Guild rules kept individual firms very small by limiting the number of looms they could own, usually fewer than five. Prices were controlled, and no bargaining was allowed, thereby limiting any benefits of increased efficiency. The weavers' guild also set the length of the working day and required all firms to comply.[3]

Wages were also fixed by the guild and strictly policed, not only for hired weavers but for everyone (other than owners) in the industry: all of the wool washers, carders, spinners, dyers, fullers, shearers, and the rest. Although wages were raised and lowered to reflect changes in the cost of living, the rates were entirely controlled by management, since only weavers with their own shops could belong to the guild. No variations in wages were allowed from one firm to another, and any and all forms of collective bargaining for higher wages were prohibited not only by guild rules but usually by local law as well. Not surprisingly, this often led to bitter and bloody civil strife, which sometimes even jeopardized the political freedom and independence of the community.

In the eleventh century the northern woolen industry began to expand rapidly. In part this was due to population growth. Another factor was the rapid expansion of international trade, via the Champagne fairs, sustained by the Italian merchants who purchased woolens at the fairs and took them south for export. But at least as important was freedom in the form of local autonomy. This is not to suggest that these cities were democratic; although they were ruled by councils, only the elite—primarily the richest merchants— were represented. But for their economic development it was sufficient that these communities had escaped from the control of local nobility, paying their taxes instead to distant rulers such as the Count of Flanders or the Holy Roman Emperor, who did not interfere in their internal affairs, as was discussed in the previous chapter. Unfortunately, when their internal affairs turned into bloody civil disturbances, a distant lord sometimes was prompted to interfere, with the result that some cities lost their independence, and with it their economic success.

In an important sense, it was affluence that destroyed some of the woolen towns and threatened the existence of the rest. As production increased and profits rose, increasingly bitter social tensions developed between the very wealthy merchant class and the skilled artisans they employed. Initially these tensions led to the organization of additional guilds: one for weavers, one for dyers, one for fullers, and so on. Each of these guilds attempted to specify and enforce work rules, limit admission to the craft, and set wages and working conditions. With guilds came the capacity for opposition. Soon, in one town after another the artisans engaged in violent uprisings, sometimes plundering the homes and property of the wealthy while attempting to organize "classless" communes. Often these rebel regimes were short-lived, falling apart because of internal conflicts when equality proved elusive. Sometimes they were successfully repressed. But almost always the losses in lives and property were very high.[4] Consequently, "the word 'Fleming' to outsiders was often synonymous with 'revolutionary.' "[5] After nearly a century of intermittent outbursts, a general revolution broke out in Flanders in 1280. In many towns and cities the lesser merchants and their guilds made common cause with the artisan guilds and together appealed to the Count of Flanders for support, which he granted. It soon became clear, however, that by siding with the rebels, the count's real motive was to regain absolute sovereignty over these cities. Faced with the potential loss of local autonomy, the lesser merchants turned against the artisans,[6] and the rebellions died. However, elites in some towns and cities appealed for help to the King of France. He too responded favorably, but only because he also wanted to make himself the master of Flanders. He soon succeeded in annexing southern Flanders, but an invasion by French troops prompted a united front in northern Flanders. They held fast and dealt a stunning defeat to the French army in the battle of Courtrai in 1302. Victory not only saved northern Flanders from French rule but it also resulted in far more democratic rule in the northern cities. Henceforth, in cities such as Bruges, Ghent, and Antwerp, the artisan guilds exerted substantial influence on political affairs. Prosperity returned.

In contrast, in the southern portion of Flanders commerce stagnated under high taxes, import and export duties, and other forms of exploitation and political repression by the French court. Soon there no longer was a significant woolen industry in Lille, Douai, Orchies, Béthune, and Cambrai. In fact, the combination of repression and a deteriorating economy in southern Flanders did further harm even to northern industry by causing large numbers of cloth makers to emigrate to Italy, where they were warmly welcomed and given many special privileges in exchange for launching a woolen industry. For example, a statute enacted in Padua in 1265 exempted "foreigners who came into the city to make cloth . . . from all tolls and customs duties and later also from personal taxes."[7]

While French repression caused many Flemish cloth makers to take their skills south to Italy, the new freedoms in northern Flanders caused large numbers of southern entrepreneurs to take their skills north. And they brought capitalism with them.

CAPITALISM COMES TO NORTHERN FLANDERS

Following the French annexation of the Walloon districts in the south, northern Flanders became the center of the European woolen industry, which was particularly concentrated in the cities of Bruges, Ghent, and Antwerp. Importing fleeces from England and trade goods from Italy in exchange for woolen cloth made Flanders a financial as well as a manufacturing giant. Having managed to overcome the most repressive effects of the local guilds, firms began to grow and to manifest the primary features of capitalism. However, this capitalism was not native to Flanders. It was imported by entrepreneurs who supplanted the merchants and weavers' guild with well-managed firms that integrated the entire woolen industry: importing the fleeces, coordinating all of the steps and hiring all of the subcontractors necessary to turn wool into cloth, and then exporting it based on market conditions. An early "market-driven" innovation was that, in addition to its more expensive, luxury woolens, Flanders soon began to produce less expensive varieties that led to an immense increase in sales.

These "Flemish" entrepreneurs were Italians, and their firms were Italian branch banks. Recall that, having not been content to continue buying cloth at the cycle of northern fairs, Italian banks had set up permanent branches in leading woolen centers in order to buy directly on a regular basis. Having done so, the bankers quickly recognized the inefficiencies of the guild system and saw that they could greatly increase their profits and better coordinate production to demand by managing the industry directly. In addition to organizing the woolen industry and selling the cloths abroad, the Italian banks imported and sold all manner of trade goods from elsewhere. Of course, they also lent money and dealt in bills of exchange. Soon, "only the trade and the credit of the Italian merchants kept the looms humming."[8]

Bruges

But if Italians kept the looms humming in Flanders, it is equally accurate to say that the looms of Flanders were so vital to Italian banking that no firm without a Bruges branch ever amounted to much. All three of the "supercompanies" did nearly as much business in Bruges as at home, and the same was true for the Medici Bank a century later. In fact, of all its branches, the Medici Bank in Bruges had the largest capitalization—higher even than that of the home bank in Florence.[9]

But why manufacture woolens? Because the poor soil of Flanders was far more suitable for grazing sheep than for raising crops. Moreover, Flanders's sheep produced good quality fleeces, and since the sheep ranches were spread out, the early cloth industry was widely dispersed in rather small villages. In time, however, Flanders's weavers became increasingly dependent upon English fleeces, which were markedly superior even to their own. Consequently, the woolen industry was concentrated in larger communities that had firms with sufficient capital to support foreign trade. Chief among these cities was Bruges, especially with the arrival of Italian bankers.

Not that Bruges ever became a manufacturing town. It lived instead from trade and transportation. Nearly all of the fleeces imported from England came to Bruges and were then sent on to inland weaving towns such as Ghent,[10] from whence finished cloth was returned to Bruges for export. Moreover, before the appearance of Italian ships, Flemish boats (mostly based in Bruges) dominated commercial transport in the channel. When Genoan and Venetian ships entered the picture, they unloaded their spices, silks, and other southern goods at Bruges and loaded cargoes of woolen cloth. Given this strategic location, Bruges (the name means "landing stage") became the dominant financial and trading center of northern Europe. It is impossible to say exactly when this was accomplished, but within several years of Genoa's victory over the Muslim fleet guarding the Strait of Gibraltar in 1291, regular voyages between Bruges and Genoa began—mostly involving large round ships although some galley traffic took place during the summer. In response to all this commercial activity, Bruges became a large city, with about forty thousand residents in 1340, rising to perhaps ninety thousand in 1500.[11]

As noted, the initial commercial development of Flanders was mainly an Italian achievement because only the Italians had mastered the necessary business methods.[12] And as they established branch banks, not only in Bruges but also in other strategic Flanders locations, the Italians negotiated remarkable treaties to protect and further their interests, which gave them substantial trading advantages and extraterritorial rights setting them legally apart from the local community. Typical clauses in these treaties, repeatedly reaffirmed by each new Count of Flanders, were (1) a prohibition on the count's ability to usurp any bank property; (2) that no Italian banker could be arrested for debt; (3) that local authorities could in no way interfere with an Italian ship captain's right to discipline his crew while in port; (4) should officials wish to expel an Italian banker from Flanders, eight months' notice must be given to allow him to dispose of his property; (5) that no additional local duties could be charged beyond those agreed upon with the count. It was not, however, a one-way street. In 1395 the Italians agreed that all their ships would stop in Bruges and offer their goods for sale before going on to England, giving the right of first refusal to the Bruges merchants. The city of Bruges sweetened the deal by paying the Italians 9,500 gold francs.[13]

Although the Italians depended upon their treaties with the Count of Flanders, the leading cities in Flanders enjoyed substantial independence and, for the times, a remarkable degree of democracy—especially after the united front against French invaders resulted in greatly extending the franchise. So, manufacturing and commerce had the freedom and the security from seizure needed to flourish and to allow the development of capitalism. Granted that, so long as it was dominated by Italians, there were colonial aspects to early Flemish capitalism, it was true capitalism nonetheless. Moreover, during the fifteenth century the Italian hegemony of commerce waned as locals gained the necessary commercial skills to manage their own firms. In fact, the very first bourse, precursor to the modern stock exchange, was originated in Bruges by Flemish merchants in 1453. No shares in companies were sold in this first bourse (the word means "exchange"), but it was a marketplace where investors gathered to buy and sell commercial paper such as bills of exchange and mortgages.

For several centuries the Italians reaped the fruits of Flemish commerce because the locals lacked sufficient knowledge of commercial techniques. During this period, the Bruges harbor would have remained a rather sleepy little port had it not been for Italian ships. But the Flemings soon learned how to do business for themselves and to capitalize on what they had understood for centuries: how to weave fine woolens.

Ghent

Bruges's leadership in trade and finance was matched by Ghent's leadership in manufacturing. Exporters from Bruges patronized the cloth market in Ghent's town hall, and importers from Ghent bought cargoes of wool, wine, grain, and hides from ships arriving in Bruges. This trade was facilitated by the fact that Ghent was (and is) linked to Bruges by the Lieve Canal. Even so, although the Italian branch banks made it possible for merchants in Bruges to engage in trade over very long distances based on written correspondence, for lack of such banks in Ghent it was difficult to buy or sell between the two cities without direct, personal contact. This impediment was tolerable because it took only about twelve hours to journey between Bruges and Ghent,[14] so businessmen from one city frequently maintained regular accommodations at inns in the other city. Even so, the local courts labored under a burden of suits brought by unpaid sellers and unhappy buyers.

Cloth making in Ghent might date from Roman times, but it is first attested to late in the tenth century. Even then it must have been on a very modest scale, since in 1100 the population numbered fewer than five thousand. Then came the booming export market. By 1340 Ghent had a population of about fifty-six thousand,[15] more than two-thirds employed in the woolen industry. Later in that decade, when the Black Death killed such large numbers in most European cities, Ghent seems to have been spared, although it suffered greatly at that same time from a political revolution that caused many deaths and disenfranchised the weavers, many of whom then moved elsewhere. This, combined with several outbreaks of plague in the 1360s, cut Ghent's population by half. Although, as with all European industries, Ghent's woolen business suffered from the immediate decline in demand caused by the Black Death, the city was too short of weavers to respond to the increased demand that soon resulted when marked increases in individual purchasing power (due to higher wages reflecting labor shortages) made it possible to sell more to fewer people. So, many "regular customers began looking elsewhere for their cloth,"[16] and this gave further stimulation to the rise of a textile industry in the Italian city-states.

Even so, the people of Ghent continued to spin, weave, full, and dye. Slowly, commercial interests reasserted themselves and Ghent's woolen industry revived. But never again was Ghent a one-industry city, nor did it any longer lack domestic capitalist firms. Ghent soon developed thriving enterprises in ironworking, bell casting, kettle making, gold- and silversmithing, leather working, furriery, shoemaking, and tailoring. Guilds still played a major role in controlling these industries, but only at the workshop level. Finances, production goals, and marketing were controlled by larger firms, managed by sophisticated capitalists. And just as Bruges continued to thrive from trade and shipping, Ghent expanded its role as an internal trading center to distribute goods—those it produced and those it shipped in from elsewhere—throughout the region. In doing so, Ghent took advantage of its location on the Scheldt River, which flows north to Antwerp.

Antwerp

To discover highly developed capitalism in northern Europe, one need only examine Antwerp, which by late in the fifteenth century "was the richest and perhaps the most famous city in Europe,"[17] described by the medieval Italian traveler and writer Ludovico Guicciardini as "Venice outdone." The volume of trade passing through Antwerp's port far surpassed anything known anywhere in previous history. "For never since has there been a market which concentrated to such a degree the trade of all the important commercial nations of the world."[18]

The Portuguese discovery of a sea route around Africa to the East Indies in 1493 made Antwerp even more important as a trade center because the King of Portugal shipped nearly everything (mostly spices, particularly pepper) arriving back in Lisbon from Asia on to Antwerp, in part because syndicates organized there were prepared to buy entire cargoes, often while the ships were still in transit. In this way it was possible for a syndicate to achieve a short-term monopoly on spices and keep prices high. The English used similar tactics in managing their woolen exports, sending all their cloths to Antwerp and doling them out from there so as to maximize profits. So too for the large volume of metals, especially copper, coming out of eastern Europe. Once Venice had been the chief outlet, but by the start of the sixteenth century the shipments went mainly to Antwerp, and from there to the rest of the world.[19]

Even so, and although there was also a substantial industrial sector within the city, the true specialty of Antwerp was finance. "For nearly a century . . . this cosmopolitan city controlled exclusively the money market of the known world . . . every important loan in Europe was negotiated here."[20] For example, in 1519 the local branch of the Fugger Company lent more than half a million gold guilders to Charles V (recently crowned King of Spain, but born and raised in Ghent) to fund his election as the Holy Roman Emperor.

Antwerp's rise to power and glory was not only rapid, but in many ways it was an act of nature. In 1375–76, and then again in 1406, severe storms struck the Flanders coast, causing huge waves and tides that scoured a deep harbor, "allowing large seagoing vessels to reach the port of Antwerp for the first time."[21] Meanwhile, nature was interfering with Bruges's access to the sea. Recall that centuries earlier storms had given Bruges a port via the Zwin River. Unfortunately the river began to silt up, and despite dredging, eventually it became necessary for ships to unload at an increasing distance from Bruges. By the 1450s seagoing ships actually harbored at Sluis and offloaded their cargoes onto small barges of shallow draft, which could be towed seven miles upriver to Bruges. Understandably, this impediment encouraged a shift in traffic to Antwerp, which enhanced its newly gained natural harbor by construction of enormous port facilities, complete with cranes to speed unloading. In addition, Antwerp had the advantage of being located at the mouth of the Scheldt River, which rises in France (as the Escaut), runs through Lille, Tournai, and Ghent on its way to the ocean, and has long served as a major artery for inland water transportation.

Politics also played a crucial role in the emergence of Antwerp. While Bruges and other northern Flemish cities endured decades of brutal civil strife and then a war to prevent annexation by France, Antwerp remained at peace, and many merchants, especially foreigners, abandoned Bruges and Ghent for the safety of Antwerp. Consequently, what had been a sleepy little village in the thirteenth century became a city of perhaps one hundred thousand, many of them foreigners, by early in the sixteenth century.[22] And when newcomers arrived they found a city steeped in freedom and tolerance. Bruges was "free compared with the restrictions prevalent in [most] other cities in the Middle Ages, but in comparison with the absolute freedom enjoyed by the foreign merchants in Antwerp, Bruges seems medieval."[23] For example, in Bruges, as in nearly all medieval towns and cities, hotels and lodging houses were subject to "many stringent regulations" closely enforced by the authorities, but there were no such regulations in Antwerp—anyone could take a room provided they could pay. As to commerce, there were practically no restrictions. As a memorandum from the foreign merchants of Antwerp to Philip II put it: "No one can dispute, they say, that the liberty granted to merchants is the cause of the prosperity of this city."[24]

As with all independent northern cities (until the advent of Spanish repression), a distant nobleman—a duke or a margrave—was acknowledged as the titular ruler, and in Antwerp he was represented by the *schout* (or sheriff), who appeared on behalf of the crown in criminal cases. "In reality Antwerp was a free commune" governed by a three-tiered representative body.[25] At the top were two burgomasters charged with administration; they were selected from a College of Magistrates, which consisted of eighteen *skepyns* (aldermen), a treasurer, a secretary, and an advocate, in addition to the other burgomasters. The College was selected from and advised by the Broad Council, consisting of all past *skepyns,* two *wijickmasters* from each of the city's twelve wards, and two representatives from each of the twelve major guilds. While the *schout* commanded a body of troops, each of the twelve wards also had its own soldiers.

This arrangement sustained a high level of individual freedom and secure property rights.

Although capitalism seems to have reached new heights in Antwerp, it was a matter only of magnitude, not innovation. Every financial and commercial technique employed there was well known.[26] What occurred in Antwerp was capitalism on a far larger, international scale. Thus, while the first bourse appeared in Bruges, this capitalist institution soon reached new heights in Antwerp. In fact there were two bourses in Antwerp. One was controlled by the English merchants and specialized in commodities. Merchants of every nationality "go morning and evening at a certain time to the Bourse of the English. There they do business with the help of brokers of every language, who are there in great numbers, chiefly as to the buying and selling of commodities of every kind."[27] Eventually, much of the activity of the English bourse was devoted to buying and selling futures, speculating on price changes over as little as an hour or as long as several months. As is true even today, trading in commodities futures was extremely risky and spawned an amazing array of systems—several of the most popular being based on astrology. In addition to the English bourse, the Antwerp bourse specialized in financial paper: bills of exchange, mortgages, and short-term bonds issued by various governments and rulers, including the Habsburgs. On both bourses, traders tended to cluster according to nationality— "the Antwerp Bourse seemed a small world wherein all parts of the great world were united."[28] In fact, the early capitalists in Antwerp were foreigners, many of them Italians, who left Bruges to escape its outbreaks of violence. Although they soon were joined by locals, the commercial community continued to become ever more cosmopolitan as the vast scope of the city's trading network drew entrepreneurs from northern and eastern Europe as well as from Spain and Portugal.

All of this was achieved well before the Reformation, while Antwerp was a profoundly Catholic community, "a city of churches and religious foundations heavily endowed by the affluent populace."[29] In fact, when Protestantism arrived it mostly recruited the least-skilled workers and nearby farmers, while the "capitalistic families for the most part remained loyal to the Church."[30] So much for claims about the Protestant ethic. Ironically, it was the Reformation that destroyed capitalism in Antwerp and in most of Flanders, as will be pursued in the next chapter.

ON TO AMSTERDAM

By late in the sixteenth century Amsterdam was replacing Antwerp as Europe's primary port and financial center. It did so largely by default, as Antwerp's economy was wrecked by war and Spanish occupiers, who destroyed its democratic practices and ate up its financial and commercial institutions.

It is remarkable that Amsterdam was able to function as a port, because entry to its shallow harbor required passage over a large mud bank. Through the fifteenth century this was accomplished by keeping the ships serving Amsterdam small and relatively flat-bottomed. Although the Dutch continued to prefer ships of shallow draft, compared with English ships, by the sixteenth century even Dutch ships became too large and too deep of draft to come over the mud bank. The dredging technology of the times could not remove such a massive barrier, so the port remained in business by use of "ships camels, huge drums filled with water and chained under the ships. When pumped dry, they elevated the ships so they could slide across the bank. This makeshift system lasted for 135 years."[31]

It is true that when Amsterdam took Antwerp's place as the leading port and financial center of western Europe, it was a Protestant city. But to use this in support of the Protestant ethic thesis ignores not only many centuries of prior Catholic capitalism but the fact that capitalism was brought to Amsterdam by an immense migration of refugees, most of them Catholics, who fled Antwerp and Flanders, bringing their firms and their sophisticated skills with them.[32] During 1585–87, perhaps as many as 150,000 refugees came north as Antwerp's population fell by half, as did the populations of Ghent and Bruges. Not all of these people came to Amsterdam. Some settled in other Dutch cities, while many stayed only briefly before moving on to Germany and England. But early in the 1600s a third of Amsterdam's one hundred thousand residents consisted of newly arrived foreigners. Not surprisingly, a new Dutch textile industry quickly developed, mostly owned and operated by newcomers. Equally quickly, the Portuguese spice merchants shifted their distribution center from Antwerp to Amsterdam. And since Amsterdam has access to the Rhine, it soon dominated imports and exports from Germany.

Nevertheless, bulky commodities remained of major importance. The Dutch had long dominated the transport of grain, timber, salt, ore, and wine in the Baltic region. With the emergence of Amsterdam as the new center of commerce, this trade boomed. For example, between 1590 and 1600 Dutch shippers displaced the English as carriers of the Muscovy trade, seasonally sailing around the top of Scandinavia to the Russian port of Archangel.[33] The reason for the virtual Dutch monopoly on bulky cargoes was lower costs. They built very wide ships of limited draft that could accommodate very large cargoes. They could sail with relatively small crews, and they devoted no significant amount of space on their ships to armaments. The Dutch also enjoyed substantially lower costs for shipbuilding materials. Hence, compared with the English they could haul much more per ship, at lower labor costs, and with a significantly lower per ship investment. The English gave priority to the fighting capacity of their ships, including their merchant ships, which greatly reduced their cargo capacity but made them especially suited for the "rich trades"—to transport light, small luxury goods that attracted pirates. Pirates had no interest in shiploads of pine logs, wheat, or salted herring, so Dutch ships had no need for the speed, the large crews, or the substantial complement of cannons, that characterized English merchant ships. The Dutch also could build ships much more cheaply because while the English had a good supply of local timber to build hulls, they were badly lacking in the tall, straight pine trees needed for masts and many other crucial naval supplies. As the remarkable Vassar College naval historian Violet Barbour explained: "Prices for timber, deals, plank, hemp, flax, pitch and tar were far higher in England than Holland. These high prices were reflected in the cost of shipbuilding, and the cost of shipbuilding was reflected in freight rates. The English merchant could not build cheaply because he could not import timber and other materials cheaply, and he could not import cheaply because he could not build cheaply."[34] Quite simply, for transporting bulky commodities, English ships cost too much and carried too little.

Many writers have linked Dutch Calvinism and capitalism as a leading example of the Protestant ethic. As R. H. Tawney put it: "An earnest, zealous, godly generation, scorning delights, punctual in labor, constant in prayer, thrifty and thriving, filled with a decent pride in themselves and their calling, assured that strenuous toil is acceptable to Heaven, a people like those Dutch Calvinists whose economic triumphs were as famous as their iron Protestantism."[35] Should one doubt the point, one merely needs to look at the sober expressions and somber dress worn by members of the Dutch bourgeoisie depicted by Rembrandt. But it simply wasn't true! Even for the times, Amsterdam was quite wild and wide open. "The sober garb of the burgher aristocracy and the clergy contrasted sharply with the colorful costumes of the lower classes and the finery of plumed gallants, both native and foreign."[36] In fact, the Calvinist preachers could not even get businesses or the pubs to shut down for the Sabbath. As it reached its economic peak, many of Amsterdam's leading capitalists remained Catholics, while many others quite openly professed themselves to be irreligious "libertines."[37] Of course, some of the foreign newcomers embraced Calvinism, since that was the official faith, and for a time the Dutch regime imposed some disabilities on religious nonconformity—Lutherans, Mennonites, and Catholics could not hold services in some parts of the Dutch Republic and Catholic priests were barred in some places. Still, there were many Catholics in most areas of the country, and in Amsterdam, "a substantial body of prominent citizens"[38] remained Catholic. To a considerable extent, "the expansion of Dutch trade and the development of the commercial spirit were carried on in spite of the Calvinist Church rather than because of it. . . . Dutch Calvinism was opposed to the working of the capitalist spirit, and . . . Calvinist Holland was quite distinct from commercial Holland."[39]

From the start, Amsterdam's commercial prominence was challenged, as was its independence. For several generations, the Dutch Republic had to fight off repeated attempts by the Spanish to make it a part of the Spanish Netherlands, and to evade covetous maneuvers by the French. Then they had to battle the English to maintain their trade and colonies. In the end, of course, the tiny Dutch Republic did not prevail; the remarkable fact was that it could play so major a role for so long. For centuries the Dutch successfully withstood Spanish and French offensives, and eventually they even battled the English to a long standoff. Dutch power finally evaporated during three decades of suppression as part of Napoleon's empire, during which England seized most of the Dutch colonies.[40] But throughout, capitalism shaped Holland's commercial landscape as completely as windmills and dikes shaped its geography.

ENGLISH CAPITALISM

While economies boomed in Flanders and Holland, capitalism took a firm hold in England as well. Here too, as in Flanders, capitalism arrived in the form of Italian semicolonialism. Italian banks proliferated in England (and Ireland) during the thirteenth century,[41] a fact acknowledged in the Magna Charta, signed in 1215, which guaranteed the rights of foreign merchants to enter the country and conduct their business without hindrance. By the start of the thirteenth century, London had foreign merchant enclaves quite similar to those formed by Western colonialists in Asia some centuries later. But here the word *"semi*colonialism" is apt because foreign merchants operated in England only at the pleasure of the crown, and were not backed by military pressure. Secure behind the channel, the English had become one of the major Western powers, soon to conduct the Hundred Years War in defense of their possessions in France.

The English were also blessed with an exceptionally productive agriculture and vast mineral resources, as well as abundant waterpower. So it was only a matter of time before they went into business for themselves, imposing unfavorable taxes and duties on foreign firms and products, meanwhile confronting them with increasingly effective competition from English firms. Even so, it was the decline of feudalism and the remarkable rise of political freedom that gave the greater impetus to English capitalism. As was made explicit in the Magna Charta, the English merchants enjoyed secure property rights and free markets, unlike early capitalists in southern Italy and those in the Walloon area of Flanders, who were destroyed by despots. Moreover, unlike those on the Continent, English industries did not need to huddle in a few crowded, expensive, independent cities but could enjoy the same political freedom in rural areas and small towns as they could in London. As a result, English industries were remarkably decentralized. Perhaps of even greater importance, freedom and the security of property greatly spurred invention and innovation, with the result that English industries developed or exploited technologies far superior to those used by their European competitors. The Industrial Revolution was not a revolution at all but an *evolution* of invention and innovation that began in England perhaps as early as the eleventh century.

As was the case in Flanders, capitalism first came to England in response to the woolen trade, and the early development of English capitalism took place almost entirely within this single industry. Therefore, close examination of how capitalism transformed the English woolen industry offers the most revealing perspective on the rise of English industrial capitalism. This will be followed by a sketch of the way that these initial lessons in capitalism were utilized and elaborated as England shifted from wood power to coal.

From Wool to Woolens

The basic contours of this story are clear in Table 5-1 (all figures have been rounded). In the thirteenth century, England was, in effect, a vast sheep ranch serving the continental woolen industry, both in Flanders and in Italy. English exports of cloth were so insignificant that no tax records exist. However, wool exports were rapidly climbing, from an annual average of 17,700 sacks in 1278–80 to 34,500 sacks a year in the first decade of the fourteenth century, or almost 9 million fleeces (the standard sack of wool contained about 260 fleeces).[42] By midcentury, the first statistics on exports of

TABLE 5-1 *English Wool Exports, 1279–1540*

YEARS	AVERAGE ANNUAL EXPORT OF CLOTHS (IN BOLTS)	AVERAGE ANNUAL EXPORT OF FLEECES (IN SACKS)
1278–80	—	17,700
1281–90	—	23,600
1301–10	—	34,500
1347–48	4,400	—
1351–60	6,400	33,700
1401–10	31,700	13,900
1441–50	49,400	9,400
1501–10	81,600	7,500
1531–40	106,100	3,500
1543–44	137,300	1,200

Constructed from Carus-Wilson and Coleman, 1963

woolen cloths become available. The annual average for 1347–48 was 4,400 cloths (bolts of woolen fabric about twenty-eight yards long). Because export duties on fleeces had been farmed out for those years, no record of fleece exports survive, but the average for the next decade was 33,700 sacks a year, or slightly below the level at the turn of the century. From then on, cloth exports rose rapidly and fleece exports declined correspondingly. At the end of that century, the English exported 31,700 cloths and only 13,900 sacks of wool. By 1543–44 annual English exports of woolen cloth amounted to 137,300 bolts, and fleece exports were down to an insignificant 1,200 sacks.

The table reflects two of the three primary features of the rise of the English woolen industry. First was the development of English cloth-making firms. Second was the imposition of taxes and export duties specifically designed to keep the superb English wool out of the hands of foreign weavers. Not shown, but no surprise, is that when the English exported most of their wool, they imported most of their cloth. During 1333–36 imports averaged about 10,000 cloths a year. Of course, as the English woolen industry grew, less was imported, so that even by 1355–57 the number of imported cloths had dropped to about 6,000 a year.[43] As these three trends ran their course, the English eventually came to dominate the world woolen market completely.

English woolen manufacturing began on a relatively small scale but took full advantage of the superiority of local wool by specializing in a luxury product—by early in the thirteenth century wealthy Europeans would buy only English cloth,[44] the very best of which was often dyed scarlet and esteemed by European royalty.

Although the volume of English woolen exports was still small, the Venetians became concerned and imposed a special import tariff on English woolens in 1265, thereby raising the price charged for English woolens by Venetian merchants in comparison with the Italian-made woolens they traded in the East and with Islam. The lesson was not lost on the English crown, and ten years later the king imposed an export duty on English fleeces. This meant, of course, that English cloth makers could buy the superior English fleeces much cheaper than could cloth makers in Flanders and Italy, and could sell the finished cloths abroad for less—only a very small export duty ever was imposed on woolens, and at first this duty was limited to foreign merchants. Even when an export duty was applied to English merchants, it was kept to a very modest rate. Thus sheltered from foreign competition and having increasingly exclusive access to the best wool, the English woolen industry eventually achieved the preeminence that it maintained for centuries.

But there was more to it than just having the best fleeces and favorable government tax policies. Just as the Italian woolen industry had benefited from substantial immigration of skilled artisans from Flanders fleeing the bloody civil disturbances that beset that region, so too did the English. In 1271 Henry III "decreed that 'all workers of woollen cloths, male and female, as well of Flanders as of other lands, may safely come into our realm, there to make cloths' and he granted them freedom from taxation for five years."[45] In 1337 Edward III further extended these benefits to Flemish cloth makers and even sent recruiters among them. It was not only weavers and fullers and dyers who came. Some entrepreneurs brought their entire firms, workers and all, to England. Nor was it simply that these people were inclined to flee Flanders; they were drawn to England because of greater freedom, political stability, lower costs, and finer raw materials. Most of all, they were drawn by far higher wages and profits because of superior technology.

Perhaps the most remarkable feature of the English wool industry, one that subsequently was imitated by many other English industries, was dispersion. There never really were any "woolen" cities in England similar to those in Flanders, or even Italy. Although English woolen firms were as large as any found on the Continent, they were scattered through the rural countryside. The reasons for this were technological and political.

The Thirteenth-Century Industrial Revolution *by water powered mills + tool*

In 1941 Eleanora Carus-Wilson pointed out that from very early days the English woolen industry had rapidly migrated from urban locations to villages and rural areas. Why? Several factors were involved, but water-powered fulling mills played such an important role that Carus-Wilson entitled her famous paper "An Industrial Revolution of the Thirteenth Century."

Fulling is major step in producing good cloth. When cloth comes from the loom it is quite loose. The process of fulling involves submerging a cloth in water (usually containing a natural clay detergent called "fuller's earth") and beating it very vigorously. When fulling is properly done, the cloth will shrink by as much as half its prefulled dimensions, making the fabric much tighter and stronger; fulling also cleans the cloth of oils and "felts" it so that the surface becomes far smoother and softer.[46] Three traditional methods of fulling were used: a submerged cloth was beaten with the feet, with the hands, or with clubs. A wall painting in Pompeii shows a nearly naked fuller standing in a trough, stomping on a cloth while holding on to the sides of the trough. These traditional methods were still used in Flanders, Italy, and, for a time, in England too. Then at some point a new method was introduced: two wooden hammers, attached to a drum and turned by a crank, were raised and dropped on the cloth in a trough—although the process still depended on muscle power. An immense breakthrough occurred when someone hooked such a device to a water mill (one probably constructed to grind grain), with the result that a very physically demanding task that often required employment of a crew of fullers could now be done mechanically by a single operator overseeing a whole series of hammers able to full a large amount of cloth quickly. An important variant on the fulling mill was the hemp mill, which used the same hammer arrangement to crush flax stalks in order to free the fibers for use in weaving linen.

Carus-Wilson pointed out that the invention of the fulling mill "was as decisive an event [for the woolen industry] as were the mechanization of spinning and weaving in the eighteenth century, but we know neither when nor where, much less by whom, the fulling mill was invented."[47] Some historians propose that fulling mills appeared in the eleventh century and some say it was not until the twelfth, but fulling mills were so common in the thirteenth century that they revolutionized the English industry, leaving Europe far behind. And it was due to the fulling mill that the woolen industry had a marked preference for villages and rural areas on good streams.[48] Such locations had several additional advantages. Moving water was also very useful for dyers, who needed to rinse excess dye from their cloths. Moreover, locating in a rural area permitted firms to escape repressive guild regulations, to pay far lower taxes than those imposed by towns and cities, and to pay lower wages because the cost of living was much lower too. Consequently, the capitalists running woolen firms avoided the cities and set up shop in small towns and villages.[49]

Why didn't this happen in Europe? Because in Europe it was only in the cities that there existed enough freedom and sufficiently secure property rights to sustain industry. In the European countryside feudalism still prevailed, and everyone had to fear the local lord's avarice. But in England, freedom and security prevailed throughout the realm, and the "proverb 'City air maketh free' could have had little meaning for an Englishman . . . least of all for an aspiring captain of industry."[50] Thus there was no need for medieval English industrialists to huddle in crowded, expensive, disorderly, filthy cities—many devoid of waterpower—as their counterparts in Flanders, Holland, along the Rhine, and in Italy were forced to do. The analogous English proverb could well have been "Country air maketh money." Nor was it the case that rural English cloth makers were thereby small, unsophisticated firms. To the contrary, fulling mills required a very substantial capital investment, and rural firms needed to maintain a sizable labor force since their locations minimized the availability of subcontractors.

It should be noted that fulling gave the English cloth a significant advantage on the international market. Of course, cloth makers on the Continent also fulled cloth—their ancestors had done so for many centuries. But the continental cloth makers fulled only *some* of their cloths, although this entailed a large sacrifice in quality[51]—clothing made of unfulled cloth would be ruined by shrinking were one caught out in the rain. Unfulled cloths reflected the lack of fulling mills—fulling by hand or foot is very labor intensive, being time-consuming and very tiring. It has been estimated that without fulling mills the number of fullers required was nearly half as many as the number of weavers, "whereas one fuller working at a mill would be able to finish the product of 40 to 60 weavers."[52]

Not only did the English profit by fully exploiting the advantages of the fulling mill; this was but the first step in their mechanization of the textile industry. Soon after the fulling mill came the gig mill, for raising the pile on fabrics. Then, in 1589, came the knitting machine; then the flying shuttle (1733), the spinning jenny (1770), the spinning mule (1779), and the power loom (1785). All of these inventions met with angry worker resistance, but when James Watt built the first practical steam engine in 1776, there they were, along with many other mechanical contrivances, waiting to be hooked up! Technological innovation was the hallmark of English capitalism.

Finally, dispersion and relatively unfettered capitalism may have entered into the international dominance of English woolens in an unexpected way, by producing more fashionable and attractive products. As A. R. Bridbury put it, to explain the success of English woolens it is not enough to invoke better fleeces or lower prices; what should be stressed is "art and skill . . . the exotic dyeing of these cloths and . . . the subtle blending of design and colour in their creation . . . the search for making cloth which would be more fashionable internationally."[53] In European textile centers the guilds often exerted the dead hand of tradition on colors and designs, and originality nearly always suffers when creative people are crowded together and fully aware of one another's work. Far greater variation in styles and quality was likely to turn up in England's dispersed woolen industry, where designers couldn't look over one another's shoulders. Moreover, the freedom of their capitalist managers to shape production with little interference meant that favorable feedback among various offerings could rapidly be reflected in production. In modern terminology, the English woolen industry was "marketing driven."

Although the woolen industry was the initial basis of England's rise to international commercial prominence, it was by applying the lessons learned from woolens to other opportunities that the English became the world's first truly industrial nation. The crucial next step was the rise of coal-powered industries, a development that helps to reveal the dynamic link between capitalism and technological innovation.

Coal Power

For most purposes, wood is an inferior fuel. But in ancient times, in most inhabited parts of the globe, it was relatively abundant and close at hand. Coal, by contrast, is a far superior fuel but was much less widely available, and as surface seams were used up, it became increasingly difficult to obtain, and very expensive to transport. So the ancients depended almost entirely on wood and charcoal not only to heat their buildings and to cook and bake but for all processes requiring heat, such as metallurgy and making bricks, glass, soap, salt, pottery, and even for brewing. The low temperatures produced by wood fires imposed severe limits on the quality of these products. For example, most weapons and armor were made of bronze and brass because these were alloys of soft metals that melted at a relatively low temperature. It was well known that iron was far superior for these purposes, but it required much higher temperatures—it could be worked with charcoal heat, but not melted so that it could be poured.

In the twelfth century, London began to grow quite rapidly, and the price of firewood began to rise too as nearby sources were used up. A century later wood prices were increasing so rapidly as to cause hardship for many London families. At Hampstead, about five miles from London, the firewood unit known as a faggot sold for about twenty pence per hundred in the 1270s. By the 1290s the price had risen to thirty-eight pence. In Surrey, about twenty miles from London, the price of firewood increased "by some 50 percent between the 1280s and the 1330s."[54] Meanwhile, since about 1180 several London industries had begun to import coal by water from Newcastle, and the price of this coal rose very little as firewood became increasingly expensive. Moreover, this English coal was of very high quality and produced far more heat per pound than did wood. As the price gap between coal and wood narrowed, more firms needing industrial heat switched to coal. The competitive price of coal in England partly reflected technical improvements in mining and transportation, but to a far greater extent, the growing market for coal *prompted* the invention and adoption of such technology. In addition, just as waterpower caused the woolen industry to cluster near streams, the switch from wood to coal caused many industries to cluster near coal mines; as a result "the size of the enterprise in a number of industries increased greatly."[55]

Even in England, where high-quality coal was abundant, it soon proved necessary to follow seams well belowground. Boring rods were invented to locate seams. Underground rather than strip-mining necessitated removal of the water that often flooded mine shafts. The Romans had dealt with seepage by hand bailing via bucket brigades. The English met the problem with a variety of pumps driven by waterpower or by horses turning a wheel. In similar fashion, the English used ventilating fans powered in the same way as the water pumps to force fresh air down mine shafts.[56] These techniques were used on the Continent too, and some probably originated there, but the English exploited them more extensively because their mines were managed on a far larger scale.

An additional problem facing mining industries was how to transport heavy loads of coal or mineral ores. Toward the end of the reign of Elizabeth I, the solution was found by unknown inventors in southern Nottinghamshire who installed metal rails to support horse-drawn wagons—later known as trams or trolleys. Two techniques were used. One was like the modern railroad in that the wagon wheels were flanged so that they stayed on the track. The second was known as a "plateway" and involved a flange attached to the rails to guide the wagon wheels. At first the latter was the preferred method since, when the wagon reached the end of the rail line, having regular wheels, it could proceed in the regular way. However, the former method was far cheaper since it cost much less to attach flanges to wagon wheels than to put one all along a track. To facilitate flanged wheels, railways often were extended from the mine to a nearby industry, such as a smelter, or to a waterway where barges awaited. The great virtue of rails was to greatly reduce friction, so that much less power was needed to move a load. A wagon set in motion on a rail will roll about five times as far after the power is removed than will one set in motion on a paved highway.[57] Consequently, a horse can pull a far heavier load along rails than down a road. So, long before steam engines, there was an extensive system of rails in the most industrial areas of England. Little wonder that the locomotive was invented in England and that England led the world in the development of railroads. In truth, the extensive horse-drawn rail system virtually demanded perfection of the locomotive once Watt's stationary engine had proved practical and reliable.

As was mentioned, it took coal to work iron properly, both to smelt the ore and to produce molten iron. This was greatly facilitated by the invention of the blast furnace, which utilized water-powered bellows to achieve intense heat. The furnaces themselves were very large, the walls being five or six feet thick. A few blast furnaces were used in Europe as early as the fifteenth century, but they were widely adopted in England by the middle of the sixteenth century. Variants on this technology were soon adopted by the English to make kilns to bake bricks. Of even greater importance was the discovery of how to close the clay crucibles in which glass was made from potash and sand. The result was the capacity to make large amounts of glass so cheaply that soon most English homes had glass windowpanes. In this respect, glass manufacturing was typical. Market after market was expanded and dominated by English products because of breakthroughs in production that resulted in high quality and low costs. By early in the sixteenth century the English were manufacturing the finest cannons in Europe, cast from iron and having much greater range and dependability, while being far cheaper, than the brass and bronze weapons cast on the Continent. Come the battle with the Spanish Armada, the English ships were outnumbered, but the Spanish were outgunned.

Capitalism was essential to England's industrialization. Well-ventilated mines, kept dry by water-powered pumps and served by rail systems, required a very substantial investment and sophisticated management. Smelters with elaborate blast furnaces served by mechanical bellows are not backyard operations. These were capital-intensive activities and required a large, dependable labor force. So, beginning in the very early days of the woolen industry, English firms had been getting larger and more complex, a trend that was surprisingly little affected by plagues, wars, or political turmoil.

It must be recognized, however, that English capitalism could develop as it did only because the English enjoyed unparalleled levels of freedom. It was no coincidence that the nation with the longest tradition of individual liberty was the nation where invention and industry thrived.

It was invention that constituted the success of the West. Large, reliable, well-armed, speedy ships let Europeans travel the globe with impunity. Compasses, mapping technology, accurate clocks, and telescopes allowed them to find their way. Effective firearms helped them dominate wherever they chose to land.

Even so, it wasn't only material inventions that sustained Western success; *cultural inventions* were of even greater importance, especially ideals and methods for organizing and motivating effective collective actions. Methods and ideals are the fundamental aspect of capitalism—rational business techniques based on faith in progress and reason. Freedom, too, is not an aura that floats over societies; it exists only where people believe in freedom and develop methods for sustaining it.

Nor is military might solely a function of weapons and numbers. Reckless New World adventurers such as Cortés and Pizarro did not succeed against seemingly impossible odds mainly because they had firearms. They did so only because their troops were so well disciplined, their officers were so well trained, and because even when only a few dozen conquistadors were surrounded by thousands of Aztecs or Incas, they believed God would give them victory.

Finally, unlike many world religions, Christianity is not a collection of folk beliefs served by wandering priests and scattered, independent temples. From earliest days it has been sustained by well-organized congregations having distinctive creeds. If that has often led to ugly conflicts, it also has generated the energetic missionizing and high levels of individual commitment that have played a major role in the success of the West, both at home and abroad.

Unfortunately, even profound cultural inventions are fragile. So, during the sixteenth century, war, repression, religious conflicts, and greedy despots rearranged the map of European freedom and capitalism.

WE HAVE SEEN HOW CAPITALISM ORIGINATED IN ITALY AND SPREAD from there to Flanders, Holland, and England. But as the seventeenth century dawned, capitalism had mostly disappeared in Italy and Flanders, while those who ruled Europe's two greatest land powers, Spain and France, were no more favorable toward capitalism than they were toward democracy or Protestantism. There they stood, solidly Catholic societies ruled by despots who taxed, looted, and regulated commerce to a virtual standstill. Meanwhile, capitalism continued to flourish in England and Holland, both predominately Protestant.

Little wonder that some jumped to the conclusion that capitalism could prosper only in Protestant contexts, ignoring the fact that it had originated in deeply Catholic societies. Even so, the fact that capitalism languished in both France and Spain, and that Spain had destroyed capitalism in Flanders and the Italian city-states, is of considerable interest. Any adequate discussion of the rise of capitalism in some parts of Europe must also explain its absence or decline in other parts. Overall, Spain probably poses the more significant issues because of its immense New World wealth, its military power, and its foreign aggression. But the role of France requires attention as well.

The theme of this chapter was expressed in Chapter 3: despotic states are avaricious and devour much of the wealth that might go into economic development. However, it would be wrong to suppose that despotic states are weak. Command economies often direct a large part of their resources to sustaining very powerful military forces, as demonstrated by imperial Spain's large, effective, and fierce army, which imposed Spanish rule on substantial sections of Europe. The French kings also fielded impressive armies, having a far larger pool of manpower to draw upon than did any other European nation. Eventually, this numerical supremacy enabled Napoleon temporarily to impose French rule on much of Europe, including Spain—despite the fact that French peasants lived in abject poverty compared with farmers in Holland or England.

But one might wonder: if capitalism was so crucial to the success of Europe, how could Spain and France compete at all? It was not simply because they were big countries, otherwise China and India would have dominated the world. An important factor was that France and Spain were both Christian societies having their full measure of faith in progress and reason, and many people in these nations were quick to recognize new technology and to import the fruits of economic progress, even if they were unable or unwilling to produce it for themselves. Hence, when the Spanish Armada set sail against England, it was a very formidable fleet, even though about the only thing aboard that came from Spain was the crews—all the provisions, arms, and even the ships themselves were imported from elsewhere, much of it from capitalist suppliers. In addition, many French and Spanish entrepreneurs emulated capitalism as best they could within the severe limits imposed by their greedy states, and often were surprisingly productive. Nevertheless, had either Spanish or French territorial ambitions prevailed, Europe would have stagnated, as will be seen. Fortunately, capitalism survived and Europe's progress continued because tiny Holland thwarted Spain's imperial ambitions and the English navy first withstood the Spanish Armada and later drove Napoleon to ruin. Because of capitalism? Perhaps.

1492: BACKWARD SPAIN

Since the start of the seventeenth century, Western historians have devoted immense effort to explaining the "decline of Spain." The English traveler Francis Willughby wrote in 1673 that Spain had fallen on bad times because of "1. A bad religion. 2. The tyrannical Inquisition. 3. The multitude of Whores. 4. The barrenness of the Soil. 5. The wretched laziness of the people very like the Welsh and Irish. 6. The expulsion of the Jews and Moors. 7. Wars and plantations."[1] Forty years later the Florentine ambassador to Spain noted that "poverty is great here, and I believe it is due not so much to the quality of the country as to the nature of the Spaniards, who do not exert themselves; they rather send to other nations the raw materials which grow in their kingdom only to buy them back manufactured by others."[2]

Even very early Spanish writers lamented Spain's decline from the Golden Age it had enjoyed during the reign of Ferdinand and Isabella. As Pedro Fernández Navarrete put it in 1600, "These glorious monarchs raised Spain to the highest state of happiness and greatness it had ever known, in which it remained until decline began." Such views persisted. As the distinguished J. H. Elliot summed up in 1961, "it seems improbable that any account of the decline of Spain can substantially alter the commonly accepted version of seventeenth-century Spanish history, for there are always the same cards, however we shuffle them."[3] But then Henry Kamen produced a whole new deck: *Spain never declined because it never rose!*[4]

Kamen's brilliant revision of the conventional wisdom turns on a crucial distinction between Spain and the Spanish empire. The empire came into being when Charles V, a Habsburg raised in Ghent, succeeded to the crown of Spain through the intricacies of dynastic marriages, and then borrowed a fortune from Jakob Fugger to finance his election as the Holy Roman Emperor, thus bringing portions of the Low Countries, and major parts of Germany, under his rule, along with Spain and its emerging New World colonies. This was a *dynastic* empire, not one built by Spanish expansion or conquest, aside from its foothold in the New World. And Spain's subsequent contributions to the empire mainly consisted of military recruits and gold and silver brought from the New World. These massive amounts of specie caused inflation throughout western Europe and financed the maintenance of large, well-equipped armies to fight the French, Protestant German princes, various Italians, the Dutch, and the English. But New World riches brought no significant benefits to Spain, which remained a very underdeveloped, feudal nation. Once Spain's backwardness was no longer obscured by the grandeur of the empire, it was incorrectly seen as a decline from better times.

It was not Spain but the Spanish empire that destroyed capitalism in Italy and the Netherlands. To set the stage for the havoc wrought by the empire, it will be useful to sketch the economic, social, and political situation of Spain in its Golden Age under Ferdinand and Isabella.

In 1492, when Columbus set sail, "Spain" hardly existed, being the very recent and rather nominal joining of two independent kingdoms, Castile and Aragon. Even today, many people think of themselves as Castilians or Aragonians rather than as Spaniards, and this probably applied to everyone in these kingdoms in 1492, including the royal couple. Isabella's Castile was by far the more important kingdom, having about 6.2 million people and two-thirds of the land area. Upon her marriage to Ferdinand, who held a relatively weak kingship over Aragon, they "unified" their kingdoms to form Spain. The new nation had a total population of about 7.2 million, or about half that of France.[5] From the very start the royal couple were celebrities, and so very popular that after 1480 the Cortes of Castile, a legislative body of the nobility, rarely met and imposed no limits on the crown. Subsequently, the Cortes found itself unable to reject an enormous tax increase imposed by Charles V, and Castile thus reverted to an absolutist state. The Cortes in Aragon continued to exert some influence on local taxes—but Aragon was only the stubby tail of the dog.[6]

In 1482 Ferdinand and Isabella launched an attack on Alhama, a city on the border of Granada, the Moorish (Muslim) nation on the southern coast of the Iberian peninsula, surrounded on three sides by Castile. The city soon fell, and, after a long series of similar attacks, Granada surrendered to Spanish forces on January 2, 1492. While the so-called reconquest of Moorish Spain added several hundred thousand Moors to the population of Spain, it brought only a negligible amount of wealth to the crown,[7] and since the war had been very expensive, victory imposed a very substantial loss. The great need for new sources of income played a major role in the decision to finance Columbus, who set sail within weeks of the return of the royal couple from their triumphant visit to Granada.

The price paid for Granada was an ominous portent of things to come. Over the next century, the costs of empire bled immense wealth from Spain, helping to preserve it as a nation of impoverished peasants, dependent on imports not only for manufactured products but even for sufficient food.

Spanish agriculture was hampered by poor soil and by the very strange institution known as the Mesta. Spanish sheep grew high-quality fleeces, not as good as those of English sheep but better than those from elsewhere. Consequently, Spain's primary export was wool fleeces, and Spain had progressively replaced England as the source of wool for the Flanders and Italian cloth industries. The Mesta was an organization of sheep owners who had royal privileges to sustain migratory flocks of millions of sheep, which they moved across Spain "from their summer pastures in the north to their winter pastures in the south, and then back"[8] north again in the spring—grazing as they went, making it impossible to farm along their routes, which covered huge areas. When conflicts arose with landowners, the crown always sided with the Mesta on grounds that nothing was more important to the economy than the wool exports. So government protection of the Mesta greatly discouraged investments in agriculture.[9] This made it necessary for Spain to import large shipments of grain and other foodstuffs.

Geography also made it difficult to unite a Spanish nation or even to carry on domestic commerce. Rough mountain ranges created easily defended enclaves (as Wellington was to demonstrate during the Napoleonic Wars), but these same natural barriers greatly handicapped commercial transport and "added terrifyingly to prices."[10] For example, it cost more to transport spices from Lisbon to Toledo than it did to buy the spices in Lisbon.

As for manufacturing, Spain had little, and most of what did exist soon perished when the flood of gold and silver from the Americas allowed far greater reliance on imports. Nor did Spain develop much in the way of an indigenous merchant class, its commercial life remaining in the hands of foreigners, most of them from Italy. This was a source of pride among leading Spanish citizens—known as the hidalgos. Manufacturing and commerce were for inferior people and nations, so let others toil for Spain, was how they put it.[11] So, while the empire dominated northern Europe, Spain itself remained frozen in feudalism and was productive mainly of young men, many of them from the nobility, with no escape from poverty except as professional soldiers. These well-trained, long-service, well-equipped Spanish soldiers were the most feared and formidable fighting force in Europe. But they fought for the empire, not Spain. Their victories were far from home, in the Low Countries, in Italy, and along the Rhine. And the means to pay them came from thousands of miles across the Atlantic.

WEALTH AND EMPIRE

At its peak in the sixteenth century, Spain controlled an immense empire that sprawled from the Philippines to Austria, including the Americas, the Netherlands, many portions of Germany, Tunis, Sardinia, Sicily, most of Italy, and all of the Iberian peninsula— Portugal, Navarre, and Roussillon having been added. To protect and control this expanse, the empire maintained regular armies totaling about two hundred thousand men, recruited from all over Europe—large numbers from Ireland, Flanders, Italy, and Germany as well as from Spain. These imperial forces were among the first long-service, standing armies in Europe since the decline of Rome.

But Spain could not arm these fine soldiers. It had no weapons factories, it made no gunpowder, it cast no cannons or even any cannonballs. When an urgent shortage of balls arose in 1572, Philip II wrote to Italy asking that two Italian experts in casting cannonballs be sent at once to Madrid because "there is no one here who knows how to make them."[12] This led nowhere, and when the huge Spanish fleet sailed against England in 1588, all its guns and cannonballs were imported, as was most everything else aboard, including the supply of ship's biscuit. Something that wasn't on board was maps; there weren't any mapmakers in Spain (the first street map of Madrid was published in the Netherlands). So the call went out for pilots who knew the channel coasts. None could be found in Spain; Admiral Medina Sidona had to rely on French pilots to navigate his fleet.[13] Of course, the ships weren't built in Spain either.

What the empire did have, or at least appeared to have, was wealth. The sources of this wealth were three. First, the emperor imposed crushing levels of taxation. For example, taxes in Castile were heavier than anywhere else in Europe—"by 1590 one-third of the average peasant's [gross] income in a good year was consumed in tax."[14] Levels of taxation imposed on all other parts of the empire were only slightly lower than in Castile. Second, huge sums were extracted from church income. Protestant rulers had gained immense wealth by expropriating church property. Given that the Spanish empire was fighting to defeat these "greedy heretics," the pope could hardly resist pressure to share his income. Thus, Charles V was granted a third of all tithes paid to the church within his domains, was allowed to tax church property, and was given other slices of church wealth.[15] The tithes were especially valuable since no one was exempt, whereas many large groups, such as the entire hidalgo class in Spain, had been exempted from imperial taxes.

Finally, and above all, the empire was funded by huge imports of gold and silver from Peru and Mexico, and by convoys of treasure ships bringing spices and silks from Asia. Between 1500 and 1650, over 180 tons of gold and 16,000 tons of silver came to Seville from the New World.[16] These imports tripled Europe's supply of silver and increased the gold supply by about 20 percent.[17] But because of its extraordinary dependence on imports, very little of this wealth stayed in Spain. As the Venetian ambassador remarked, "This gold that comes from the Indies does on Spain as rain does on a roof—it pours on her and it flows away."[18] Substantial amounts flowed to Genoa, whose many merchants residing in Spain controlled much (perhaps most) of its commerce.[19] Much more wealth was dispersed across the empire to pay the soldiers, finance the local administrations, and support allies. Huge sums also went for special undertakings—the direct costs of the Armada sent against England amounted to more than 10 million ducats, about twice the empire's total annual budget and many times more than Queen Elizabeth's income.

Even so, the wealth of the empire was largely illusory when account is taken of its truly staggering debts. It began with Ferdinand and Isabella, who never managed to balance their budgets, so that Charles V assumed their very substantial debts at his coronation. Charles expanded these debts on a properly imperial scale, starting with a sum of more than half a million gold guilders borrowed from Jakob Fugger to gain the Holy Roman emperorship. This too was but a drop in the bucket. During his reign Charles secured more than five hundred loans from European bankers, amounting to about 29 million ducats.[20] Much of this amount still had not been repaid when his son Philip II ascended to the throne in 1556, and a year later Philip declared bankruptcy. Nevertheless, only five years later imperial debt was again so high that 1.4 million ducats, more than 25 percent of the total annual budget, was paid out as interest on current loans.[21] Worse yet, by 1565 the imperial debt in the Low Countries alone stood at 5 million ducats, and interest payments plus fixed costs of governing produced an additional deficit of 250,000 ducats a year.[22] The same pattern held for the empire as a whole—debt dominated everything. During the first half of the 1570s, Phillip II's revenues averaged about 5.5 million ducats a year, while his total expenditures often nearly doubled that amount, with interest on his debts alone exceeding 2 million ducats a year.[23] No one was too surprised when again in 1575 Philip disavowed all his debts, amounting to about 36 million ducats. By doing so, however, he left his regime in the Netherlands penniless. As his governor general complained, "Even if the king found himself with ten millions in gold and wanted to send it here, he has no way of doing so with this Bankruptcy."[24] To send it by sea was far too risky. Only a few years before, in 1568, the Spanish had tried to sneak four small coasters with 155 chests of ducats to Antwerp to pay the Duke of Alva's soldiers. But the boats were intercepted by the English and most of the cash ended up in Queen Elizabeth's treasury.[25] To send money by a letter or bill of exchange also was impossible because there was no Spanish banker in the Netherlands any longer able to pay such an amount, and other bankers would not honor Spanish credit. Eventually, the northern Netherlands was lost in large part for lack of money to pay the troops on time as the empire struggled through many subsequent bankruptcies, the next one coming in 1596.

From the days of Ferdinand and Isabella onward, the empire hemorrhaged money. Eventually, having spent nearly every day of his long reign sitting at his desk in the Escorial reading and writing letters to officials throughout his vast realm, trying in vain to balance his accounts, endlessly seeking new loans and trying to defer repayments, and wondering why God ignored his pleas, Philip II finally faced this brutal truth. In 1598, just before his death, he signed a peace treaty with France and began to cut the ties between Spain and the Netherlands.

This left the English and the Dutch as the major economic forces in Europe, each having achieved advanced levels of capitalism and each in the process of building a colonial empire. By now they faced no serious competition from Italy or Flanders.

SPANISH ITALY

Having been the cradle of advanced capitalism, by the end of the sixteenth century the Italian city-states were no longer major economic powers. What had happened? Many things: extremely aggressive competition from England and northern Europe in their home Mediterranean market, as well as the loss of some of their Middle Eastern commerce to Muslim aggression; a drift toward oligarchy, resulting in less freedom and more precarious property rights. But the final blow was struck by the expansion of the Spanish empire.

It all began when Sicily and Sardinia were subsumed by the crown of Aragon in 1295. Two centuries later they became part of Spain when Ferdinand and Isabella united Castile and Aragon. Then, in 1504, after a decade of battles between French and Castilian troops, the Kingdom of Naples, consisting of all of Italy south of the Papal States, was joined to Aragon. When Charles V became King of Spain in 1516, these large hunks of Italy were his. But he wanted more. To meet this potential threat, France, Venice, Milan, and the Vatican formed the League of Cognac in 1526 to oppose Spanish expansion. The league proved to be a paper tiger when Charles led an army of Spanish veterans and German mercenaries against the pope in 1527. Unfortunately, being short of funds as usual, Charles had not paid his troops for some time, so when they entered Rome unopposed they broke ranks and engaged in a spree of "looting, killing, and burning."[26] Although Charles expressed his most sincere regrets for the Sack of Rome, as it became known all across Europe, it must be said that never again did he, or his son Philip, face open opposition from a pope. To the contrary, the Vatican became a willing and substantial source of imperial funding.

Of course, the French also had designs on the northern city-states. In 1499 Louis XII seized **Milan.** Fourteen years later French rule was overthrown in Milan and the Sforzas took control, only to be ousted after the French defeated them at the battle of Marignano in 1515. In 1529 the French signed a new treaty that restored the Sforzas to power. But in 1535 Milan became part of the Spanish empire. Five years later Charles V appointed his son Philip to be Duke of Milan. Under Spanish rule, which lasted until 1706, the economy stagnated and soon Milan was just another sleepy community with a remarkable past.

As for **Genoa,** in 1396 it submitted to French rule. This continued intermittently, with several eras of rule by Milan, until 1528, when the famous Genoese admiral Andrea Doria broke off his service to France and allied himself with Charles V. This ended French influence in Genoan affairs and greatly strengthened the position of Genoese bankers and merchants in Spain. But it also imposed an oligarchic government in Genoa, one given to high taxes, favoritism, monopolies, and the occasional usurpation, and subject to Spanish control.

Florence retained its independence only by acknowledging a Medici as grand duke and by a web of brilliant marriages linking the Medici to the major European royal dynasties. But unlike their illustrious ancestors, these Medici were not content to rule through an elected body on which they exerted only a soft touch. Instead, these Medici presumed to be monarchs. This eventually aroused republican opposition, and in 1529 the city rebelled against its masters. The Medici appealed for aid, whereupon Spanish forces, joined by papal troops, laid siege to the city. After eleven months the defenders (including Michelangelo) surrendered. A year later Charles arranged the marriage of his half sister Margaret to the newly restored duke. From then on Florence, although technically an independent duchy, was controlled by the empire. Freedom was but a memory and capitalism languished.

Venice was the only one of the four major Italian city-states that did not succumb to Spain. But, surrounded on three sides by Spanish possessions, Venice also slipped into oligarchy and then, overtaxed and overregulated, lost its ability to compete with the English, and to a lesser degree with the Dutch, even in its home Mediterranean market. It is a cautionary tale worth telling.

In the early 1500s Venetians still dominated the fine glass industry. Their textiles were still luxurious, Spanish fleeces having proved an adequate substitute for the now unavailable English wool. Their mirrors were in a class by themselves. So was their soap, their lace, and their porcelain. And Venetian printers, using secret techniques for casting lead type, were the best and most affluent in the world. Things had never been better. Fifty years later the Venetian economy was in shambles and still rapidly declining.

The first phase in the decline of Venice came when some of its most valuable master craftsmen deserted, most of them to England, taking their trade secrets with them.[27] For example, some Venetian master glass makers earned more per day in England than they could earn in a week at home. They allowed the English to become competitive in the fine glass market, augmenting their rapidly expanding dominance of the manufacture of cheap glass.

The question arises as to how the English could be price competitive with Venice when they bribed their master craftsmen to immigrate and also had to ship their goods much farther to compete in the Mediterranean market. This question becomes even more compelling when it is recognized that the English overwhelmed Venice and other competitors by selling goods of equal or superior quality for *far lower* prices! For centuries all European capitalists had embraced the principle of "selling dear"—charging the highest possible prices. But English capitalists, in "a fundamental departure in economic thought . . . [adopted] a new way of thinking about competition and prices . . . [to sell] as cheaply as possible."[28] That is, they took *volume* into account when computing potential returns. And when they did so they realized that they had unbeatable cost advantages, especially vis-à-vis Venice and other Italian industries.

One of these advantages was lower production costs. This was partly a result of lower labor costs, greater mechanization, and better organized and managed industries that were very receptive to technical innovations. In contrast, the Venetian state gave unwavering support to the various trade and craft guilds, and these, in turn, kept labor costs very high and blocked all efforts to innovate. For example, after the English found the bow dyeing method and thereby cut their costs of dyeing cloth by two-thirds, Venetian woolen firms were forbidden to adopt it. "The episode is entirely typical of dozens of other attempts at cost-cutting which were rejected by [the] government."[29] In addition, the English had discovered mass markets for goods of lower quality, such as cheap woolens. These returns soon far exceeded those earned by luxury items. But the Venetians were forbidden to enter these markets; the government felt it far more important to maintain the city's reputation for excellence.

Even so, taxation played by far the major role in pricing Venetian goods out of the market—the government imposed excessive, and ever-increasing, taxes and duties. During the period 1588–1630, Venice's taxes on its woolen industry averaged more than 40 percent of the selling price of cloths. This included import duties on raw materials, various taxes on all manufactured goods, and export duties. The import duty alone allowed the English to price their woolens 15 percent below Venice.[30] And since English taxes on industries were very low and export duties minimal, in combination with lower production costs English merchants often could make excellent profits while charging half the Venetian prices. Of course, Venetian merchants made many attempts to convince the government to reduce taxes and to permit adoption of cost-cutting technologies. Unfortunately, when despots begin dipping into golden eggs, the goose is soon cooked.

In 1635 the Venetian bailiff at Constantinople wrote: "The English devote their attention to depriving our people of the little trade that remains to them in the mart of Constantinople."[31] But it was not the English who overwhelmed Venetian capitalism, it was the Venetian state.

So much for the glories of medieval Italy.

THE SPANISH NETHERLANDS

Since capitalism in the Low Countries far predated the Reformation, it is nonsense to invoke Calvinism as the source of Dutch capitalism. It might be more accurate to suggest that Calvinism caused the destruction of capitalism in the portions of the Netherlands that remained under Spanish control, but only because Philip II rejected any degree of religious toleration and therefore scuttled several well-drawn settlements of what came to be known by some historians as the Eighty Years War and by others as the Dutch Revolution. Even so, this was not so much a war of religion as a war over political and economic freedom, as demonstrated by the fact that Dutch Calvinists and Catholics often united to oppose Spain, and that Calvinists were never a majority even in Holland. However, our primary interest in this war concerns the destruction of capitalism in the Spanish Netherlands. That purpose is adequately served by a brief case study of Antwerp.

The Destruction of Antwerp

In 1555, Charles V made his son Philip ruler of the Netherlands. At that time Antwerp was the fulcrum of international capitalism, the commercial and financial center of the world. Thirty-four years later the city had lost more than half of its population, its harbor was empty because of a Dutch blockade, it had been raped and looted by Spanish troops, and its commercial and financial firms had fled—most of them to Amsterdam.

The Reformation came very early to Antwerp. Even before Luther nailed up his ninety-five theses, a Flemish translation of the Bible had been printed in Antwerp and the city's booming printing industry was circulating accounts of misconduct of the Roman Curia. Antwerp also pioneered in producing Lutheran martyrs. In

1522 the Augustinians were expelled from the city and their prior fled to Germany, where he joined with his fellow former Augustinian Martin Luther. The next year two Augustinian fathers from Antwerp were burned in Brussels for fostering Lutheran ideas. In 1525 a monk was drowned in Antwerp for Lutheranism. No doubt many were deterred thereby from all thoughts of heresy. But many were not. Lutheranism, Anabaptism, and then Calvinism continued to gain adherents. Worse yet, the harsh religious intolerance alienated many Catholics, especially among the nobility. These sentiments were reinforced by the fact that the persecutors, both religious and civil, were Spanish and the victims were Flemish or Dutch. These divisions were exacerbated in 1566, when Calvinist radicals struck back.

The *Beeldenstorm,* or Iconoclastic Fury, involved roving bands of radical Calvinists who were utterly opposed to all religious images and decorations in churches and who acted on their beliefs by storming into Catholic churches and destroying all artwork and finery. Numerous efforts have been made to explain this frenzy of image breaking that spread across the southern Netherlands as caused by the dislocation of many textile workers and a sudden rise in the price of food. If so, how is one to account for the fact that only churches were attacked? Why no attacks on government officials or town halls, why no looting of shops and food stores?[32]

The *Beeldenstorm* reached Antwerp on August 21. As the iconoclasts proceeded they drew large, cheering crowds and no opposition. "All forty-two churches in the city were ransacked, the images, paintings, and other objects hauled into the streets, smashed, and the plate pilfered, the work continuing at night under torches."[33] But there was no cheering in the Escorial. Philip II decided that the time had come to impose serious governance on the Netherlands, in the form of Don Fernando Alvarez de Toledo, third Duke of Alba (sometimes spelled Alva). At the head of ten thousand troops (and hundreds of attractive mounted "courtesans"),[34] Alba marched from Milan (now a Spanish province) through the Alpine passes and into the Rhine valley, along what then was known as the "Spanish Road," arriving in Brussels on August 22, a year and a day after the *Beeldenstorm* had hit Antwerp. Then the bloodbath began. It is not clear how many, if any, iconoclasts Alba rounded up, for his wrath was directed against treason far more than against heresy. He defined treason as ever having favored any degree of local sovereignty. Hence, no one was safe, not even solidly Catholic nobility—a number of whom were beheaded for treason.[35] The main effect of Alba's brutality was to drive the upper classes, including William of Orange, into opposition.

Meanwhile, the Calvinist radicals had launched a fearsome opposition from the sea. The "Sea Beggars" (also known as Gueux) were formed in 1568 by Hendrik, Count of Brederode, and a number of Protestant nobles intent on an independent Netherlands. They were ridiculed as beggars when they petitioned the governor general of the Netherlands for religious toleration, and when their petition was denied, took up the name as a badge of honor. They soon assembled a fleet of very fast, small, shallow-draft fighting ships able to ply the complex waters off the Dutch and Flanders coasts, almost with impunity. Their raids caused Alba to station large garrisons at major ports, including Antwerp, where he also had built a very large fortress. But while the Spanish troops provided some protection for dockyard areas, they were useless against attacks on shipping, and the Sea Beggars soon had imposed an effective blockade of Antwerp and other southern Netherlands ports. An exodus of import and export firms began.

In the wake of rapidly spreading anger caused by Alba's imposition in 1572 of a new and onerous tax, the Sea Beggars began not only to raid but to take ports and hold them. Brill was the first, but within weeks other ports were taken and the locals reinforced with rebel troops brought by boat. This was, of course, war. Alba proceeded via a series of sieges, taking Haarlem in 1573. Later in the year Alba was replaced by Don Luis de Requesens, who went north with instructions from Philip II to attempt a negotiated settlement. The talks dragged on and on. Often enough the participants found a basis for agreement, but each time their efforts were rejected by Philip on the grounds that there could be no toleration of Protestants.

Meanwhile, Philip neglected to pay his troops. In November the imperial army mutinied, and after sacking several minor towns, a horde of troops arrived at Antwerp, at that time still a loyal outpost of the empire. What followed became known as the "Spanish Fury." Thousands died, seldom without great suffering. "The Spaniards hanged men up by their legs and arms and women by their hair; they flogged people and burnt the soles of their feet to extort the hiding place of their wealth."[36] Young women were dragged screaming to the newly built fortress. No one was safe. Not the poor (who often were killed because they had no money to give), not even the clergy, who also were forced (even tortured) to reveal where their valuables, including altar chalices and plate, were hidden.[37] The factor of the Fugger Company estimated that the Antwerp merchant community lost at least 2 million crowns in gold and silver coins.

Once the troops departed, Antwerp switched sides, joining the Protestant Union of Utrecht, thus becoming the major center of resistance in the southern Netherlands. Now rather than being blockaded by the Sea Beggars, Antwerp's shipping enjoyed their protection. Still, its commercial life had been severely curtailed.

In 1578 Don Alessandro Farnese, Duke of Parma, replaced Requesens as governor general of the Netherlands. Parma was a distinguished general, and he resumed the campaign to crush the Dutch revolt. This involved several unsuccessful attacks on Antwerp, before Parma got serious in 1584, laying siege to the city. A year later it fell and Antwerp was back in Spanish hands to stay. But it no longer was much of a prize. Once again it was cut off from the sea by blockade. Once again Protestants were outlawed, only this time they were given four years to leave. Most did not risk staying nearly that long, and so, with its population already greatly reduced, Antwerp declined rapidly again, as can be seen in Table 6-1. The emigrants took the remnants of capitalism with them.

Fighting Dutchmen

Most of them took their capitalism north to Amsterdam. Economic historians date the boom in Amsterdam as beginning in 1585, the very year when Antwerp fell to the Duke of Parma. In Amsterdam there was freedom and toleration, taxes required citizen approval, and access to the Rhine and the Meuse allowed the Dutch

TABLE 6-1 *Population Profile of the Rise and Fall of Antwerp*

1437	20,000
1480	33,000
1526	55,000
1555	100,000
1584	(City falls to the Duke of Parma)
1585	80,000
1589	42,000

Constructed from Limberger, 2001, and Van Roey, 1981

to dominate the rich and very active Baltic trade. Foreign merchants and traders—especially the English—who once clustered in Antwerp now clustered in Amsterdam.

If Holland had once been reclaimed from the Atlantic, now the ocean rescued the Dutch by providing superb defensive water barriers. Fighting at home and for their homes, using arms of their own manufacture, funded by a booming commercial economy, having unimpeded access to the sea and a stalwart English ally, the Dutch could afford to fight on and on and then some more. To oppose them, the Spanish empire depended on very expensive foreign troops, using arms of foreign manufacture, and mainly supplied from abroad. Because Spain lacked control of the sea, everything had to come overland, following the Spanish Road just as had Alba's battalions. The costs of all this were staggering.

DEFEAT

As the 1580s began, things were not going well for Philip II. The Dutch had not been dislodged by repeated onslaughts. Then, in 1585, Queen Elizabeth I sent her small but effective army—6,350 infantry and 1,000 cavalry, commanded by the Earl of Leicester—to Holland in support of the Dutch cause. Elizabeth also bought shares in stock companies organized to finance raids on Spanish shipping—especially on the treasure ships from the Orient and the Americas. To make things worse, the French continued to connive against Spain, always ready to attack from the rear. Something had to be done. Putting first things first, Philip II and his advisers decided to remove England from the equation. They would transport their invincible battalions from the Netherlands across the channel, overrun the irregular forces Elizabeth could muster against them, replace her with a Catholic monarch, and that would be that.

It was a wonderful design. It might well have succeeded had England also been ruled by a despot—but it was doomed against a free nation "of shopkeepers," where technology blossomed, enterprise was cultivated, and the queen was a devoted capitalist.

The Armada

In 1587 the Spanish began to assemble the great fleet needed for the invasion of England. The plan was to sail north into the English Channel and inflict such damage to the opposing English ships that the Armada could then protect a vast flotilla of barges and small ships conveying the Duke of Parma's veterans from Bruges and other ports to the English coast. Special arrangements were even well in hand for barges capable of carrying cavalry units with their horses, ready to ride through the surf and attack all comers. The main assembly ports for the Armada were to be Cádiz (just west of the Strait of Gibraltar) and Lisbon—Portugal had been annexed by Spain in 1581.

Fully aware of Spanish intentions, the English decided to make a disruptive raid, a plan that bore "all the signs of Elizabeth's personal intervention."[38] The English force was commanded by Sir Francis Drake, famous for his daring and devastating attacks on Spanish shipping. Although he was one of Elizabeth's favorites, Drake was not an officer in the Royal Navy. In keeping with the English affinity for free enterprise, private citizens could command the queen's ships, and in fact, English battle fleets often were a mixture of royal and privately owned ships. Drake achieved his fame, as did the other English sea dogs, by campaigns as a privateer, acting under partnership contracts with the queen. On the Continent, the sea dogs were regarded as pirates.

Drake planned to strike against both Cádiz and Lisbon, hoping to find their harbors jammed with ships not yet ready to fight. The makeup of his fleet reveals much about a truly capitalist approach to warfare and about the unique nature of the English merchant fleet. Drake began with four powerful ships of his own. Then Elizabeth put four of her best royal galleons under Drake's command and authorized him to complete his fleet by recruiting as many merchant ships as the London merchants would agree to furnish. Of what use could merchant ships be to a battle fleet? None, if they were the wide, deep, lightly gunned, cumbersome ships that sailed for continental merchants. But English merchants built fighting ships and overcame the commercial deficiencies of these vessels by scorning bulky cargoes in favor of light, valuable goods. They also benefited from not having to sail in convoys for protection or to buy insurance against pirates. Thus, while continental merchant vessels could support a battle fleet only by bringing supplies or serving as fireships, major English merchant ships were a superb naval reserve, built to take their place in the line of battle. They had narrow bottoms for speed, and their hulls spread to their greatest width above the water in order to provide for gun decks. As Violet Barbour pointed out, the only way to distinguish between a large English merchant ship and a royal man-of-war was not on the basis of shape, number of gun ports, or rigging, but only "by the decoration lavished upon her."[39] The queen's ships had a great deal of scrollwork and carving, and always an impressive figurehead, while the merchants took a more frugal approach to these matters. Merchant ships therefore were of great military value to Drake, and he convinced the London merchants associated with the Levant Company to provide him with nine, plus a number of frigates and pinnaces for scouting, communication, and inshore service. The merchants did not take part out of purely patriotic motives. Drake's fleet was in fact commissioned as a stock company, and participants (including the queen) were to receive shares in all prizes and loot acquired by the expedition, giving "the voyage some of the aspects of a private commercial venture."[40]

When the fleet arrived at Cádiz on April 29, 1587, everything went as Drake had hoped. The harbor was crowded. The Spanish ships were mostly without crews, and many lacked guns and sails. Drake sailed in, sank some thirty ships, and sailed out again with a large number of prize vessels, which he dispatched for England. Drake then sailed for Cape Saint Vincent, where he positioned his fleet to harass the coastal trade and to intercept squadrons trying to reach Lisbon (which he had judged as too strong to attack once surprise was lost). Again he wreaked havoc on the Spanish, taking many prizes and supplies.[41] Although these were minor blows compared with the immense scale of the planned Armada, they were sufficient to cause the sailing date for the Armada to be postponed until the next year. Drake kept it all in perspective, writing to Elizabeth's spy master Francis Walsingham, "Prepare in England strongly and most by sea!"[42]

When the Armada did sail the following year, several extreme flaws in the Spanish plan were revealed. The English fleet could not in fact be defeated because it refused to fight in the traditional manner. Rather than closing for deck-to-deck infantry battles, the nimble English vessels stood off and relied on their powerful broadsides. The Spanish ships were stuffed with troops eager to put the English sailors to the sword, but their cannons were somewhat lacking in weight and number, and soon began to run short of powder and shot. Fighting so close to home that crowds on the shore often could see some of the battle, the English were constantly resupplied with powder and shot carried out on lighters.

Even so, the Armada did well enough as it battled its way up the English Channel so that it remained mostly intact and was still a potent naval force as it passed the coast of Flanders, where the Duke of Parma awaited. Now a second major tactical flaw was revealed. The Armada was capable of sheltering the barge flotilla, had it come out from shore. Indeed, that might have forced the English to close in for deck-to-deck fighting. So why didn't Parma's veterans come out? Because the Dutch Sea Beggars were blockading Flanders and their ships could sail in the shallow coastal waters, out of reach of the Armada. In the face of Dutch opposition, had the barges pushed out, the sea soon would have been full of drowning Spanish soldiers and riderless cavalry horses.

So the troops sat on the beach and the Armada continued north, pounded all the way by long-range English guns. Eventually, having passed to the north of Scotland, the Armada decided to swing west to circle around Ireland and hence back to Lisbon. Now came terrible storms, and dozens of Spanish ships were wrecked along the Irish coast; for many weeks bodies kept washing up on Irish beaches.

That it was storms that had done the worst damage to the Armada revealed much about the two navies. English naval construction was so superb and England's seamen so adept that during the entire forty-five-year reign of Elizabeth I, "not a single English warship was lost through shipwreck; while over the same term of years, entire squadrons of Spaniards were overwhelmed by the sea."[43]

Crumbling Empire

Although the defeat of the Armada was a terrible blow to Spanish pride, no one in Seville or cloistered in the Escorial recognized it as decisive. Instead, Philip and his advisers planned to regroup and fight again. So, nine years later the Spanish sent a second Armada against England. A fleet of about a hundred ships set out in October, a stormy time of year. This time the English had no advance warning, and most of their fleet was in port undergoing maintenance. But after four days at sea, this second Armada ran into a gale. Once again Spanish ships proved less than seaworthy, and the crews seemed "raw and untrained." After the storm passed it was revealed that "about a third of the vessels, including some of the best warships, had foundered or gone to pieces on the neighbouring sands; thousands of Spaniards had perished."[44] Even so, in 1602 the Spanish managed to land troops in Ireland. Outnumbered and poorly supported, they soon surrendered.

Meanwhile, far more important defeats of Spanish imperialism were taking place elsewhere. In 1594 the Dutch began to intrude in the Caribbean, and in 1595 they began to colonize the East Indies. The English soon did likewise, and in 1605 they laid claim to Barbados in the West Indies. The New World no longer was uncontestedly Spanish. Nor was it any longer an unlimited source of silver. Costs of mining had risen very substantially as it became necessary to work deeper veins. In addition, the demand for Spanish imports began to fall sharply in the Americas. The problem was that Spanish colonists had essentially re-created the Spanish economy. They now produced their own grain, wine, oil, and coarse cloth equal to what they had long imported from home. Spanish merchants, who had long prospered from trading with the Americas, soon found themselves overstocked. "The goods which Spain produced were not wanted in America; the goods that America wanted were not produced in Spain." Beginning in the 1590s, Spain became increasingly less important to the economies of its American colonies, and Dutch and English interlopers became more active.[45]

Of course, the Spanish empire didn't just drop dead, or even stop fighting. In 1590 and again the next year imperial troops in the Netherlands turned south and fought unsuccessful campaigns against the French. And soon these same northern armies were embroiled in the Thirty Years War. But the news, both economic and military, continued to be mostly bad. In 1596 the empire once again declared bankruptcy, then again in 1607, 1627, 1647, and 1653. In 1638 the French captured the fortress at Breisach on the Rhine, thus closing the Spanish Road from Italy to the Netherlands. Thereafter, Spanish troops and supplies could reach the Netherlands only by sea, subject to attack by both the English and the Dutch navies.

By this time the tide had so irrevocably turned that people began to publish treatises to explain the "decline of Spain." But it was the empire that declined; Spain had never risen. As Douglas C. North explained in a book that helped win him the Nobel Prize in economics, Spain's "economy remained medieval throughout its bid for political dominance. Where it retained political sway, as in the Spanish Netherlands, the economy of the area withered."[46]

FRANCE: TAXATION, REGULATION, AND STAGNATION

France was also a relatively underdeveloped nation. After the divisive traumas of the Hundred Years War, a highly centralized, absolutist regime evolved. This new regime, which historians prefer to call the "Old Regime," soon sustained an astonishingly large and unprincipled bureaucracy. The king had uncontested power to levy taxes, in no way checked by any legislative body. As would be expected, taxes on both agriculture and commerce soon rose to disabling levels. In addition, the state cooperated with the guilds to so overregulate industry and invention that capitalism barely existed.

Creating an Absolutist State

Like Spain, France was a relatively recent creation. For centuries, a substantial slice of the territory belonged to the English crown and the remainder was cut up into many relatively sovereign units. In 1453, when the Hundred Years War ended, no more than half of the area that became France was part of the royal domain. Major duchies such as Burgundy, Brittany, Provence, and the huge Bourbonnais in the center of France, along with many smaller regions, all stood outside the realm. Beginning in 1461, it took three French kings—Louis XI, Charles VIII, and Louis XII—more than fifty years to bring it all together. But of course, quite intense localism prevailed, as did local dialects and even languages, and while this always posed some political problems, it greatly increased the power of the central state by diffusing the power of representative bodies.

Beginning as early as the tenth century, a national assembly often played a significant role in the affairs of France. In 987 Hugh Capet was elected king by this body, representing the nobility, the clergy, and the towns.[47] The assembly took the name Estates-General when it met in Paris in 1302. Although the Estates-General had played an "important role . . . in bringing the Hundred Years War to a successful conclusion,"[48] soon after it fell into disuse. Louis XI called it into session once, in 1468. It met again in 1483 to greet the boy king Charles VIII. After that it did not gather again until 1560. Having gathered once more in 1614, the Estates-General was "ingloriously dismissed, not to assemble again until 1789,"[49] in a last-minute effort to head off the French Revolution.

It wasn't only the king's doing that the Estates-General seldom met. Efforts to sustain a national assembly for the whole of France were always resisted, not only by the crown but even more vigorously by those eligible to take part. Since France had by far the largest area of any western European state, many objected that it was too far and too expensive to come, especially since their local concerns always were ignored by the huge majority of outsiders with whom they had little in common. In response, French kings began to deal directly with the small, provincial estates and ceased trying to sustain a nationwide body. But of course, any given local estate was in a very weak position vis-à-vis the king. Hence, the power of the state was virtually unchecked. Moreover, as Louis XIV put it so frankly, the king was the state (*"L'état, c'est moi"*). But the most significant aspect of this absolutist state was the king's ability to impose taxes without seeking any consent.[50]

Taxation

Once the absolutist state was established, French taxes soon became exorbitant, as they always do when those who tax are the primary beneficiaries of state largess. Even so, the French crown fell progressively deeper into debt. Even when taxes had been pushed to a maximum level of 200 million livres a year, the king owed 2 billion livres.[51] Part of this was because France spent a great deal on its armed forces—although these expenses could have been substantially reduced had the crown not persistently pursued unsuccessful expansionist policies. But as seems inevitable under despotic rule, an enormous annual sum went for court life. It is estimated that in the reign of Louis XVI, at least 6 percent of all state revenues were consumed by the glitteringly extravagant court in Versailles.[52] Even more taxes were spent to support a huge and unproductive hierarchy of relatives and cronies, and probably even more was eaten up by corrupt officials. Cardinal Richelieu was remarkable for being the de facto ruler of France during the reign of Louis XIII, and for surviving repeated assassination plots. But perhaps he ought to have become equally famous for his magnificent talent for corruption, which made him far wealthier even than the king. His successor, Cardinal Mazarin, grew even richer.[53]

The basic French tax was on property and known as the *taille*. It was a mess of inconsistency and exemption. The clergy and the nobility paid no taxes on their land. Villages paid as a whole, and often their assessment was "a relic of bygone days," assuming that the population had neither grown nor declined.[54] In addition, the French imposed taxes on an array of commodities: salt, wine, liquors, tobacco, candles, and soap being among those bringing in the greatest revenue. Finally, the French collected a head tax known as the *capitation,* the amount depending on which of twenty-two status groups one was assigned to. Initially, as with the *taille,* the clergy and the nobility were exempt from the *capitation.* That changed on January 18, 1695, with this proclamation: "None of our Subjects of whatever quality and condition shall be exempt from the Capitation." Henceforth, "clergymen, nobles, officeholders, and residents of privileged cities . . . were now to join the mass of peasants in paying direct taxes." In modern perspective this seems only fair, but at the time the elites affected saw it as an extraordinary grievance, which led them to support political challenges to the state that unwittingly helped to bring on the Revolution.

Crushing tax burdens caused dreadful dislocations and harmful tactics in French life. Nowhere was this more evident than among the peasants. Not only were they satisfied with low levels of productivity due to the negative incentives imposed on them by taxes but they pretended to be much poorer than they really were, and to sustain this pretense French peasants made no investments in visible means of increased productivity. Adam Smith pointed out that because of taxes the French farmer was "afraid to have a good team of horses or oxen, but endeavors to cultivate with the meanest and most wretched instruments of husbandry that he can." In contrast, writing back to France during a visit in England, Voltaire expressed surprise that the English peasant "is not afraid to increase the number of his cattle, or to cover his roof with tile, lest his taxes be raised next year."[55]

Although nearly everyone in France was substantially overtaxed, the most destructive effects on French industry and commerce were not from taxes per se but from the sale of "privileges." Virtually everything was prohibited except by royal license. Did someone wish to start a mine? The king claimed all rights to all minerals below the surface, no matter who owned the land above. Therefore, to mine anything, anywhere, in France it was necessary to purchase a royal license. Even more amazing is that, having purchased such a license, the mining firm could search for minerals on anyone's property, and having found a vein they could mine without any payment to the owner of the land, nor need they observe any restrictions on access.[56] Clearly, then, private property was a very problematic matter in France. Or, suppose one wished to import a spice.

One must buy a specific license from the king, and use only ships licensed by the king for that purpose. Although the crown sometimes sold multiple licenses for some particular commercial activity, the primary basis for French commerce was a monopoly purchased from the crown.

After buying a license, one still had all of the start-up and operating costs required for that specific venture, and of course, those with close ties to the state were at a considerable advantage in obtaining the desired license. As a result, the aristocracy dominated French industry. Of 601 investors in the metal industry in 1771, 305 were nobles and 55 were clergy.[57] Because of limitations on royal licenses, which often created a monopoly, there was little commercial or industrial competition within the nation, and precious little direct competition from without, since nearly all French goods were sold on the domestic market and high import duties sheltered the producers from foreign products.[58] The crown preferred monopolies because it was a simple matter to sell an exclusive license to engage in some activity and then collect renewal fees; it was far more difficult to determine what aspects of a firm's activities or assets to tax and then to collect those taxes from a large array of firms. So too, the crown nearly always took the side of the guilds in any dispute because they were a lucrative and regular source of revenue from license renewal fees and the sale of guild offices, and also because it was far easier to charge each guild an annual fee based on membership than to try to tax each workshop or each guild member on some other basis.

By the same token, rather than attempt to impose a tax on officials and bureaucrats, who inevitably were well placed to evade them, the crown resorted to selling all of these positions.

Bureaucracy

Prerevolutionary France sustained a huge bureaucracy. Some bureaucratic positions were offices having great power and importance. Some were "useless offices with no duties."[59] But all of them are referred to by historians as "venal offices" in that all of them were for sale—all incumbents had purchased their positions from their predecessors. In addition, each officeholder was required to pay the crown an annual set fee (*droit annuel*), based on the declared annual income of the position (which mostly came from fees charged to the public). These declarations were "notoriously under-valued."[60] Even so, on the eve of the Revolution there were tens of thousands of venal officeholders in France, probably amounting to 2 to 3 percent of the adult male population.[61] Most of them did nothing. Most of the rest helped to clog and misdirect the machinery of government.

The legitimate returns from venal offices were quite small given their cost. Some of the more lucrative positions may have returned as much as 5 percent a year on the investment, but more earned in the 1–2 percent range, and many people bought offices knowing full well that they would lose money on the deal. So, what was the attraction? *Status!* French society was "afflicted with a mania for prestige." In return for the prestige of being an official, many would "settle for a low return and even a loss on capital."[62] The result was not good government. Many were very negligent of their duties. Many acted only for the benefit of their friends or those more powerful. And just as their offices were for sale, so were they.

Intransigent Guilds

For generations it was recognized that intransigent guilds stifled capitalism in some parts of Europe, particularly in France. Then, in the middle of the twentieth century the harmful effects of guilds on capitalism were reinterpreted as a good thing.[63] Marxist scholars and their many sympathizers stressed that guilds were an early form of labor union that protected their members from exploitation by greedy capitalists, whether by inadequate pay or from being displaced by new methods. It also became an article of faith that guild rules protected society from inferior goods—everyone assuming that traditional hand methods resulted in better quality than could be achieved by machines or assembly lines. And, the argument went, if this hobbled the rise of capitalist industries, so much the better, since everyone knew that capitalism was the enemy of social justice.

Somehow it didn't seem to matter that free and independent unions existed only in capitalist societies. Nor was it often mentioned that one of the first acts of the French revolutionaries was to destroy all guilds or that real unions were illegal in the Soviet Union. Nor did these scholars grasp that old-fashioned hand methods usually produced inferior goods, and that guild rules exploited everyone else by imposing artificially high prices and an unproductive economy. Fortunately, reality has set in and fantasies about guilds as engines of social justice have mostly run their course. Granted, guilds often did serve the interests of workers and sometimes did help to oppose despots and oligarchs, but at least as often guilds were hand in hand with an oppressive state and served as barriers to liberty as well as commerce. That certainly was the case in France before the Revolution.

Supported by industrial officials (who purchased their positions from the state as did guild leaders), the French guilds imposed extremely detailed restrictions on every facet of the manufacturing processes and management. For example, in France the dyeing of cloth was subject to 317 regulations. As to enforcement, every cloth was inspected again and again during the manufacturing process by guild officials.[64] Moreover, guild regulations, reinforced by royal edicts, discouraged inventions and innovations—"innovation was everywhere stifled or prohibited by the minute regulation of the production process that did not permit deviation from custom."[65] For example, just as the textile guilds in Venice had prohibited adoption of the English bow-dyeing method, so too was it prohibited in France.

Guild rules also kept firms very small. For example, a weaving company could have "no more than six looms, a measure destined to prevent enterprising manufacturers from gaining too much control over production"[66] since small firms usually were unable to pursue capital-intensive innovations. In addition, where guilds were strong, as in France, workers were hired or employed not by a firm but by the guild. In 1751, when an entrepreneur in Lille attempted to hire workers directly, the city council forbade it, ruling that "it has never been permitted in Lille for [manufacturers] to have workers working directly under and for them. This is a right that has always belonged to the masters of the guild."[67] Then as now, this practice made it difficult, if possible at all, for a firm to dismiss unreliable or inefficient workers, or to offer bonuses to superior workers. Finally, in collusion with the state bureaucracy, guilds often set the prices at which goods must be sold, keeping them high so as to facilitate high wages and high taxes, without taking any account of market forces.[68]

Practices such as these helped to destroy capitalism in Venice, and they prevented all but the most rudimentary capitalism from developing in France.

French "Capitalism"

Capitalism rests upon three factors: secure property rights, free markets, and free labor. France was quite deficient on all three. The state treated property rights as a privilege to be sold or ignored. Markets were so highly constrained by royal regulations and licenses that firms could not freely move into areas of opportunity. The sale of monopolies closed many markets and removed incentives for efficiency or effort. And the power of the guilds greatly restricted free labor: it was very difficult for individuals to pursue new opportunities and equally difficult for firms to offer such opportunities. For the most part, the French commercial and industrial economy consisted of licensed firms limited to given markets, subject to usurpation, and employing not workers but a guild. Under these circumstances it is surprising that any trace of capitalism existed in France at all.

In fact, although there did exist some semblance of rational firms, especially in mining and metallurgy, French commerce was stunted by the classic economic weakness of all despotic regimes: that wealth is seen not as a tool but as a badge of superior status. Just as many French investors eagerly purchased an office having no income or duties, so too they were very reluctant to invest in commercial or industrial enterprises, since these were considered degrading; most who did invest in such things could hardly wait to draw out their capital and put it in something respectable, such as land, urban property, venal office, or annuities, despite the fact that the return on these investments was extremely low (often around 1 percent, seldom as high as 5). However, these investments also involved virtually no risk.

Respectable investments in France were defined by the aristocracy. Others accepted their definition because they were avid seekers of social status and had no choice but to play the game as those already having high status defined the rules. Consequently, they willingly purchased land that yielded a return of less than 2 percent in preference to earning 5 percent or more from commercial investments.[69] Those who owned land or urban real estate not only were taxed at a reduced rate but qualified as *somebody*, even if they were not of the nobility. The Abbé Coyer explained ruefully in 1756: "The Merchant perceives no luster in his career, & if he wants to succeed in what is called in France *being something*, he has to give it up. This . . . does a lot of damage. In order to be *something*, a large part of the Nobility remains nothing."

The preferred circumstance was to live from rents paid by tenant farmers. And the appropriate outlook was that when more revenues were needed or desired, one thought not of increasing agricultural productivity but only of raising the rents. No wonder that a careful estimate made in 1788 by the father of modern chemistry, Antoine-Laurent Lavoisier, found that English farms were almost three times as productive as French farms, because the French seldom reinvested in capital improvements.[70]

The same lack of reinvestment hobbled French industry. Huge sums that would have been reinvested in any truly capitalist economy were consumed or diverted to a properly aristocratic form of wealth since the primary motive for gaining wealth was to live like a gentleman.[71] Weber could rightly claim that France lacked the "spirit of Capitalism." Indeed, the conversion of commercial capital into investments conferring higher status was so common that on the eve of the Revolution more than 80 percent of the wealth in France was invested in land, buildings, and venal offices, rather than in commerce or industry.[72]

There were, of course, some industries in France—although there were few enough that George Taylor could legitimately claim that, when authors offer examples, "always the same ones are named."[73]

Nor were most of these examples of much significance. Metalworking is always cited as a leading French industry in this era, but in reality its output was "slight, scattered, of poor quality and very expensive . . . [and none of it] was genuine steel." One reason for this was that in this era the French mined very little coal.[74] Compared with the English, the Dutch, or even the long-suffering Italian city-states, France's industries were small, backward, and little appreciated. The same could be said of its capitalism, and for the same reasons.

But then, from whence came modern France? Not from the Revolution, which replaced one tyranny with another. Not from Napolean, another tyrant who turned a generation of Frenchmen into war casualties. But ironically, modern France arose from its weak, unstable governments in the post-Napoleonic era and from being nearly surrounded by booming capitalist economies—especially to the north, where a new and frightening Great Power was being assembled from the archipelago of German principalities. Finally, ambitious French entrepreneurs gained the freedom needed to become true capitalists.

It was not Catholicism but tyranny that impeded capitalism in France and Spain, and suppressed it in Italy and the southern Netherlands. Ironically, perhaps no monarchs in history were more conscientious, honest, or hardworking than Charles V and his son Philip II. Between them they built the Spanish empire and ruled it for more than eighty years. Nearly every day they rose early and worked diligently at administering this sprawling entity. Had they been wastrels or playboys, they might have done much less damage to the economies in their charge. In contrast, the French kings were relatively lazy and far less sincere, and under their regime France fared rather better than Spain in terms of economic progress. That is the greatest irony of all: given despotic rule, rampant government corruption provides for degrees of freedom that do not exist under honest and dedicated tyrants.

CHAPTER SEVEN

Feudalism and Capitalism in the New World

CHRISTIANITY: TWO RELIGIOUS ECONOMIES

A Captive Monopoly
Counter-Reformation Catholicism
Indolent State Churches
Religion in a Free Market

FREEDOM: PATTERNS OF RULE

Colonization
Colonial Governance and Control
Independence
Ending Slavery

CAPITALISM

Industry and Labor
Investing in Human Capital

LATIN AMERICAN PROTESTANTISM: OPIATE OR ETHIC?

IT REQUIRES NO DEEP INSIGHTS TO EXPLAIN WHY HUGE NUMBERS OF illegal immigrants enter the United States from Mexico each year. Who wouldn't want to escape grinding poverty for an opportunity to participate in *Norteamericano* affluence? Not much greater insight is needed to explain why the New World north of the Rio Grande eventually eclipsed even Europe in terms of economic might, while everything south languished: because North America was modeled on England while Latin America re created Spain.

It was far more than symbolic that the first British settlements were called New England, while the first Spanish colonies were known as New Spain. As British colonists, North Americans inherited extensive freedom and a capitalist economy. In contrast, the Spanish colonists in Latin America inherited a repressive and unproductive feudalism. Both continents were colonized by Christians—Catholics in the south and mainly Protestants in the north. But that wasn't the important religious difference. What mattered was that the Catholic Church in Latin America was remarkably weak, both politically and in terms of popular support, a fact long obscured by its status as a legal monopoly. In contrast, the extensive pluralism that developed in North America, and the competition it fostered among denominations, produced an unmatched level of individual religious commitment and cultural influence. And rather than relying on government support, all of the competing denominations in North America learned to keep their distance from the state and each made huge investments in independent educational institutions, meanwhile preaching the virtues of honesty, hard work, thrift, and self-reliance.

Strangely, in the enormous literature on differences in the economic development of North and South America, far less attention has been paid to religion and to the legacies of Spanish colonialism than would seem appropriate. In fact, Latin American writers have too often placed most of the blame for their plight on *Norteamericano* colonialism, while ignoring the deeply embedded impact of their Spanish heritage, religious and political, as well as economic.[1] Major aspects of this story remain to be told. Telling it permits extension and reapplication of the arguments developed in previous chapters: that Christian faith in progress and reason, in combination with political freedom and the productive energy of capitalism, turned the North American colonies into an economic giant.

Of course, Brazil was not a Spanish colony, having been awarded to Portugal under the Treaty of Tordesillas (1494). However, Portugal was ruled by Spain for nearly a century after the Duke of Alba led an invasion in 1580, which made Philip II of Spain (confusingly) Philip I of Portugal. Although an independent Portuguese crown was reestablished in 1668, Portugal closely resembled Spain. Both were feudal, Catholic kingdoms and both established feudal, Catholic colonies. Hence, there seldom is any need to treat Brazil as a separate case.

CHRISTIANITY: TWO RELIGIOUS ECONOMIES

Religion is not just a matter of individual commitment, nor can it be fully comprehended on the basis of individuals and their membership in various religious groups. Religion always is embedded in societies and is greatly shaped by the conditions imposed on religious expression and organization by the state. To encompass this reality fully, the term "religious economy" was introduced.[2] A religious economy consists of all of the religious activity going on in any society: a "market" of current and potential religious adherents, a set of one or more organizations seeking to attract or retain adherents, and the religious culture offered by the organizations.

Because individual religious tastes always vary considerably within any society, and because no single "firm" can offer both an intense and a lax religious "product," if left to its own devices the *normal* condition of any religious economy would be *pluralism*, wherein a set of distinctively different religious firms appeal to various market segments. But because it requires a high level of religious freedom, the normal religious economy has not been typical, at least not within the confines of monotheism. Instead, religious economies usually have been distorted by state regulations that either impose a monopoly firm or constrain the market by subsidizing a state church and making it difficult for other religious groups to compete.[3] But religion languishes in a monopolized religious economy, not only because so many find their religious tastes unserved but because, as with commercial monopolies, monopoly religious firms become lazy and inefficient. In contrast, religion thrives in a free market, where many religious groups vie for followers and those firms lacking energy or appeal fall by the wayside. By now there is a very large research literature that supports these conclusions,[4] and nowhere do they fit the historical record so snuggly as in comparisons between the Americas. Since European settlement began far sooner in Central and South America than in the north, the story starts with the Latin church.

A Captive Monopoly

Discussions of church and state in Catholic nations usually stress the power of the church. Political figures are depicted as bowing to bishops who always favored authoritarian policies and feudal social structures. This is a fantasy popularized by Protestant historians. The pope did not invade Spain and sack Madrid. It was Charles V of Spain who invaded Italy in the sixteenth century and sacked Rome.

A far more accurate perspective on the relative powers of church and state can be gained from examining the connections between the Reformation and royal self-interest—the relative stakes that various kings and princes had in remaining Catholic or embracing Protestantism. Henry VIII reaped enormous profit and power by deposing England's Catholic bishops and religious orders. The same was true for the kings of Norway and Denmark as well as for many German princes. Rather than continuing to have local bishops sending large sums off to the pope and allowing the church to own huge, untaxed tracts of their realms, by becoming Protestants, kings and princes could claim the tithes and by expropriating church lands they could greatly expand their holdings and those of their noble supporters.[5]

However, other kings and princes had very little to gain by joining the Reformation because they already had imposed very favorable terms upon the pope. For example, in 1516 (a year before Martin Luther nailed up his ninety-five theses) the Concordat of Bologna, signed by Pope Leo X and Francis I, the King of France, gave the king the right to appoint all of the higher posts in the church in France: the ten archbishops, eighty-two bishops, and all of the priors, abbots, and abbesses of the many hundreds of monasteries, abbeys, and convents. Through these appointments, the king gained complete control of church property and income. As Owen Chadwick put it, "When he wanted ecclesiastical money, his methods need not even be devious."[6] Nevertheless, the Spanish crown had an even more favorable deal with the Vatican. Late in the fifteenth century, Ferdinand and Isabella had gained the right not only to make all important church appointments but to impose taxes on the clergy and church property. Moreover, they got the pope to agree that it would be illegal to publish papal bulls and decrees in Spain or its possessions without prior royal consent. The subordination of the church to the Spanish crown increased even more during the reign of Charles V—among other things the pope agreed to let him take one-third of the tithes paid to the church (from which no one was exempt, as many were from royal taxes).

These arrangements played a major role in keeping Spain and France Catholic, but they made the church relatively subservient to the state. This soon had dire consequences when the pope sought to prevent the introduction of slavery in the New World.

Recall that as early as the sixth century the church began to oppose slavery, and that by the end of the tenth century it had managed to eliminate slavery from most of Europe. Then, during the 1430s, the Spanish colonized the Canary Islands and began to enslave the native population. When word of this reached Pope Eugene IV, he immediately issued a bull, *Sicut dudum*. The pope didn't beat around the bush: under threat of excommunication he gave everyone involved fifteen days from the receipt of his bull "to restore to their earlier liberty all and each persons of either sex who once were residents of said Canary Islands. . . . These people are to be totally and perpetually free and are to be let go without exaction or reception of any money."[7] But the pope's bull was ignored, as were similar bulls by his next two successors.

With the successful Spanish and Portuguese invasions of the New World, enslavement of native peoples continued, soon to be augmented by increasingly large shipments of slaves from Africa. Some of those involved in slavery proposed that it was not a violation of church teachings since these were not "rational creatures" but a species of "animals." The church would have none of it. In 1537, Pope Paul III issued three decrees against New World slavery (these were ignored by historians until recently). In his initial bull the pope declared that "the Indians themselves indeed are true men" and therefore "by our Apostolic Authority [we] decree and declare . . . that the same Indians and *all other peoples*—even though they are outside the faith— . . . should not be deprived of their liberty or their possessions . . . and are not to be reduced to slavery, and whatever happens to the contrary is to be considered null and void." In the second bull the pope invoked the penalty of excommunication on anyone, regardless of their "dignity, state, condition, or grade," who engaged in slavery.[8]

Church opposition did end the blatant enslavement of the Indians, although many exploitative practices continued. But papal bulls had no impact on the flow of slaves from Africa. True enough, for a long time Spanish colonies lagged far behind the British and the French in using African slaves—the island colonies of the latter two powers being rapidly transformed into slave-based plantation economies. But this was due to a difference in economic approaches, not to religious considerations, even though, as the volume of slavery in the New World continued to rise, the church continued to reassert its opposition. In 1639, at the request of the Jesuits of Paraguay, Pope Urban VIII issued a bull reaffirming Paul III's imposition of excommunication on all who traded or kept slaves.

As with Paul III's bulls, so too Urban's opposition to slavery had no effect and went almost unnoticed. Rome's position was not supported by many of the local bishops, all of whom had been appointed by the King of Spain. Recall too that it was illegal to publish these antislavery bulls, or any papal statements, in Spain or in the New World colonies without royal consent, which was not given. When Urban VIII's bull was illegally read in public by Jesuits in Rio de Janeiro, the result was that a mob sacked their local college and injured a number of priests. In Santos another mob trampled the Jesuit vicar general when he tried to publish the bull. Having continued to oppose slavery, and for building remarkably advanced and successful Indian communities, in 1767 the Jesuits were brutally expelled from the New World.[9]

Nevertheless, the bishops in Spanish America were not entirely without influence. By appealing to the Spanish court that enslavement of the Indians interfered with efforts to convert them to Christianity, the bishops obtained "New Laws" in 1542 that prohibited enslavement of the Indians, and as mentioned, these laws were generally observed. Somewhat later, when substantial numbers of African slaves were introduced into Spanish areas in the New World, the bishops managed to have the Spanish court accept the Código Negro Español (Spanish Black Code), which greatly mitigated the actual conditions of slavery.[10] Both of these actions provoked "intense conflicts between civil and religious authorities."[11] Keep in mind that while the king chose the bishops, he could do so only from the pool of eligible nominees and that these were men trained and selected by the Vatican. And since their appointments were for life, bishops often simply outlasted their noble opponents. But they never were nearly as powerful as were the secular rulers. Unfortunately too, in response to the Reformation, at this same time the Catholic Church was undergoing substantial changes that made it far less favorable to progress and commerce.

Counter-Reformation Catholicism

Soon after the conversion of the Roman Emperor Constantine in 312, there came to be essentially two Catholic churches. Prior to Constantine, the church was led by a dedicated, poorly paid, and rather ascetic clergy, who sometimes knowingly risked martyrdom. This group, and its heirs, constituted the *church of piety*. But when Constantine began to shower the church with privileges and subsidies, he "precipitated a stampede into the priesthood"[12] by the sons of the upper classes, since church offices now produced high incomes and had substantial political influence. Soon, church positions, even lowly parish pastorships, were bought and sold as investments—higher offices often carrying enormous price tags. This new church hierarchy formed the *church of power*. As pointed out in Chapter 2, a clergy of "investors" was unlikely to be hostile to commerce, and during the formation and rise of capitalism, the church of power led the way to accommodate traditional ascetic religious predilections to economic realities. Put another way, had the church of piety prevailed, Christianity probably would have continued to denounce usury and to oppose profit and materialism in general, just as Islam still does.

The brutal shocks caused by the rapidly spreading Reformation disorganized the church, so much so that at the Council of Trent (1562–63) the church of piety was able to resume leadership. The sale and purchase of church offices ended and many worthy reforms were instituted, including the formation of a vast network of seminaries to properly train priests. But there was a dark side too. The Counter-Reformation church displayed an anti-intellectual streak that had long been deflected by the church of power. New alarms about heresy now caused the church to suppress scholarship, thereby fostering misconceptions about religious opposition to science. Moreover, like their Puritan Protestant counterparts, the clergy of the church of piety were very ambivalent about wealth and were very suspicious of commerce. And just as Puritan divines expressed contempt for "ambition" and decried "covetousness," the ascetic faction now in control of the church had a deep disdain for "progress" and "modernity." Far better that people remain on farms and in villages, leading simple, humble, pious lives.

The irony of all this is, of course, that in recovering the lost virtues of the church, the leaders of the Counter-Reformation also restored a faith best suited for a far earlier time, a faith compatible with command economies but completely out of touch with democracy, let alone capitalism. It was this church that prevailed in southern Europe and in the New World colonies. And it was from these sources that came the recent expression by some Latin American church leaders of misguided anticapitalism and the left-wing fantasies of "liberation theology."

Indolent State Churches

In keeping with treaties in effect in Spain and France, the church surrendered substantial control of its affairs in the New World. For the Spanish colonies, not only did the King of Spain appoint all the bishops but the crown and its administrators even determined the establishment of new dioceses and set their boundaries. In return, the crown outlawed any and all faiths other than the Roman Catholic Church. The state also took charge of collecting the *diezmo* (or tithes), a 10 percent religious tax on income. On the one hand, the bishops favored this arrangement because the state had the power to collect the tax far more effectively than could the clergy. On the other hand, state collection of the tithes forced the bishops to lobby unceasingly to be paid their full share, as inevitably "the colonial administrators skimmed" from the receipts.[13]

Even so, the circumstances of the church in the New World were exceedingly comfortable. From the tithes, frequent bequests, huge land grants, and income from its agricultural estates, the Latin church grew very rich. And as in medieval Europe, here too the church excelled at long-term planning and careful management. Hence, the church "had become the dominant economic force in colonial society by the end of the seventeenth century."[14] By the end of the eighteenth century, in Peru "there was scarcely an estate of any size that did not belong in whole or in part to clerics. In Lima, out of 2,806 houses, 1,135 belonged to religious communities, secular ecclesiastics, or pious endowments."[15] At this same time, the church owned half of all productive real estate, both rural and urban, in the huge colony of New Spain, including almost two-thirds of the houses in Mexico City.[16]

But despite its immense material wealth, the church in Latin America was poor in terms of popular support. For as Adam Smith recognized so clearly, religious organizations are not immune to the shortcomings that soon beset all monopolies. Rather, when fully supported by state establishment, "the clergy, reposing themselves

upon their benefices," give "themselves up to indolence" and neglect "to keep up the fervour of faith and devotion in the great body
of the people."[17] This surely was the case in Latin America. As a monopoly church imposed by the state, the Catholic hierarchy was
content to claim everyone as a member while making little effort actually to generate active participation.[18] Centuries of illusions to the
contrary, Latin America never became a "Catholic continent." In
many places it wasn't even Christianized—indigenous faiths persisted, and travelers often reported that many large areas seemed to
be entirely without priests.[19]

That situation remains true even today, despite the recent appearance of a more vigorous Catholicism in Latin America. In 1995,
for example, one diocesan Catholic priest was said to serve 29,753
Catholics in Guatemala, 20,552 in Bolivia, and 17,835 in Brazil (compared with 1,822 in the United States and 1,956 in Canada). These
figures are, of course, nonsense. While the number of priests in each
nation is known and accurately reported, the number of Catholics
reported for any Latin American nation is absurdly exaggerated.
The practice has been that, when calculating the number of
Catholics, local officials have paid no attention to church attendance or even to baptismal statistics. They have merely subtracted a
tiny portion from the total population and claimed everyone else
for the church. Until quite recently, official publications such as the
Catholic Almanac reported that well over 95 percent of all inhabitants of most Latin nations were Catholics.

But the lack of priests strongly testifies otherwise. First of all, the
general level of Catholic commitment has not been sufficient to
prompt many to seek ordination. Even today a substantial number
of the priests in Latin America are foreigners—87 percent of those
serving in Mexico and Guatemala, 75 percent in Venezuela, and
55 percent in Chile. In contrast, only 12 percent of the Catholic
priests in India are foreign-born.[20] Second, these small numbers
of priests seem to have been adequate to meet the demands upon
their services. Mass attendance has always been very low, and even
baptism has been far from universal—despite the fact that many get
their infants baptized only to ensure their "good luck." As the very
distinguished David Martin noted, "The culture of the people has

been quite resistant to Catholic teaching. . . . Perhaps less than 20 percent of Latin Americans are regularly involved in the [Catholic] church."[21]

However, Latin American irreligiousness does not stem from any sort of secular modernity; faith in magic and superstition flourish. No, Latin Americans *remain* unchurched because a subsidized clergy were content, as Adam Smith put it, to rest upon their benefices, while relying on the state to suppress all potential competitors. Nothing could be more obvious, given what has happened since most Latin nations dropped their laws against non-Catholic religions a few decades ago: vigorous Protestant groups are sweeping over the continent! In many Latin nations the great majority of those now in church on Sunday mornings are Protestants, and in many of these same nations foreign missionaries substantially outnumber Catholic priests. And as recent theories based on the idea of religious economies predict,[22] competition has rapidly been invigorating Latin Catholicism. Where the proportion of Protestants is greater, the rate of Catholic attendance at mass is higher too![23] For the first time in history, Catholic seminary enrollments are rising in many Latin nations[24] and the Catholic Charismatic Movement is growing very rapidly[25]—more evidence that religion thrives in a pluralistic religious economy.

Religion in a Free Market

Religious freedom is not easily achieved. Even though they fled Europe to escape persecution, the Pilgrims learned nothing about tolerance from this experience; they learned only about the use of power. From the start, the Massachusetts Bay Colony embraced a monopoly state church and persecuted all hints of nonconformity. Whenever they detected the presence of Quakers, for example, even if only aboard ships anchored in the harbor, the Congregationalists subjected them to public whippings and expulsion. Between 1659 and 1661, four Quakers who had previously been whipped and driven out of Massachusetts were hanged for having returned. Other colonies were not so intolerant, but most of them also established state churches—the Church of England in New York, Virginia, Maryland, North and South Carolina, and Georgia, and the Congregationalists in the New England colonies.

Surprisingly, from the start local observers recognized that religion was stronger in colonies without a subsidized church. As Colonel Lewis Morris, former colonial governor of New Jersey, put it in a letter he wrote from retirement in New York to a friend:

If by force the salary is taken from [the people] and paid to the ministers of the Church, it may be a means of subsisting those Ministers, but they wont make many converts. . . . Whereas [without establishment] the Church will in all probability flourish, and I believe had at this day been in a much better position, had there been no act [of legal establishment passed by the New York assembly] in her favor; for in the Jersies and Pennsylvania, where there is no act, there are four times the number of church men than there are in the province of N. York; and they are soe, most of them, [religious] upon principle, whereas nine parts in ten, of ours, will add no great credit to whatever church they are of; nor can it be expected otherwise.[26]

However, American religious tolerance and the constitutional ban on religious establishment were not the result of insights like these, nor were they rooted in liberal thought. Freedom of religion was a matter of necessity. Like it or not, pluralism existed. So many colonists had brought their faiths with them that in 1776, on the eve of the Revolution, the religious makeup of the colonies was as shown in Table 7-1—even the Congregationalists had only 20 percent of the congregations. Of course, state churches did not vanish overnight, since the prohibition in the federal Constitution against establishing religions was not interpreted as binding on the states: Connecticut disestablished the Congregational Church in 1818, followed by New Hampshire in 1819, but Massachusetts did not cease to collect church taxes in support of an established Congregationalism until 1833.

Despite one church congregation for every 650 inhabitants in 1776, actual church membership in America was low by current standards. While nearly everyone professed to be a Christian, slightly fewer than 20 percent belonged to a specific congregation.

TABLE 7-1 *Number of Congregations in the Thirteen Colonies by Denomination, 1776*

DENOMINATION	NUMBER OF CONGREGATIONS
Congregational	668
Presbyterian (all divisions)	588
Baptist (all divisions)	497
Episcopal (Church of England)	495
Quakers	310
German Reformed	159
Lutheran (all synods)	150
Dutch Reformed	120
Methodist	65
Roman Catholic	56
Moravian	31
Separatist and Independent	27
Dunker	24
Mennonite	16
Huguenot	7
Sandemanian	6
Jewish	5
TOTAL	**3,228**

Sources: Paullin, 1932; Finke and Stark, 1992, 2005

Even in Puritan Boston there probably were more people in the taverns on Saturday night than there were in church on Sunday morning. This was, of course, a holdover from Europe, where the prevalence of established churches had always suppressed participation, just as Colonel Morris thought it must. But once all churches were placed on equal footing and had to compete effectively for supporters, the "miracles" of pluralism began to appear. Nearly a century later, in 1860, more than a third (37 percent) of Americans actually belonged to a local congregation. The 50 percent mark was passed at the start of the twentieth century. And for the past thirty years, slightly more than 60 percent have belonged, which probably is about the maximum rate that can be sustained (90 percent of Americans claim a denominational affiliation, but many do not actually maintain a local membership).[27] Church membership followed a very similar trend in Canada.

But even early in the nineteenth century, when local church membership probably did not include more than one American in four, European travelers were marveling at American piety. In 1818, the English intellectual William Cobbett wrote to friends back home, in the town of Botley, about his amazement at the density and popularity of churches in America: "Here are plenty of Churches. . . . And, these, mind not poor shabby Churches; but each of them larger and better built than [those in] Botley."[28] Writing of his travels in the United States during 1830–31, Alexis de Tocqueville noted that "there is not a country in the world where the Christian religion retains a greater influence over the souls of men than in America."[29] At midcentury, the Swiss theologian Philip Schaff observed that attendance at Lutheran churches was far higher in New York City than in Berlin.[30] And each of these foreign observers knew that the reason for this was pluralism. As Cobbett explained, "It is the circumstance of the church being established by law that makes it of little use as to real religion . . . establishment forces upon the people, parsons whom they cannot respect, and whom indeed, they must despise. . . . When our Parsons . . . talk about religion or the church, being in danger [without tithes] . . . they mean that they are in danger of being compelled to work for their bread."[31] The Austrian journalist Frances Grund wrote in 1837 that establishment makes the clergy "indolent and lazy," while in America, because of competition there is "not one idler amongst [the clergy]; all of them are obliged to exert themselves for the spiritual welfare of their respective congregations."[32]

But not all of the clergy exerted themselves equally, with the result that the profile of American religion today is extremely different from that of 1776. Of the five largest denominations back then, four have become small and continue to shrink: the Congregationalists (now the United Church of Christ), the Presbyterians, the Episcopalians, and the Quakers. Meanwhile, over the next century the Methodists grew from small beginnings to become by far the largest denomination in America, enrolling a third of all church members in 1850, trailed by the Baptists with 21 percent. Then, during the next century, the Methodists became a complaisant denomination, which soon led to a serious membership decline, especially during the past forty years. Meanwhile, the Baptists continued to grow, and the Southern Baptist Convention is today the largest Protestant body in the nation. One reason the Baptists surpassed the Methodists is that, as increasing numbers of Methodist clergy embraced "modern" theology, they were protected by powerful bishops who shared these views, which were not nearly so popular with the membership. In contrast, the Baptist clergy remain at the beck and call of congregations, and those who offend or are uninspiring get the sack. Also growing very rapidly, as can be seen in Table 7-2, are other evangelical Protestant groups as well as the Mormons. Clearly, a free market religious economy favors robust, energetic organizations.

Although competitive churches and diligent clergy are in keeping with basic principles of capitalism, it was freedom that allowed both North American religion and commerce to flourish.

FREEDOM: PATTERNS OF RULE

Alexis de Tocqueville wrote of the United States early in the nineteenth century as "one of the freest and most enlightened nations

TABLE 7-2 *Some Growing and Declining American Denominations*

| DENOMINATION | AMERICAN MEMBERS PER 1,000 U.S. POPULATION | | |
	1960	2000	% CHANGE
United Church of Christ	12.4	5.0	−71
Episcopal Church	18.1	8.2	−55
United Methodist Church	58.9	29.8	−49
Presbyterian Church (USA)	23.0	12.7	−45
Evangelical Lutheran Church in America	29.3	18.2	−39
Unitarian Universalist	1.0	0.8	−20
Quakers (all meetings)	0.7	0.6	−14
Roman Catholic	233.0	221.7	−5
Southern Baptist Convention	53.8	56.3	+5
Church of the Nazarene	1.7	2.2	+35
Seventh-day Adventist	1.8	3.1	+72
Foursquare Gospel	0.5	0.9	+80
Latter-day Saints (Mormons)	8.2	18.2	+122
Assemblies of God	2.8	9.1	+225
Church of God (Cleveland, Tenn.)	0.9	3.1	+244
Church of God in Christ	2.2	19.5	+786

Source: *Yearbook of American Churches, 1962,* and *Yearbook of American and Canadian Churches, 2001*

in the world."[33] No one wrote anything like that about any nation south of the Rio Grande.

A comparison as of 1770 reveals many of the reasons why. In that era the North American colonies were rapidly being populated by waves of immigrant smallholders and were administered by governors in cooperation with active, elected colonial assemblies. Final political authority was vested in the elected British Parliament, the king's authority having become quite circumscribed. In contrast, the Spanish colonies were sparsely settled by upper-class hidalgos or those aspiring thereto, who owned immense estates granted by royal decree. These *estancias* were based primarily on an indigenous, semicoerced labor force, with hired Europeans serving as foremen and overseers—there were very few European smallholders.

The Spanish colonies were ruled by a viceroy in conjunction with a supreme administrative body known as the Audienca, made up of senior officials sent over from Spain. Moreover, there were no provisions for any legislative action in the Spanish Americas, and all laws imposed on the colonies were decided upon in Spain.[34] Nor were there a democratic regime back home in Spain; the nation remained a feudal kingdom. In fact, all of the colonial administrative positions were *sold* by the King of Spain! Although some attention was paid to qualifications, more weight was given to family background and the ability to pay. The number of official positions sold in the colonies greatly proliferated under Philip II as he attempted, unsuccessfully, to avert repeated bankruptcies. Positions that were largely honorific were bought by those seeking status, but most positions were purchased as investments to be made back from the many opportunities to sell influence and services. Given that until well into the eighteenth century nearly all appointees were residents of Spain who had no previous familiarity with the colonies and who returned to Spain upon leaving office, their decisions often were not well advised.[35]

Finally, nearly all of the British colonists had come to stay; many Spanish colonists were only sojourners. The British colonies were founded on production, the Spanish colonies on extraction.

Colonization

Perhaps the most remarkable aspect of Spanish settlement of the New World, especially from early in the sixteenth century until well into the nineteenth, is how few came over. Spanish emigrants to the New World were required to register at the House of Trade in Seville, and during the course of the entire sixteenth century only about fifty-six thousand did so. At one time historians assumed that this total was exceeded many times over by illegal immigrants, but it is now accepted that the number of unregistered emigrants was small.[36] In similar fashion, an estimate that somewhat more than three hundred thousand Spaniards went to the New World from 1500 to 1640[37] is now thought to be much too high.[38] But even this figure would have left most of Latin America utterly unsettled by Europeans.

There were many reasons why the Spanish did not voyage west in large numbers. For one thing, unlike England, Spain was not abundant in "shopkeepers" or people having the outlook required to become successful smallholders—Spain was itself a land of huge estates and of agricultural laborers only slightly above serfdom. Nor were there glittering prospects of becoming a successful shopkeeper or smallholder in a New World that was also dominated by feudal landowners—although the prospects were far more promising even for very poor emigrants than seemed credible to those in Spain.

A second reason for not coming was that the voyage was extremely dangerous. Not only did many die aboard ship from various diseases or from running out of water but large numbers of ships were lost. The Atlantic was wide and stormy, and the Spanish had inferior ships, poor maintenance, and relatively unskilled sailors—recall the fates of both Armadas. Many surviving letters and diaries dwell on the horrors of the passage across. In addition, the attractions of emigration were minimized by the fact that most of those few who went did not plan to stay but merely to sojourn in pursuit of sudden wealth. Many, perhaps most, of those who hit it rich did return to Spain, where they expressed their immense relief to be back. Those who were less fortunate often expressed regrets over having come when corresponding with relatives back home.

Finally, the authorities in both Spain and the colonies imposed restrictions on immigration in order to keep the numbers down. Since in those days the Spanish colonial economies were fueled mainly by mining and exporting gold and silver, additional population was regarded as an expensive surplus that merely added to the costs of subsidizing life in the colonies. To limit newcomers, whenever possible the authorities refused entry permission unless one had relatives already established in a colony. All non-Catholics were excluded, as were nearly all non-Spaniards. Initially, only single men were allowed to emigrate, but eventually married men were allowed to take their families to the New World—single women were never allowed (which resulted in increasingly large creole and mestizo populations).

In contrast, emigrants from Britain came to the British colonies in North America in far greater numbers than came to Latin America from Spain—an estimated total of more than six hundred thousand came from Britain between 1640 and 1760,[39] and many others came from Holland, France, Germany, and other parts of Europe. Many of the colonists came as whole families or married couples. But many singles came too, women as well as men. They did not come in search of feudal estates or to mine gold and silver. Most of them came because of the high wages prevailing in the colonies and the extraordinary opportunities to obtain fertile farmland or to set up a workshop or store. They had no interest in going back. Moreover, because they came in British ships, and began coming a century later, their voyages were far safer and much less debilitating, as well as being much shorter. Although most became smallholders, the droves of immigrants to the northern colonies did not mainly become subsistence farmers.[40] Their family farms were huge by comparison with European peasant plots, and they shared in the substantial and regular profits from exporting their crops and hides to Britain as well as feeding the nonagricultural colonists. In contrast, the Spanish colonies imported not only manufactured goods but large amounts of food, paid for mainly with precious metals from mines, many of which were owned outright by the

Spanish crown. An additional source of rapid colonization in the north was the result of British policies allowing relatively free immigration from most European nations as well as by religious dissenters and even Roman Catholics. In 1776 there already were fifty-six Catholic parishes in the thirteen colonies as well as five synagogues.

Colonial Governance and Control

In principle, the Spanish colonies were ruled by authoritarian regimes imposed by the Spanish court. In reality, Spain was far away—an exchange of messages often took a year or more—so the local elites usually did as they wished. For example, the "New Laws" imposed in 1542 from Spain to protect Indians from slavery and ruthless exploitation often were ignored—in Mexico the viceroy officially suspended these laws in order to head off a rebellion. But the fact that the colonies could not be governed without the help of the colonists did not lead to democracy but merely appended local oligarchies to those nominated by the crown.

British colonies provided much greater individual freedom and substantial amounts of democracy. From the earliest days, the British colonies had elected popular assemblies to consult with "and often handicap their English governors."[41] Of course, only property owners could vote in assembly elections, but since large numbers of colonists owned their own farms and shops, the franchise was relatively widely held.

Aside from governance per se, probably the chief aspect of control imposed on their colonies by European nations was a set of economic policies that Adam Smith named *mercantilism*. The fundamental feature of the system is that the nations attempt to profit from their colonies. The mechanism for achieving this is to require a colony to trade only with the colonial power, exchanging raw materials for manufactured goods, with the balance of trade favoring the colonial power.

Following mercantilist policies, the British imported agricultural products, furs and skins, millions of pounds of dried fish and whale oil, and raw materials from North America in exchange for manufactured products, fixing the prices charged and the prices paid in order to ensure a favorable balance of trade. This was always a source of friction and encouraged North Americans to do a great deal of smuggling and illegal trading, and to found many small, local manufacturing firms—modeled on British capitalism. As time passed, North American exports to Britain became less and less "raw," reflecting local economic development. For example, in 1770 American colonies exported more flour to England than they did unmilled grain, large amounts of soap and candles, far more barrel staves, masts, and finished boards than logs, an immense amount of rum (rather than undistilled molasses), and even 3,149 pairs of shoes.[42] Another source of economic stimulation to North America was that, although the British used their naval superiority to prevent ships flying other flags (especially the Dutch) from carrying cargoes to their colonies, they permitted colonial vessels to operate freely. Since ships could be built far more cheaply in New England than in Britain (many essential shipbuilding materials and marine supplies were major imports from the New World), this gave an immense stimulus to colonial marine industries as well as to an American merchant marine: in 1773 American shipyards built 638 oceangoing vessels.[43] Having such a large merchant marine made it so easy to engage in smuggling and illegal trading that in 1770 American colonial exports to Europe and the West Indies yielded as much as did exports to Britain.[44]

Even so, looking only at trade statistics, Britain did seem to profit from its mercantile policies with the colonies. In 1772, exports from the American colonies to England were valued at 1.3 million pounds sterling, while imports from England totaled 3 million.[45] However, the bill for maintaining colonies far exceeds the price the colonial power pays for its imports. Governments also incur costs to administer, defend, and sometimes to control their colonies. In the case of North America, Britain had to defend its colonies, especially during three expensive wars with France. Given the remarkable affluence of the colonies (per capita income being far higher than in Britain), Parliament decided to impose taxes on them to help offset the heavy costs of their defense. This met bitter resistance and helped prompt the Revolution, thereby imposing staggering new costs on Britain.

Initially, Spain seemed to profit immensely from its New World colonies. Treasure ships sailed east, while ships loaded with food and manufactured goods sailed west. Because of the dangers from British and Dutch raiders and pirates, and to minimize smuggling, the Spanish organized their trade into two annual convoys between Seville and ports in the Caribbean: the outgoing fleet carrying Spanish exports and the return trip bringing back imports—including shipments of gold and silver from New World mines and cargoes transferred across Panama from Pacific treasure ships. But as was noted in Chapter 6, Asian treasures and colonial gold and silver did little more than allow Spain to live far beyond its means and helped to prevent economic development in both Spain and its colonies. In fact, unlike Britain, Spain could not supply its colonies with its own manufactured products but had to buy them from other European nations (they often were of British origin) and then resell them to the colonies at a marked-up price. This made smuggling extremely profitable and widely pursued. It did not, however, stimulate manufacturing in the Spanish colonies. Not only would this have been opposed by the Spanish crown but it was incompatible with the rural feudalism on which the colonies were based. Spanish colonies were unable to export much in the way of raw materials to Spain, their estates being largely subsistence enterprises, nor would raw materials have been of much use to an unindustrialized Spanish economy.

To sum up: The British colonies enjoyed a very high level of local political autonomy based on relatively democratic institutions. The Spanish colonies were ruled by oligarchies, whether Spanish or domestic. Both sets of colonies were exploited and their economies somewhat distorted and controlled by mercantilism. But this stimulated domestic economic development in the north and reinforced feudalism in the south.

Independence

This is not the place to summarize the American Revolution or the various campaigns that liberated continental Latin America. Instead, the focus will be on several crucial differences between north and south that had lasting consequences.

The Revolutionary War was not nearly so unequal as it sometimes is presented. The colonies were relatively densely settled and able to supply substantial military forces—in 1776 the thirteen colonies had a total population of about 2.5 million, compared with 8.3 million living in Great Britain (not including Ireland). The colonies were contiguous and closely knit by culture, trade, outlook, circumstance, and personal relationships. Unity was increased by the exigencies of war and subsequently by the departure of many colonists who had supported the British. It is true, however, that the American colonists were opposed by the world's leading economic power, a nation able to hire and sustain large armies across the sea and to capture and hold some major cities. But their supply line was more than three thousand miles long, and the British efforts to blockade the colonies were thwarted not only by the colonial merchant fleet but by French and Dutch interference. In the end, the British lacked the troops and the popular support to prevail in the countryside against an elusive foe, and eventually the costs of continuing the war could not be justified—especially not to an elected Parliament. After the war, the new nation was easily united, and the long heritage of British political culture sustained the establishment of lasting democratic institutions.

Liberation movements in Latin America did not involve the colonies in a long, demanding, and unifying battle against a powerful European nation. When it was conquered by Napoleon in 1808, Spain had its weakness exposed for all to see, and the liberation of Spain's New World colonies was essentially unopposed from abroad—opposition came from local interests who preferred to remain colonists rather than to embrace the "revolutionary" rhetoric of the "liberators." Even the defeat of Napoleon in 1815 did not leave Spain in any position to reassert its claims over the southern continent. By early in the 1820s, Spain's only remaining New World possessions were Cuba and Puerto Rico—the rest had been "liberated." Brazil became an independent kingdom in 1822.

Independence brought both gains and losses for the church. For one thing, the subordination of the church to the Spanish (and Portuguese) crowns was no longer in effect. Henceforth, the Vatican chose the bishops and papal pronouncements no longer were subject to censorship. For another, the liberators found it expedient to retain church support and extended many privileges in order to obtain it.[46] However, later in the century, church lands were expropriated (in the name of *liberación*) in some nations and the legal prohibitions against non-Catholic faiths were relaxed somewhat. But the church remained a major factor in secular affairs.

Once they gained their freedom, optimism ran high among Latin Americans. Most influential citizens believed that all that was needed was sufficient capital and some additional skilled labor in order to exploit the many natural resources of the continent, for now they would not be hindered by Spain and would enjoy access to European markets.[47] Of course, as will be seen, skilled labor remained in short supply. But a more serious lack was something too many took for granted: freedom.

The newly liberated colonies did not constitute a well-settled, relatively integrated, contiguous group of settlements but were widely scattered and isolated by major geographic barriers, and local areas were dominated by isolated cliques and opportunists. Many wars erupted. Larger political units were dismembered into many smaller ones. By 1823 Central America had separated from Mexico. "Gran Colombia—the union of Venezuela, Colombia, and Ecuador created by Simón Bolívar—finally broke up in 1830 after the Liberator's death, and the short-lived union between Peru and Bolivia in the 1830s collapsed following a Chilean invasion."[48] Out of all this turmoil came repressive, often greedy regimes. Military rule was common, as were one-party republics, and whatever the form of government, the old caste systems prevailed relatively intact, the fears of the liberators' revolutionary rhetoric proving to have been unfounded. Even in nations holding elections, very few citizens actually had the right to vote.[49]

Ending Slavery

However, the overthrow of Spanish colonial rule did bring an end to slavery. There were several factors involved. First, with the exception of Brazil and the island colonies, most of Latin America never developed plantation economies, and the utilization of African slaves was always on a small scale. Second, slave owners usually opposed the liberation movements, so that by proclaiming emancipation, these movements were able to enlist slaves to their cause—albeit revolutionary leaders were probably sincere in their opposition to slavery. In any event, emancipation was accomplished in most of Latin America well before the American Civil War: Argentina in 1813, Columbia in 1814, Chile in 1823, Mexico in 1829, and Ecuador, Peru, and Venezuela in the 1850s.

That left Brazil, Cuba, and Puerto Rico. The defeat of the Confederacy sealed their fate—early in the Civil War some anticipated a union of the American South with Cuba and Puerto Rico and possibly even with Brazil. After the war, as the British navy intercepted most attempts to ship new slaves from Africa to these remaining slave societies, and under intense economic as well as diplomatic pressure from Europe and the United States, the slaves were emancipated in Puerto Rico in 1873, in Cuba in 1886, and in Brazil in 1888.

It is not clear to what extent slavery stymied the economic development of Latin America; emancipation did not result in any substantial bursts of development. It is clear, however, that slavery greatly influenced economic development in North America. By 1860 the northeastern United States had become a major world industrial power, but the South remained a somewhat feudal, agricultural region lacking both cities and industries. It is not true that the slave-based plantation economy was unprofitable and about to collapse of its own lack of productivity—although several generations of historians embraced that fiction.[50] The plantations were very profitable and were operated in accord with basic capitalist principles. But they did not fund development; instead they sustained political elites who were militant in their defense of a "Southern way of life" that was hostile to industry and change.

CAPITALISM

In 1620, when the *Mayflower* set sail, Britain was the world's foremost economic power, denigrated by antagonistic and envious Europeans as a "nation of shopkeepers." Britain's booming capitalism was outperforming any economy in all previous history, sustaining seemingly endless and rapid industrial growth and innovation—soon to be widely referred to as the Industrial Revolution. These same basic capitalist economic practices and perspectives came to the British New World as colonies sprang up and were populated by emigrants drawn not in search of cities of gold but by the virtually unlimited opportunities presented by an "inexhaustible" supply of fertile farmland and natural resources. This rapidly developing, affluent new civilization had need for large numbers of merchants, artisans, and skilled craftsmen as well as farmers. And because all of these occupational groups came in large numbers, especially to the northern colonies,[51] British America became a land of ambitious smallholders, infused with the spirit of capitalism, who quite naturally enjoyed the aphorisms in favor of work and thrift so well expressed by Benjamin Franklin (and so overinterpreted by Max Weber). Even in the earliest Puritan communities, ostensibly founded on communal principles, entrepreneurs flourished, land speculation was rife, and most new towns were founded and developed in anticipation of real estate profits.[52]

Industry and Labor

In 1776 there was very little manufacturing in North America. There were many small workshops making needed items such as shoes, harnesses, kettles, nails, pails, and simple hand tools, but their products were sold only in the local market. Larger-scale production tended to be limited to refining food and drink for export (for example, milling flower and distilling rum). A bit more sophisticated were plants making candles and soap or preparing furs and hides for export. There were also many small shops making rifles (in contrast with the muskets in use in Europe) and, as noted, some very busy shipyards. Nevertheless, most manufactured items sold in colonial America were imported from Great Britain—in 1770 Americans imported 5,928 scythes and 5,603 axes.[53]

A century later, in 1870, the United States was a manufacturing giant, second only to Great Britain and towering above Germany and France in terms of manufacturing output. In contrast, there was essentially no manufacturing in Spain or in Latin America (see Table 7-3). In another thirty years (1900) the United States had far surpassed Britain and was creating more than a third of the world's manufactured goods, more than twice as much as Britain. By 1929 the United States dwarfed the world as a manufacturing power, producing 42.2 percent of all goods, compared with Germany's 11.6 percent and Britain's 9.4. Spain still failed to gain a separate entry, but for the first time Latin America as a whole was sufficiently productive to be listed, the entire continent manufacturing only about 80 percent as much as Canada.

One reason for the extraordinary progress by the United States was abundant natural resources, especially large, easily mined deposits of iron and coal. There was also a considerable amount of conveniently located waterpower. Another advantage was an extremely productive agriculture, which sustained rapid urbanization as well as producing large amounts of cotton for the northeastern textile mills. Industrialization also benefited from a large, rapidly growing domestic market. But a primary reason for the rapid industrialization of the United States was very high labor costs.

One might think that high labor costs would have impeded the growth of factories, given the need to compete in the international market. In fact, high labor costs impelled American capitalists to invest in technology to make their workers so productive as to offset their high wages, from which everyone benefited. It worked this way.

American wages were high because employers had to compete with the exceptional opportunities of self-employment in order to attract adequate numbers of qualified workers. As Alexander Hamilton explained shortly after the American Revolution, "The facility with which the less independent condition of an artisan can be exchanged for the more independent condition of a farmer . . . conspire[s] to produce, and, for a length of time, must continue to

TABLE 7-3 *Percentage Shares of the World's Manufacturing Output*

NATION	PERCENTAGE OF WORLD'S MANUFACTURING OUTPUT		
	1870	1900	1929
Great Britain	31.8	14.7	9.4
United States	23.3	35.3	42.2
Germany	13.2	15.9	11.6
France	10.3	6.4	6.6
Russia	3.7	5.0	4.3
Belgium	2.9	2.2	1.9
Italy	2.4	3.1	3.3
Canada	1.0	2.0	2.4
Sweden	0.4	1.1	1.0
India	—	1.1	1.2
Japan	—	0.6	2.5
Finland	—	0.3	0.4
Latin America	—	—	2.0
China	—	—	0.5
All others	11.0	12.3	10.7

Source: League of Nations, 1945

occasion, a scarcity of hands for manufacturing occupation, and dearness of labour generally."[54] Good farmland was so abundant and so cheap that even those who arrived in America without any funds could, in several years, save enough to buy and stock a good farm. Consider that in the 1820s the federal government sold good land for $1.25 an acre while wages for skilled labor amounted to between $1.25 and $2.00 a day.[55] It didn't take long to save enough for a farm sufficiently large to raise cash crops yielding solid returns, which then often enabled an owner to aquire additional acreage. Consider too that in America there were no mandatory church tithes, and taxes were very low.

The situation of the British manufacturer was dramatically different. The average worker had little choice but to work for wages—whether as a hired farm laborer or as an industrial worker. Farmland was very expensive and seldom for sale. There were few new opportunities to become a merchant or even a skilled worker. Since the population was growing, there was at all times a large, available labor pool, albeit there was a constant emigration of the most ambitious to America. So, British employers could set wages very low and still attract the needed workers. How could American manufacturers possibly compete on price, given their far higher labor costs? Through better technology.

British manufacturers were relatively reluctant to invest in new machines and processes because these increased their costs and cut into profits unless they also raised their prices. But Americans eagerly embraced promising new technology if they anticipated a sufficient increase in worker productivity. For if workers equipped with a new technology could produce more than could the less mechanized workers in Britain and Europe, this reduced the relative cost of American labor *per item*. In this way technology made it irrelevant that American workers were paid, say, three times as much an hour as British and European workers (as they often were), when American workers produced five or six times as much per hour, thus offsetting both their own higher wages and the capital investments in new technology made by their employers. Throughout the nineteenth century, Americans led the way in developing and adopting new techniques and technologies. And they did so without provoking the reactionary labor opposition to innovation so often faced by nineteenth-century British capitalists—no Luddites smashed machines in the United States. Why not? Because, given the constant shortage of labor, American manufacturers continued to compete with one another for workers and used a significant portion of their productivity gains to increase wages and to offer more attractive conditions. In contrast, "even when labour-saving devices were introduced, many English employers were so habituated to the idea of low money wages that they were not prepared to concede to their labour the higher money earnings which the new devices warranted and which would have reconciled labour to their introduction."[56]

Far greater worker productivity was the basis for the incredible growth of American manufacturing shown in Table 7-3, and the reason why it came largely at the expense of the British. Americans were not more humane employers. They were more sophisticated capitalists who recognized that satisfied, productive workers are the greatest asset of them all. This attitude toward labor played a major role in continuing to bring many of the most skilled and motivated British and European workers to America, thereby expanding the labor force sufficiently to sustain ever more industrial growth. Unfortunately, far too many published discussions of the rise of American industry (especially in textbooks) denounce the "robber barons" and "plutocrats" for their "vicious exploitation" of labor, and especially for abusing "unsophisticated" immigrants. Such tracts are anachronistic, comparing labor practices back then with those of today, almost as if factory latrines in 1850 should have had flush toilets. The proper comparison is between the situation of American labor and labor in the other industrializing nations in the same era.

In addition to being highly paid and equipped with the latest technology, American workers were notable in another way. They were far better educated than workers anywhere else in the world (excluding Canada).

Investing in Human Capital

The same William Cobbett who wrote home to England in 1818 about the high level of religious activity in the United States also wrote: "There are very few really *ignorant* men in America. . . . They have all been *readers* from their youth up" (his italics).[57] From the earliest days of settlement, the American colonists invested heavily in "human capital," as modern economists would put it. And in this, religion played a primary role.

A major point of contention during the Reformation had to do with reading the Bible. For centuries the church had thought the best way to avoid endless bickering and disagreement about God's word was to encourage only well-trained theologians to actually read the Bible. To this end, the church opposed all translations of the Bible into contemporary languages, thus limiting its readers to those proficient in Latin or Greek, which even most of the clergy were not. Moreover, in the days before the printing press there were so very few copies of the Bible that even most bishops did not have access to one. Consequently, the clergy learned about the Bible from secondary sources written to edify them and to provide them with suitable quotations for preaching. What the public knew about the Bible was only what their priests told them.

Then came the printing press. The Bible was the first book Gutenberg published. It was written in Latin, but very soon Bibles were being printed in all of the major "vulgar" languages (hence "vulgate" Bibles), making the Bible the first-ever best seller. As had been feared, a great deal of disagreement and conflict quickly arose as one reformer after another denounced various church teachings and activities as unbiblical. And the one doctrine most widely shared among the various dissenting Protestant movements was that everyone must consult scripture for themselves. So, when the Pilgrims arrived in 1620, one of the very first things they did was to concern themselves with educating their children.

In 1647 the Massachusetts Colony enacted a law asserting that all children must attend school.[58] It required that in any township having fifty households, one person must be appointed to teach the children to read and write, and the teacher's wages were to be paid either by parents or by the inhabitants in general. Furthermore, in any township having a hundred or more households, a school must be established, "the master thereof being able to instruct youth so far as they may be fitted for the university." Any community that failed to provide these educational services was to be fined "till they shall perform this order." Other states soon followed suit, and free public schools became a fixture of American life. As the nation spread west, one-room schoolhouses were among the first things the settlers constructed (along with a saloon, a jail, and several churches). Much the same took place in Canada and by the end of the eighteenth century North America had by far the "most literate population in the world."[59]

Notice that the Massachusetts school law required that schoolmasters be qualified to prepare students for college. This was not as unreasonable as it might appear. A decade before they passed this law and only sixteen years after landing at Plymouth Rock, the Puritans had founded Harvard. This initiated three centuries of intense competition among the religious denominations to found their own colleges and universities. As can be seen in Table 7-4, prior to the Revolution, ten institutions of higher learning had already begun operating in the American colonies (compared with two in England). Of these, only the University of Pennsylvania, instituted by Benjamin Franklin to train businessmen, was not affiliated with a denomination. Following the Revolution, at least twenty more colleges were founded before 1800, including Georgetown University, founded by Jesuit scholars in 1789. During the next century literally hundreds of colleges and universities arose in the United States, and most of these were also of denominational origin (although many abandoned their denominational ties during the twentieth century).

Meanwhile, the impact of religion on education was quite negative south of the Rio Grande. As it had in medieval Europe, the church claimed authority over education throughout Latin America but lacked the resources to provide schools for more than the upper classes. The governments were content to leave education up to the church as it saved them money and leaders could see no particular need for peasants to be literate anyway. Congruent with this posi-

TABLE 7-4 *U.S. Colleges Founded Before 1776*

INSTITUTION	YEAR	DENOMINATION
Harvard	1636	Congregational
William and Mary	1693	Episcopal
Yale	1701	Congregational
Moravian	1742	Moravian
Princeton	1746	Presbyterian
Pennsylvania	1751	nonsectarian
Columbia	1754	Episcopal
Brown	1764	Baptist
Rutgers	1766	Dutch Reformed
Dartmouth	1769	Congregational

tion, until well into the twentieth century there were legal bans against the sale of Bibles in most nations of Latin America.[60] Consequently, in 1860, on the eve of the Civil War, African-Americans had a literacy rate (21 percent) almost as high as did the population of Argentina (24), and higher than the people of Brazil (16), Chile (18), Guatemala (11), Honduras (15), and Puerto Rico (12). Literacy rates in Spain and Portugal probably were no higher, given their very low rates of school enrollment. In contrast, 89 percent of white Americans were literate in 1860, as were 83 percent of Canadians,[61] and most illiterates were first-generation immigrants.

Nearly 150 years later, these huge educational differences persist. If we look only at persons aged twenty-five and older, as of the year 2000, the average American had completed 12.3 years of school and the average Canadian 12.1 years. In Argentina the average person had completed 8.8 years of schooling, in Chile and Peru 7.6, in Mexico 7.2, in Venezuela 6.6, in Ecuador 6.4, in Columbia 5.3, in Brazil 4.9, in Nicaragua 4.5, and in Guatemala 3.5. These Latin American rates are similar to Spain's, where the average person has 7.3 years of schooling, while Portugal's rate is 5.9 years.[62]

This lag in education has been absolutely critical for the lack of economic progress in Latin America. In recent years, study after careful study has found that by far the most important factor in economic development is education.[63] Moreover, education is a factor within local control. As even some very poor nations have shown, substantial educational gains can be achieved by unassisted local efforts. Keep in mind that there probably were a number of illiterates in the first generation of Puritan settlers. But not in the second. It is a matter of perspective and commitment.

The sad fact is that today many Latin American nations are spending heavily on education and getting almost nothing in return. As a report by the Inter-American Development Bank put it in 1998, "despite adequate public spending . . . the distribution of education has hardly improved over time."[64] The money gets soaked up by an educational bureaucracy, with "little attention to priorities and accounting, extensive corruption, and political manipulation of the system."[65]

LATIN AMERICAN PROTESTANTISM: OPIATE OR ETHIC?

Protestantism is growing extremely rapidly in Latin America. Revivalists routinely fill huge soccer stadiums, and in many nations a majority of churchgoers are Protestants—most of them belonging to various Pentecostal groups.[66] Many social scientists, both North and South Americans, have denounced this as a new, more potent "opium of the people." Rowan Ireland asked whether it was true that these newly converted Protestants "are apolitical conservatives who leave the injustices of the world to the Lord's care, privatizing public issues and giving implicit support to authoritarian political projects." Having interviewed two converts, his answer was "Yes." Ireland explained that the moral vision of their religion could not extend beyond efforts to "right small wrongs in anticipation of the Lord who alone achieves justice."[67] In similar fashion, Pablo Deiros charged that Latin American Protestants are "fundamentalists" whose "social conscience is subdued, and their organizations reinforce this oppressed conscience by supplying a sociocultural structure which attributes a sacred character to state oppression."[68]

Many of these same social scientists not only sneer at Latin American Protestants but do so in the context of extolling radical Catholic "Liberation Theology" and its efforts to organize the poor into "base communities" from which to take radical political action. Having begun in the wake of the Second Vatican Council in the middle 1960s, Catholic author-activists, especially Father Gustavo Gutiérrez, made *liberación* such a popular buzzword among leftist intellectuals that even some dedicated Marxist groups, including the Sandinistas, claimed to have been inspired by these religious views. Many conferences were held. Many Marxist-Christian dialogues took place. Very little else happened, except that the "masses" embraced Pentecostalism. By now, Liberation Theology is widely recognized as a naïve clerical fantasy, although many academics refuse to concede the point.[69] Meanwhile, of course, many voices continue to condemn *all* religion, Catholic as well as Protestant, as an opiate. However, others propose that, rather than being an opiate, Latin Protestantism is a stimulant to progress. Citing Max Weber's Protestant ethic thesis, and noting that Latin Protestants tend to preach thrift and personal responsibility, these social scientists suggest that the spread of Protestantism in Latin America may spur the development of capitalism or, at the very least, increase the number willing to act as responsible citizens in pursuit of democracy.[70] Which view is correct—if either?

A number of case studies conducted in small Latin American communities have revealed that conversion to Protestantism does in fact relate to individual economic behavior—that converts tend to combine thrift with financial responsibility and to display some degree of entrepreneurialism.[71] However, some of these studies also suggest that these economic behaviors tended to precede the conversion—that Protestantism appealed to those who already displayed the so-called Protestant ethic. Unfortunately, none of the studies was based on proper samples or used adequate statistical methods.

Recently, Anthony Gill published a statistically sophisticated study based on large, national samples of Mexico, Argentina, Brazil, and Chile.[72] The results are compelling. Gill found that highly committed Protestants and Catholics do not differ in their economic or political attitudes or activities. Both groups have more liberal economic views, more conservative political attitudes, a higher level of civic participation, and greater trust in government than do less religious people. Citing the lack of Protestant-Catholic differences, Gill wrote: "It is clear that Weber is not at work in Latin America." But neither is Marx: religion is not causing political apathy or alienation.

Finally, Latin America may be pursuing the North American recipe for success. New levels of freedom have stimulated religious pluralism as well as the emergence of independent political parties. One-party rule seems to be going the way of the monopoly church. Perhaps, then, Latin Americans finally are developing the necessary basis for effective capitalist economies—but only if they do not revert to their old command economies under new, democratic-sounding labels, as they so often have done in the past.

Globalization and Modernity

Christianity created Western Civilization. Had the followers of Jesus remained an obscure Jewish sect, most of you would not have learned to read and the rest of you would be reading from hand-copied scrolls. Without a theology committed to reason, progress, and moral equality, today the entire world would be about where non-European societies were in, say, 1800: A world with many astrologers and alchemists but no scientists. A world of despots, lacking universities, banks, factories, eyeglasses, chimneys, and pianos. A world where most infants do not live to the age of five and many women die in childbirth—a world truly living in "dark ages."

The modern world arose only in Christian societies. Not in Islam. Not in Asia. Not in a "secular" society—there having been none. And all the modernization that has since occurred outside Christendom was imported from the West, often brought by colonizers and missionaries. Even so, many apostles of modernization assume that, given the existing Western example, similar progress can be achieved today not only without Christianity but even without freedom or capitalism—that globalization will fully spread scientific, technical, and commercial knowledge without any need to re-create the social or cultural conditions that first produced it. A brief assessment of these matters will properly conclude *The Victory of Reason*.

It seems doubtful that an effective modern economy can be created without adopting capitalism, as was demonstrated by the failure of the command economies of the Soviet Union and China. The Soviets could get rockets into orbit, but they couldn't reliably get onions to Moscow. As for China, millions had to die to prove that collectivized agriculture is unproductive. Today, with capitalism thriving in many nations recently freed from Soviet oppression, and with the Chinese having taken to heart that they have long been outproduced by Taiwan, both Russia and China now seek to build capitalist economies. It remains to be seen whether either nation can provide freedom, without which effective capitalism is impossible. Indeed, for want of both freedom and capitalism, Islamic nations remain in semifeudalism, incapable of manufacturing most of the items they use in daily life. Their standards of living require massive imports paid for with oil money just as Spain enjoyed the fruits of other nations' industry so long as it was kept afloat by gold and silver from the New World. Without secure property rights and substantial individual freedom, modern societies cannot fully emerge.

But if modernization still requires capitalism and freedom, what about Christianity? On the one hand, a strong case can be made that although Christianity was necessary for the rise of science, by now science has become so well institutionalized that it no longer requires a Christian warrant. The same may be true for belief in progress. The conviction that we can deeply penetrate nature's secrets and achieve advanced technology may no longer need to be based on faith, since all one really needs to do now is look around.

On the other hand, if Christianity is now irrelevant to modernization, why is it still spreading so rapidly? The fact is that Christianity is becoming globalized far more rapidly than is democracy, capitalism, or modernity. The religious revolution going on in Latin America is not merely Protestantization but Christianization—most new Latin Protestants not really ever having been Catholics. Africa is turning Christian so rapidly that there are far more Anglicans south of the Sahara than in Britain or North America, not to mention the tens of millions of new Baptists, Pentecostals, Roman Catholics, and members of Protestant sects of local origin—about half of sub-Saharan Africans now are Christians.[1] Even so, the Christianization of the Southern Hemisphere may soon be dwarfed by what is going on in China.

When the Communists took power in 1949, there were perhaps

2 million Christians in China. At the time, not only Marxists but even American liberal church leaders dismissed these as mainly "rice" Christians—people who put up with missionary efforts only in exchange for handouts. Fifty years later we have discovered that these Chinese rice Christians were so "insincere" that they endured decades of draconian repression, during which their numbers doubled again and again—there might be as many as 100 million Christians in China today![2] Moreover, conversion to Christianity is concentrated not among the peasants and the poor but among the best-educated, most modern Chinese.

There are many reasons people embrace Christianity, including its capacity to sustain a deeply emotional and existentially satisfying faith. But another significant factor is its appeal to reason and the fact that it is so inseparably linked to the rise of Western Civilization. For many non-Europeans, becoming a Christian is intrinsic to becoming modern. Thus it is quite plausible that Christianity remains an essential element in the globalization of modernity. Consider this recent statement by one of China's leading scholars:

One of the things we were asked to look into was what accounted for the success, in fact, the pre-eminence of the West all over the world. We studied everything we could from the historical, political, economic, and cultural perspective. At first, we thought it was because you had more powerful guns than we had. Then we thought it was because you had the best political system. Next we focused on your economic system. But in the past twenty years, we have realized that the heart of your culture is your religion: Christianity. That is why the West is so powerful. The Christian moral foundation of social and cultural life was what made possible the emergence of capitalism and then the successful transition to democratic politics. We don't have any doubt about this.[3]

Neither do I.

Acknowledgments

As must anyone writing a historical study of substantial scope, I have relied on hundreds of specialists to educate me about their areas. It has been remarked that there is a valuable role to be played by someone willing to stroll from one scholarly encampment to another in pursuit of larger designs. Those are my intentions. I also intend this book for the general reader. This has entailed no loss of scholarship, only a ban on jargon and on needless academic paraphernalia.

Besides other writers, I am indebted to my agent, Giles Anderson, for useful suggestions about the book I planned to write, and especially for selecting Random House as my new publisher. This enabled me to work with Will Murphy, whose taste and sense of structure transformed this into a very different and far better book. Originally, I ended the book with a very brief conclusion following what is now Chapter 5. Will suggested bringing the story across the Atlantic, to finish with developments in the New World. But of course! Will also suggested that I begin the book with the chapter on rational theology, originally placed second behind a long chapter on how despots destroy commerce. He was quite right, and the chapter on despots disappeared (several fragments having been placed in other chapters). How nice to work with a real professional.

I also must acknowledge the contributions of several friends and fine scholars: Daniel Chirot, Anthony Gill, Laurence R. Iannaccone, David Lyle Jeffrey, and Arthur Wu.

Corrales, New Mexico
August 2004

Notes

INTRODUCTION

1. Weber [1904–5] 1958.
2. See Lenski, Nolan, and Lenski 1995; Smelser 1994; also the summary in Hamilton 1996.
3. With one minor exception, Weber took it as self-evident that throughout Europe Protestants far surpassed Catholics in educational and occupational achievement and that Protestant areas were, and had been, well ahead in the Industrial Revolution. The exception was his rather offhand citation of a study by his student Martin Offenbacher of educational attainment in Baden, which purported to show that Protestant students were more likely to enroll in schools offering mathematics and science, as opposed to schools specializing in the classics. Not only is this astonishingly slim evidence for a thesis of immense historical scope, it wasn't even correct—the shortcomings of Offenbacher's "findings" have been fully exposed (Becker 2000, 1997; Hamilton 1996). In any event, Weber's starting point seems to have reflected nothing more scholarly than the smug anti-Catholicism of his time and place. Daniel Chirot has suggested to me that Weber's deep anti-Catholicism also explains his disregard for French scholarship.
4. Trevor-Roper [1969] 2001: 20–21.
5. Pirenne was refuting not Weber, whom he may not yet have read, but Sombart 1902 and other Marxists who equated capitalism with the Industrial Revolution.
6. Braudel 1977: 66–67.
7. Gilchrist 1969: 1.
8. Great Britain did, of course, lead the Industrial Revolution.
9. Delacroix and Nielsen 2001; Samuelsson [1961] 1993.
10. Charanis 1953; Chirot 1985; Ostrogorsky 1957; Schluchter 1981; Weber [1921] 1951, [1917–19] 1952, [1921] 1951.
11. Waldron 2002.
12. Stark 2003a.
13. Ibid.

CHAPTER ONE

1. *Essay Concerning Human Understanding:* book 3, ch. 10.
2. Rahner 1975: 1687.

3. Clough 1997: 57.
4. *City of God:* book 5, ch. 1.
5. Bauckham 1990.
6. I have relied on the translations of Aquinas's *Summa Theologica* provided by Monroe 1975: book 14, ch. 28.
7. *On Repentance:* ch. 1.
8. *Recognitions of Clement:* book 2, ch. 69.
9. In Lindberg and Numbers 1986: 27–28.
10. Southern 1970a: 49.
11. Ozment 1980.
12. Saint Bernard of Clairvaux (1090–1153).
13. Colish 1997.
14. Reform Judaism rejected the authority of scripture and embraced a very vague image of God, too impersonal and remote to sustain theology.
15. Denny 1993: 612.
16. In Ayoub 1996: 414.
17. Macmurray 1938: 113.
18. Jeffrey 1996: 12.
19. I Corinthians 13:9, RSV.
20. Pickthall translation.
21. In Lindberg 1986: 27.
22. *City of God:* book 22, ch. 24.
23. In Gimpel 1961: 165.
24. In Gimpel 1976: 149.
25. In Hartwell 1971: 691.
26. Grant 1986; Meyer 1944.
27. Southern 1970: 50.
28. In Lindberg 1986: 27–28.
29. *Confessions:* book 12, ch. 18.
30. In Benin 1993: 68.
31. Calvin [c. 1555] 1980: 52–53.
32. For a summary see Stark 2003a.
33. Bloch [1940] 1961: 83.
34. Darwin and Seward 1903: I:195.
35. *On the Heavens.*
36. Cohen 1985; Collins 1998; Dorn 1991; Grant 1994, 1996; Huff 1993; Jaki 1986; Kuhn 1962; Lindberg 1992, 1986; Mason 1962; Neugebauer 1975.
37. In Crosby 1997: 83.
38. Whitehead [1925] 1967: 13.
39. Ibid., 12.
40. Ibid., 13.
41. Jeffrey 1979: 14.
42. *Oeuvres:* book 8, ch. 61.
43. Russell 1922: 193.
44. The quotation from Russell continues: "I have no doubt that if the Chinese get a stable government and sufficient funds, they would, within the next thirty years, begin to produce remarkable work in science. It is quite likely that they might outstrip us."
45. Needham 1954: 581.
46. Lang 1997: 18.

47. In Mason 1962: 36–37.
48. Grant 1994, 1996; Jaki 1986; Lindberg 1992; Mason 1962, as well as the cited original sources.
49. Lindberg 1992.
50. Mason 1962.
51. Lindberg 1992: 54.
52. In Jaki 1986: 114.
53. Full text in Danielson 2000: 14–15.
54. In *Timaeus*.
55. Jaki 1986: 105.
56. Lindberg 1992; Mason 1962.
57. Southern 1953: 64.
58. Farah 1994; Hodgson 1974; Jaki 1986; Nasr 1993.
59. Farah 1994: 199.
60. Nasr 1993.
61. Morris [1972] 2000: 2.
62. Ibid.
63. Finley 1973: 28.
64. Morris [1972] 2000: 4.
65. *Julius Caesar,* Act I, Scene 2.
66. For example, Gurevich 1995; Morris [1972] 2000; Ullman 1966.
67. *De libero arbitrio* III:I, translated and quoted in Kehr 1916: 602.
68. *City of God:* book 5, ch. 9.
69. *Summa contra gentiles*, Lib. III, Cap. 113.
70. Nisbet, 1973: 482.
71. *City of God:* book 11, ch. 26.
72. Henry 1927.
73. Schlaifer 1936.
74. Davis 1966: 66.
75. Schlaifer 1936.
76. *Politics* I: 1254.
77. Bensch 1998: 231.
78. Fogel 1989: 25.
79. Bloch [1940] 1961, 1975; Davis 1966.
80. In Bonnassie 1991: 6.
81. Duby 1974: 32.
82. For a summary of these views see Bonnassie 1991; Dockès 1982.
83. Lopez 1979: 138.
84. Conrad and Meyer 1958; Easterlin 1961; Fogel and Engerman 1974; Stark 2003a.
85. Bloch 1975: 13.
86. Bonnassie 1991: 30.
87. Bloch 1975: 14.
88. In Bonnassie 1991: 54.
89. *Via Regia,* my translation.
90. Bloch 1975: 11.
91. Ibid., 30.
92. Lopez 1952: 353.
93. Stark 2003.
94. Ibid.
95. Benedict 1946.

96. Finley 1973: 28.
97. Lewis 1990; Watt 1961, 1965.
98. In Gordon 1989: 19.
99. I should qualify this assertion by noting the ability of many Protestant theologians to get around the fact that Jesus drank wine.

CHAPTER TWO

1. For an analysis of why the Dark Ages were invented, see the chapter on the rise of science in Stark 2003a.
2. Gimpel 1976: viii, 1.
3. *Works* XII.
4. The second edition of *Webster's Unabridged Dictionary* (1934) defined "Dark Ages" as the "earlier part of [the Middle Ages] because of its intellectual stagnation," and the college edition of *Webster's New World Dictionary* of 1958 defined "Dark Ages" as "1. the period from the fall of the Western Roman Empire (476 A.D.) to the beginning of the modern era (c. 1450). 2. The earlier part of the Middle Ages, to about the end of the 10th century . . . the medieval period in Europe, especially the earlier part, [that] was characterized by widespread ignorance."
5. *The New Columbia Encyclopedia* (1975) suggested that the term "Dark Ages" is no longer used by historians because this era "is no longer thought to have been so dim." In its entry for the "Dark Ages," the 15th edition of *Encyclopaedia Britannica* (1981) reported that this term "is now rarely used by historians because of the unacceptable value judgment it implies," being a "pejorative" incorrectly claiming that this was "a period of intellectual darkness and barbarity."
6. Gibbon [1776–88] 1994: II:1443.
7. Bridbury 1969: 533.
8. Vogt 1974: 25. Despite his concern for the "masses," Friedrich Engels took the same position; see Finley 1980: 12.
9. Bairoch 1988: 109–10; Nicholas 1997.
10. Chandler and Fox 1974.
11. Southern 1953: 12–13.
12. Lopez 1976: 43.
13. This is an undercount since the book is known to be incomplete. Gies and Gies 1994: 113.
14. Gimpel 1976: 13.
15. Ibid., 16.
16. Gies and Gies 1994: 117.
17. Landes 1998: 46.
18. Gimpel 1976: 14.
19. Ibid., 25–27.
20. Ibid., 32.
21. Smil 2000; White 1962.
22. Lopez 1976: 44.
23. Bairoch 1988: 125; Gimpel 1976: 43.
24. White 1962.
25. Tobin 1996: 128.
26. Hunt and Murray 1999: 17.
27. Gies and Gies 1994; Gimpel 1976; White 1962.
28. Gimpel 1976: 44–45.
29. Ibid., 46.

30. Carcopino 1940: 36.
31. Ibid.
32. Landes 1998: 46.
33. Macfarlane and Martin 2002.
34. Mumford 1939: 14.
35. Jones 1987; Gimpel 1976.
36. Lewis 2002: 118.
37. Gimpel 1976: 169.
38. Montgomery 1968; White 1962.
39. Hyland 1994.
40. Needham 1980.
41. Hime 1915; Manucy 1949; Partington [1960] 1999.
42. Barclay and Schofield 1981: 488.
43. Especially Cipolla 1965; Howarth 1974; McNeill 1982.
44. McNeill 1974: 50.
45. Cipolla 1965; Gies and Gies 1994.
46. Beeching 1982; Hanson 2001.
47. Lane [1934] 1992: 35–53.
48. Hitchins and May 1951; May and Howard 1981; Needham 1962.
49. McNeill 1974: 50–51.
50. Nicholas 1997: 3.
51. Bridbury 1969: 532.
52. Lopez 1952, 1976.
53. Lopez 1976: 8.
54. Leighton 1972: 59.
55. Ibid., 74–75.
56. Ibid., 71.
57. Translation in Leighton 1972: 121.
58. Postan 1952: 147.
59. Usher 1966: 184.
60. Daniel 1981: 705.
61. Gardner and Crosby 1959: 236.
62. De la Croix and Tansey 1975: 353.
63. Johnson 2003: 190.
64. Lopez 1967: 198.
65. Colish 1997: 266.
66. Cohen 1985; Gingerich 1975; Jaki 2000; Rosen 1971.
67. In Clagett 1961: 536.
68. White 1967.
69. Gimpel 1976: 148.
70. Although some authors actually remark that "everyone knows" what capitalism is. Cf. Rosenberg and Birdzell 1986: vi.
71. The orthodox Marxist definition is plain and simple: capitalism exists where the actual producers are wage laborers who do not own their tools, and these, as well as the raw materials and finished products, are owned by their employer (see Sombart 1902 as well as Hilton 1952). Taken seriously, this definition would make capitalists out of all owners of small craft shops such as potteries and metal smithies in ancient times. That seems especially odd since Marxists cling to their belief that capitalism first appeared during (and caused) the Industrial Revolution, a necessary assumption for those who accept Marx's theory of social change, wherein all history rests on changes in modes of production. Thus, Marxists condemn all "talk about

capitalism before the end of the eighteenth century" (Braudel 1979: 2:238), equating capitalism with "the modern industrial system" (Gerschenkron 1970: 4). But for those of us who associate capitalism with particular kinds of firms and markets, the Marxist definition is not useful.

72. Braudel 1979: 2:232–48.
73. For all of his fulminating about "wage slavery," Marx opened his study *Pre-Capitalist Economic Formations* with the statement that "one of the historic conditions for capital is free labour."
74. 1 Timothy 6:10.
75. Little 1978: 38.
76. Baldwin 1959: 15.
77. Mumford 1966: 266.
78. Collins 1986: 47.
79. Ibid., 55.
80. Ibid., 52.
81. Hayes 1917; Herlihy 1957; Ozment 1975.
82. Dickens 1991.
83. Little 1978: 62.
84. Johnson 2003: 144.
85. Gimpel 1976: 47.
86. Gilchrist 1969; Russell 1958, 1972.
87. Little 1978: 93.
88. Dawson 1957: 63.
89. Duby 1974: 218.
90. Little 1978: 65.
91. Ibid.
92. Fryde 1963: 441–43.
93. De Roover 1948: 9.
94. Duby 1974: 216.
95. Ibid., 91.
96. Ibid.
97. Gimpel 1976: 47.
98. Mumford 1967: I:272.
99. Dawson 1957; Hickey 1987; King 1999; Mayr-Harting 1993; Stark 2003b.
100. Collins 1986: 54.
101. Ch. 40, "The Daily Manual Labor."
102. Hilton 1985: 3.
103. Friedrich Prinz, as translated in Kaelber 1998: 66.
104. In Nelson 1969: 11; also Little 1978: 56–57.
105. Gilchrist 1969: 107.
106. Nelson 1969: 9.
107. Olsen 1969: 53.
108. In his *Commentary on the Sentences of Peter Lombard,* quoted in de Roover 1958: 422.
109. *Summa Theologica.*
110. Little 1978: 181.
111. Gilchrist 1969; Little 1978; Raftus 1958.
112. Gilchrist 1969: 67.
113. Hunt and Murray 1999: 73.
114. Dempsey 1943: 155, 160.
115. De Roover 1946b: 154.
116. Little 1978: 181.

117. Southern 1970b: 40.
118. For a summary see Stark 2003a.
119. Lopez 1952: 289; 1976.
120. Rodinson 1978: 139.
121. Esposito 1980; Mills and Presley 1999; Saeed 1996; Udovitch 1970.

CHAPTER THREE

1. Hartwell 1966, 1967, 1971; McNeill 1982.
2. Reade 1925: 108.
3. Beeching 1982; Hanson 2001.
4. Hanson 2001: 262.
5. Grossman 1963.
6. Some unrepentant Marxists still promulgate the slogan "Not a free market society, but a market-free society."
7. Lopez 1976: 65–66.
8. Lewis 2002: 69.
9. In Finley 1970: 21–22.
10. Finley 1970: 23.
11. Andreau 1999.
12. In MacMullen 1988: 61.
13. *Life of Marcellus* 17.3–4.
14. Childe 1952: 53.
15. Hayek 1988: 33.
16. For an excellent discussion of this see Waldron 2002.
17. Pennock 1944: 859.
18. Dworkin 1977; Howard and Donnelly 1986.
19. Waldron 2002.
20. Galatians 3:27–28.
21. Ephesians 6:7.
22. *Divine Institutes*, excerpted in O'Donovan and O'Donovan 1999: 52–54. Italics in the original.
23. Excerpted in O'Donovan and O'Donovan 1999: 256.
24. Ibid., 368.
25. Ibid., 408.
26. In Little 1978: 176.
27. *Summa Theologica* II: 66:1–2.
28. Moorman 1968: 307–19; Southern 1970a: 54–55.
29. In Shepard 1933: 25–26.
30. Lewis 2002: 99.
31. Lewis 2002: 96.
32. Matthew 22:21; also Mark 12:17 and Luke 20:25.
33. *City of God:* book 4, ch. 4.
34. Deane 1973: 423.
35. Southern 1970b: 37.
36. Excerpted in O'Donovan and O'Donovan 1999: 492.
37. *On Kingship:* book 1, ch. 6.
38. Waterbolk 1968: 1099.
39. Jones 1987: 105–6.
40. Ibid., 106.
41. Chirot 1985: 183.

42. Lopez 1976: 99.
43. Lane 1973: 4.
44. Lopez 1967: 129.
45. Wickham 1989: 90.
46. Waley 1988: 35.
47. Lane 1973: 95-101; Nicholas 1997: 248-55.
48. Lane 1973: 91.
49. Bairoch 1988.
50. Epstein 1996: 14.
51. Lopez 1976: 101.
52. Greif 1994: 280.
53. Ibid., 282.
54. Waley 1988.
55. Greif 1994: 284.
56. Lopez 1964: 446-47.
57. Russell 1972; Chandler and Fox 1974.
58. Epstein 1996.
59. Burckhardt [1860] 1990: 65.
60. Brucker 1983: 248; Nicholas 1997.
61. Nicholas 1997: 308-10.
62. Machiavelli [1525] 1988: 105.
63. Hibbert [1974] 2003.
64. Hale 1977; Hibbert [1974] 2003.
65. Nicholas 1997: 46.
66. Ibid., 118.
67. Waley 1988.
68. Chandler and Fox 1974: 11.
69. Citarella 1968: 533.
70. Hutchinson 1902: 416.
71. Citarella 1968: 534.
72. Kreutz 1991: 87.
73. Matthew 1992: 371.
74. van Werveke 1963: 19-24.
75. Witt 1971.
76. Nicholas 1997.
77. Moeller 1972: 41.
78. Rörig 1967: 27.
79. In Moeller 1972: 46.

CHAPTER FOUR

1. Lopez 1952: 289.
2. Lopez 1976.
3. Lopez 1952: 334.
4. Weber 1961, 1958, 1946.
5. Weber 1946: 197.
6. Spufford 2002: 30.
7. Ibid., 29.
8. Gies and Gies 1969.
9. Sapori [1937] 1953: 57-58.

10. Ibid., 63.
11. Hunt and Murray 1999: 108-9.
12. Ibid., 108.
13. de Roover 1966: 45.
14. Swetz 1987: 21-23.
15. In Sapori [1937] 1953: 61.
16. Swetz 1987: 17.
17. Hunt and Murray 1999: 109.
18. de Roover [1942] 1953.
19. Hunt and Murray 1999: 62.
20. Sapori [1937] 1953: 60.
21. de Roover 1946a: 39.
22. Both in Sapori [1937] 1953: 56.
23. Lopez 1956: 219.
24. Spufford 2002: 37.
25. Holmes 1960: 193.
26. Hunt and Murray 1999: 65.
27. Usher [1934] 1953.
28. Edler de Roover 1945.
29. Act I, Scene 1.
30. Spufford 2002: 32.
31. Edler de Roover 1945: 188.
32. Ibid., 181.
33. de Roover 1948; Hunt 1994; Kaeuper 1973; Lloyd 1982.
34. de Roover 1948: 88.
35. Along with the Bardi and Peruzzi Banks.
36. Kaeuper 1973; 1977: 164.
37. Kaeuper 1973: 121.
38. Kaeuper 1977: 170.
39. Sapori 1970: 23.
40. Ibid., 21-28.
41. Kaeuper 1977: 169.
42. Brentano 1916; Fanfani [1934] 2003; Robertson 1933; Samuelsson [1961] 1993; Tawney 1926.
43. Andrews 1999; Bolton 1983; Grundmann [1961] 1995; Moore 1994.
44. Bolton 1983: 63.
45. Moore 1994: 227.
46. Grundmann [1961] 1995: 70.
47. So far as I know, all of this Marxist literature is in Italian. The classic work is by Luigi Zanoni (1911) summarized in Andrews 1999, Ch. 1.
48. Grundmann [1961] 1995: 71.
49. Moore 1994: 227.
50. Stark 2003b.
51. In Killerby 2002: 41.
52. Ibid., 28-29, 36.
53. Hibbert [1974] 2003; 21.
54. Ziegler 1971: 17.
55. Nicholas 1999.
56. Hunt and Murray 1999; Miller 1963.
57. Gray 1924: 17-18.

CHAPTER FIVE

1. Hunt and Murray 1999: 39.
2. Carus-Wilson 1952: 389–90.
3. Carus-Wilson 1952: 386.
4. Nicholas 1987; TeBrake 1993.
5. Murray 1970: 29.
6. Carus-Wilson 1952: 400.
7. Ibid., 392.
8. de Roover 1948: 9.
9. de Roover 1963: 84.
10. Van Houtte 1966: 30.
11. Russell 1972; de Roover 1948.
12. de Roover 1948: 12.
13. Ibid., 14–16.
14. Nicholas 1987: 183.
15. Russell 1972: 117.
16. Nicholas 1987: 291.
17. Murray 1970: 3.
18. Ehrenberg [1928] 1985: 234.
19. Ibid., 233–35.
20. Wedgewood, 1961: 142.
21. Hunt and Murray 1999: 233.
22. Chandler and Fox 1974.
23. Ehrenberg [1928] 1985: 236.
24. Ibid.
25. Murray 1970: 32.
26. Limberger 2001.
27. Ehrenberg [1928] 1985: 238.
28. Ibid.
29. Murray 1970: 34.
30. Ibid.
31. Ibid., 6.
32. Israel 1998: 308.
33. Ibid., 312.
34. Barbour 1930: 267.
35. Tawney 1926: 211.
36. Murray 1970: 7.
37. Pollman 1999; Israel 1998; Murray 1970; Robertson 1933.
38. Israel 1998: 381.
39. Robertson 1933: 173.
40. O'Brien 2001: 15.
41. Lloyd 1982.
42. Carus-Wilson and Coleman 1963: 13.
43. Gray 1924.
44. Carus-Wilson 1952: 374.
45. Ibid., 415.
46. Carus-Wilson 1941: 40.
47. Carus-Wilson 1952: 409.
48. Bridbury 1982; Gray 1924; Miller 1965.
49. Carus-Wilson 1952: 422.

50. Ibid.
51. Usher 1966: 270.
52. Ibid., 269.
53. Bridbury 1982: 103.
54. Galloway, Keene, and Murphy 1996: 449.
55. Nef 1934: 102.
56. Reynolds 1983: 77–79.
57. Shedd 1981: 477.

CHAPTER SIX

1. In Kamen 1978: 26.
2. In Cipolla 1994: 238.
3. Both quotes from Kamen 1978: 24–28.
4. Kamen 1978, 2002.
5. Russell 1958.
6. Elliot 1966; North and Thomas 1973.
7. Elliot 1966: 49.
8. Ibid., 33.
9. North and Thomas 1973: 130.
10. Elliot 1966: 120.
11. Cipolla 1994: 239.
12. Kamen 2002: 169.
13. Ibid., 160, 171.
14. Parker 1970: 188.
15. Elliot 1966: 197–98.
16. Kamen 2002: 287.
17. Elliot 1966: 180.
18. In Cipolla 1965: 36.
19. Pike 1962.
20. Kamen 2002: 89.
21. North and Thomas 1973: 129.
22. Parker 1970: 75.
23. Ibid., 85.
24. Ibid., 86.
25. Read 1933.
26. Kamen 2002: 61.
27. Rapp 1975: 506.
28. Supple 1964: 147.
29. Rapp 1975: 518.
30. Ibid., 510.
31. In Rapp 1975: 510.
32. Israel 1998: 148.
33. Ibid.
34. Kamen 2002: 178.
35. Israel 1998: 156–57.
36. Wegg 1924: 202–3.
37. Ibid.
38. Mattingly 1962: 88.
39. Barbour 1930: 263.
40. Mattingly 1962: 88.

41. Marcus 1961: 89.
42. In Mattingly 1962: 109.
43. Marcus 1961: 84.
44. Ibid., 121.
45. Elliot 1966: 289.
46. North and Thomas 1973: 131.
47. Myers 1975.
48. Ertman 1997: 91.
49. Wesson 1978: 138.
50. North and Thomas 1973; Wesson 1978.
51. De Vries 1976: 203.
52. Root 1994: 39.
53. Ibid.
54. De Vries 1976: 200.
55. Both quotations in Root 1994: 62.
56. Miskimin 1984: 108.
57. Taylor 1964: 496.
58. North and Thomas 1973: 123.
59. Ibid., 122.
60. Taylor 1967: 477.
61. Ibid.
62. Both quotations in Taylor 1967: 479.
63. For a very influential example and summary, see Thrupp 1963.
64. North and Thomas 1973: 126.
65. Ibid., 126–27.
66. Bossenga 1988: 695.
67. Ibid.
68. North and Thomas 1973: 127.
69. Taylor 1967: 473.
70. Ibid., 476.
71. Ibid., 485.
72. Ibid.
73. Taylor 1964: 493.
74. Goubert 1997: 56.

CHAPTER SEVEN

1. See Amin 1976; Cardoso and Faletto 1978. Also see Frank 1967, 1972.
2. Stark 1983, 1985; Stark and Finke 2000.
3. Stark and Finke 2000; Stark 2001.
4. For a summary, see Stark and Finke 2000.
5. Stark 2003a: ch. 1.
6. Chadwick 1972: 26.
7. In Panzer 1996: 8.
8. My italics. In Panzer 1996: 19–21.
9. For a complete account, see Stark 2003a: ch. 4.
10. Stark 2003a.
11. Rodríguez León, quoted in Gill 1998: 22.
12. Fletcher 1997: 38.
13. Chesnut 2003: 19.
14. Ibid., 22.

15. Mecham [1934] 1966: 38.
16. Ibid., 39.
17. Smith [1776] 1981: II:789.
18. Gill 1998: 68.
19. Robinson 1923.
20. Gill 1998: 86.
21. Martin 1990: 57–58.
22. Stark and Finke 2000.
23. Gill 2004.
24. Gill 1999.
25. Chesnut 2003: ch. 4.
26. In O'Callaghan 1855: 322–23.
27. Finke and Stark 1992.
28. Cobbett [1818] 1964: 229.
29. Tocqueville [1835–39] 1956: 314.
30. Schaff [1855] 1961: 91.
31. Cobbett [1818] 1964: 229–32.
32. In Powell 1967: 80.
33. Tocqueville [1835–39] 1956: 319.
34. Kamen 2002: 142.
35. Burkholder and Johnson 2001.
36. Kamen 2002: 130.
37. Engerman and Sokoloff 1997: 264.
38. Jacobs, in Kamen 2002: 130.
39. Engerman and Sokoloff 1997: 264.
40. Breen 1986.
41. Webster 1981: 888.
42. *Historical Statistics of the United States,* vol. 2: table: Z 294.
43. Ibid., Z 510–15.
44. Ibid., Z 294.
45. Ibid., Z 213–26.
46. Mecham [1934] 1966: esp. 96.
47. Bulmer-Thomas 1995: 2.
48. Ibid., 20.
49. Mariscal and Sokoloff 2000: 206.
50. See Stark 2003a: ch. 4.
51. Anderson 1985.
52. Martin 1991.
53. *Historical Statistics of the United States,* vol. 2: table: Z 406–17.
54. In Habakkuk 1967: 11–12.
55. Habakkuk 1967: 12–13.
56. Ibid., 199.
57. Cobbett [1818] 1964: 195–96.
58. Stark 2003c.
59. Mariscal and Sokoloff 2000: 161.
60. Gill 1998. As late as 1880 the Italian police searched the baggage of all tourists to prevent them from taking "Protestant" Bibles into Rome (Bainbridge 1882).
61. Mariscal and Sokoloff 2000.
62. *Nations of the Globe,* an electronic database distributed by Wadsworth/Thomson Learning, 2002.
63. Delacroix 1977; Firebaugh and Beck 1994; Hage, Garnier, and Fuller 1988.

64. In Ratliff 2003: 8.
65. Ratliff 2003: 9.
66. Chesnut 2003, 2004; Martin 1990, 2002; Stoll 1990.
67. Ireland 1993: 45, 64.
68. Deiros 1991: 175.
69. See Smith 2002.
70. Brusco 1995; Gooren 2002; Putnam 1993.
71. For an extensive summary see Martin 1990; ch. 11; also O'Connor 1979 and Turner 1979.
72. Gill 2004.

CONCLUSION

1. Barrett, Kurian, and Johnson 2001; Jenkins 2002.
2. Aikman 2003.
3. In Aikman 2003: 5.

Bibliography

Aikman, David. 2003. *Jesus in Beijing: How Christianity Is Transforming China and Changing the Global Balance of Power*. Washington, DC: Regnery.

Amin, Samir. 1976. *Unequal Development: An Essay on the Social Formation of Peripheral Capitalism*. New York: New York University Press.

Anderson, Virginia Dejohn. 1985. "Migrants and Motives: Religion and Settlement of New England." *New England Quarterly* 58:339-83

Andreau, Jean. 1999. *Banking and Business in the Roman World*. Cambridge: Cambridge University Press.

Andrews, Frances. 1999. *The Early Humiliati*. Cambridge: Cambridge University Press.

Arberry, A. J. 1955. *The Koran Interpreted*. New York: Macmillan.

Arnott, Peter. 1970. *The Romans and Their World*. New York: St. Martin's Press.

Ayoub, Mahmoud M. 1996. "The Islamic Tradition." In Willard G. Oxtoby, ed., *World Religions,* 352-491. Oxford: Oxford University Press.

Baillie, John. 1951. *The Belief in Progress*. New York: Charles Scribner's Sons.

Bainbridge, William E. 1882. *Along the Lines at the Front: A General Survey of Baptist Home and Foreign Missions*. Philadelphia: American Baptists Publication Society.

Bairoch, Paul. 1993. *Economics and World History: Myths and Paradoxes*. Chicago: University of Chicago Press.

———. 1988. *Cities and Economic Development: From the Dawn of History to the Present*. Chicago: University of Chicago Press.

Baker, Herschel. 1952. *The Wars of Truth*. Cambridge, MA: Harvard University Press.

Balazs, Etienne. 1964. *Chinese Civilization and Bureaucracy*. New Haven: Yale University Press.

Baldwin, John W. 1959. *The Medieval Theories of the Just Price*. Philadelphia: The American Philosophical Society.

Barbour, Violet. [1950] 1966. *Capitalism in Amsterdam in the 17th Century*. Ann Arbor: University of Michigan Press.

———. 1930. "Dutch and English Merchant Shipping in the Seventeenth Century." *The Economic History Review* 2:261-90.

Barclay, Brig. Cycil Nelson, and Vice Adm. Brian Betham Schofield. 1981. "Gunnery." *Encyclopaedia Britannica,* 488-98. Chicago: University of Chicago Press.

Barnes, Harry Elmer. 1948. *Historical Sociology: Its Origins and Development*. New York: Prentice Hall.

Barrett, David B., George T. Kurian, and Todd M. Johnson. 2001. *World Christian Encyclopedia,* 2nd ed. New York: Oxford University Press.

Bauckham, Richard. 1990. *Jude and the Relatives of Jesus in the Early Church*. Edinburgh: T & T Clark.

Baumol, William J. 1990. "Entrepreneurship: Productive, Unproductive, and Destructive." *Journal of Political Economy* 98:893–921.

Bautier, Robert-Henri. 1971. *The Economic Development of Medieval Europe*. New York: Harcourt Brace Jovanovich.

Beard, Miriam. 1938. *A History of the Business Man*. New York: Macmillan.

Becker, Carl. 1932. *The Heavenly City of the Eighteenth-Century Philosophers*. New Haven: Yale University Press.

Becker, George. 2000. "Educational 'Preference' of German Protestants and Catholics: The Politics Behind Educational Specialization." *Review of Religious Research* 41:311–27.

———. 1997. "Replication and Reanalysis of Offenbacher's School Enrollment Study: Implications for the Weber and Merton Theses." *Journal for the Scientific Study of Religion* 36:483–96.

Beeching, Jack. 1982. *The Galleys at Lepanto*. New York: Charles Scribner's Sons.

Benedict, Ruth. 1946. *The Chrysanthemum and the Sword: Patterns of Japanese Culture*. Boston: Houghton Mifflin.

Benin, Stephen D. 1993. *The Footprints of God: Divine Accommodation in Jewish and Christian Thought*. Albany: State University of New York Press.

Bensch, Stephen P. 1998. "Historiography: Medieval European and Mediterranean Slavery." In Seymour Drescher and Stanley L. Engerman, eds., *A Historical Guide to World Slavery*, 229–31. New York: Oxford University Press.

Bloch, Marc. 1975. *Slavery and Serfdom in the Middle Ages*. Berkeley: University of California Press.

———. [1940] 1961. *Feudal Society*. 2 vols. Chicago: University of Chicago Press.

Bolton, Brenda. 1983. *The Medieval Reformation*. London: Edward Arnold.

Bonnassie, Pierre. 1991. *From Slavery to Feudalism in South-Western Europe*. Cambridge: Cambridge University Press.

Bossenga, Gail. 1988. "Protecting Merchants: Guilds and Commercial Capitalism in Eighteenth-Century France." *French Historical Studies* 15:693–703.

Botterill, Steven, ed. 1996. *Dante: De vulgari eloquentia*. Cambridge: Cambridge University Press.

Braudel, Fernand. 1979. *Civilization and Capitalism, 15th–18th Century*. 3 vols. Vol. 1, *The Wheels of Commerce*; vol. 2, *The Perspective of the World*; vol. 3, *The Structures of Everyday Life*. New York: Harper & Row.

———. 1977. *Afterthoughts on Material Civilization and Capitalism*. Baltimore: Johns Hopkins University Press.

———. 1976. *The Mediterranean and the Mediterranean World in the Age of Philip II*. 2 vols. New York: Harper & Row.

Breen, T. H. 1986. "An Empire of Goods: The Anglicization of Colonial America, 1690–1776." *Journal of British Studies* 25:467–99.

Brentano, Lujo. 1916. *Die Anfänge des modernen Kapitalismus*. Munich: Verlag der K. B. Akademie der Wissenschaften.

Brett, Stephen F. 1994. *Slavery and the Catholic Tradition*. New York: Peter Lang.

Bridbury, A. R. 1982. *Medieval English Clothmaking: An Economic Survey*. London: Heinemann Educational Books.

———. 1969. "The Dark Ages." *The Economic History Review* 22:526–37.

Brooke, John Hedley. 1991. *Science and Religion: Some Historical Perspectives*. Cambridge: Cambridge University Press.

Brucker, Gene Adam. 1983. *Florence: The Golden Age, 1138–1737*. New York: Abbeville Press.

Brusco, Elizabeth. 1995. *The Reformation of Machismo: Evangelical Conversion and Gender in Colombia*. Austin: University of Texas Press.

Bulmer-Thomas, Victor. 1995. *The Economic History of Latin America Since Independence*. 2nd ed. Cambridge: Cambridge University Press.

Burckhardt, Jacob. [1860] 1990. *The Civilization of the Renaissance in Italy*. New York: Penguin Books.

Burkholder, Mark A., and Lyman L. Johnson. 2001. *Colonial Latin America*. 4th ed. New York: Oxford University Press.

Calvin, John. [c. 1555] 1980. *John Calvin's Sermons on the Ten Commandments*. Grand Rapids, MI: Baker Bookhouse.

Carcopino, Jerome. 1940. *Daily Life in Ancient Rome*. New Haven: Yale University Press.

Cardoso, Fernando Henrique, and Enzo Faletto. 1978. *Dependency and Development in Latin America*. Berkeley: University of California Press.

Carus-Wilson, Eleanora. 1952. "Chapter VI: The Woollen Industry." In *The Cambridge Economic History of Europe*, vol. 2, *Trade and Industry in the Middle Ages*, 355–428. Cambridge: Cambridge University Press.

———. 1950. "Trends in the Export of English Woollens in the Fourteenth Century." *The Economic History Review* 3:162–79.

——— 1941. "An Industrial Revolution of the Thirteenth Century." *The Economic History Review* 11:39–60.

Carus-Wilson, Eleanora, and Olive Coleman. 1963. *England's Export Trade, 1275–1547*. Oxford: Clarendon Press.

Chadwick, Owen. 1972. *The Reformation*. Rev. ed. London: Penguin.

Chandler, Tertius, and Gerald Fox. 1974. *3000 Years of Urban Growth*. New York: Academic Press.

Charanis, Peter. 1953. "Economic Factors in the Decline of the Byzantine Empire." *The Journal of Economic History* 13:412–24.

Cheetham, Nicolas. 1983. *Keeper of the Keys: A History of the Popes from St. Peter to John Paul II*. New York: Charles Scribner's Sons.

Chesnut, R. Andrew. 2004. "Pragmatic Consumers and Practical Products: The Success of Pneumacentric Religion Among Women in Latin America's New Religious Economy." *Review of Religious Research* 45:20–31.

———. 2003. *Competitive Spirits: Latin America's New Religious Economy*. Oxford: Oxford University Press.

Childe, V. Gordon. 1952. "Chapter I: Trade and Industry in Barbarian Europe till Roman Times." In *The Cambridge Economic History of Europe*, vol. 2, *Trade and Industry in the Middle Ages*, 1–32. Cambridge: Cambridge University Press.

Chirot, Daniel. 1985. "The Rise of the West." *American Sociological Review* 50:181–95.

Chorley, Patrick. 1987. "The Cloth Exports of Flanders and Northern France During the Thirteenth Century: A Luxury Trade?" *The Economic History Review* 40:349–79.

Cipolla, Carlo M. 1994. *Before the Industrial Revolution: European Society and Economy, 1000–1700*. 3rd ed. New York: W. W. Norton.

———. 1965. *Guns, Sails and Empires: Technological Innovation and the Early Phases of European Expansion, 1400–1700*. New York: Minerva Press.

Citarella, Armand O. 1968. "Patterns in Medieval Trade: The Commerce of Amalfi Before the Crusades." *The Journal of Economic History* 28:531–55.

Clagett, Marshall. 1961. *The Science of Mechanics in the Middle Ages*. Madison: University of Wisconsin Press.

Clough, Bradley S. 1997. "Buddhism." In Jacob Neusner, ed., *God,* 56–84. Cleveland: Pilgrim Press.

Cobbett, William. [1818] 1964. *A Year's Residence in the United States of America.* Carbondale, IL: Southern Illinois University Press.

Cohen, I. Bernard. 1985. *Revolution in Science.* Cambridge, MA: Belknap Press.

Colish, Marica L. 1997. *Medieval Foundations of the Western Intellectual Tradition, 400–1400.* New Haven: Yale University Press.

Collins, Randall. 1998. *The Sociology of Philosophies: A Global Theory of Intellectual Change.* Cambridge: Harvard University Press.

——. 1997. "An Asian Route to Capitalism: Religious Economy and the Origins of Self-Transforming Growth in Japan." *American Sociological Review* 62:843–65.

——. 1986. *Weberian Sociological Theory.* Cambridge: Cambridge University Press.

Conrad, Alfred H., and John R. Meyer. 1958. *The Economics of Slavery and Other Studies in Econometric History.* Chicago: Aldine.

Crosby, Alfred W. 1997. *The Measure of Reality: Quantification and Western Society, 1250–1600.* Cambridge: Cambridge University Press.

Cummings, John Thomas, Hossein Askari, and Ahmad Mustafa, 1980. "Islam and Modern Economic Change." In John L. Esposito (1980), *Islam and Development: Religion and Sociopolitical Change,* 25–47. Syracuse: Syracuse University Press.

Daniel, Ralph Thomas. 1981. "Music, Western." *Encyclopaedia Britannica,* vol. 12, 704–15. Chicago: University of Chicago Press.

Danielson, Dennis Richard. 2000. *The Book of the Cosmos: Imagining the Universe from Heraclitus to Hawking.* Cambridge, MA: Perseus Publishing.

Dantzig, Tobias. 1954. *Number: The Language of Science.* New York: Macmillan.

Darwin, Francis, and A. C. Seward, eds. 1903. *More Letters of Charles Darwin.* 2 vols. New York: Appleton and Co.

Davis, David Brion. 1966. *The Problem of Slavery in Western Culture.* Ithaca: Cornell University Press.

Davis, R. H. C. 1970. *A History of Medieval Europe from Constantine to Saint Louis.* London: Longman.

Dawson, Christopher. 1957. *Religion and the Rise of Western Culture.* New York: Doubleday Image Books.

——. 1929. *Progress and Religion.* New York: Sheed & Ward.

Deane, Herbert A. 1973. "Classical and Christian Political Thought." *Political Theory* 1:415–25.

Deiros, Pablo A. 1991. "Protestant Fundamentalism in Latin America." In Martin E. Marty and R. Scott Appleby, eds. *Fundamentalisms Observed,* 142–96. Chicago: University of Chicago Press.

De la Croix, Horst, and Richard G. Tansey. 1975. *Gardner's Art Through the Ages.* 6th ed. New York: Harcourt Brace Jovanovich.

Delacroix, Jacques. 1977. "The Export of Raw Materials and Economic Growth: A Cross-National Study." *American Sociological Review* 42:795–808.

Delacroix, Jacques, and François Nielsen. 2001. "The Beloved Myth: Protestantism and the Rise of Industrial Capitalism in Nineteenth-Century Europe." *Social Forces* 80:509–53.

De Vries, Jan. 1976. *The Economy of Europe in the Age of Crisis, 1600–1750.* Cambridge: Cambridge University Press.

Dempsey, Bernard W. 1943. *Interest and Usury.* Washington, DC: American Council on Public Affairs.

Denny, Frederick M. 1993. "Islam and the Muslim Community." In H. Byron

Earhart, ed., *Religious Traditions of the World*, 605–718. San Francisco: HarperSanFrancisco.

de Roover, Raymond. 1966. *The Rise and Decline of the Medici Bank, 1397–1494*. New York: W. W. Norton.

———. 1963. "Chapter II. The Organization of Trade." In M. M. Postan, E. E. Rich, and Edward Miller, eds., *The Cambridge Economic History of Europe*, vol. 3, *Economic Organization and Policies in the Middle Ages*, 42–118. Cambridge: Cambridge University Press.

———. 1958. "The Concept of the Just Price: Theory and Economic Policy." *The Journal of Economic History* 18:418–34.

———. [1942] 1953. "The Commercial Revolution of the Thirteenth Century." In Frederic C. Lane and Jelle C. Riemersma, eds., *Enterprise and Secular Change: Readings in Economic History*, 80–85. Homewood, IL: Richard D. Irwin.

———. 1948. *Money, Banking and Credit in Bruges*. Cambridge, MA: The Medieval Academy of America.

———. 1946a. "The Medici Bank Organization and Management." *The Journal of Economic History* 6:24–52.

———. 1946b. "The Medici Bank Financial and Commercial Operations." *The Journal of Economic History* 6:153–72.

Dickens, A. G. 1991. *The English Reformation*. University Park: Pennsylvania State University Press.

Dobbs, Darrell. 1985. "Aristotle's Anticommunism." *American Journal of Political Science* 29:29–46.

Dockès, Pierre. 1982. *Medieval Slavery and Liberation*. Chicago: University of Chicago Press.

Dorn, Harold. 1991. *The Geography of Science*. Baltimore: Johns Hopkins University Press.

Duby, Georges. 1974. *The Early Growth of the European Economy: Warriors and Peasants from the Seventh to the Twelfth Century*. Ithaca: Cornell University Press.

Dworkin, Ronald. 1977. *Taking Rights Seriously*. Cambridge: Harvard University Press.

Earle, Peter. 2001. "The Economy of London, 1660–1730." In Patrick O'Brien, Derek Keene, Marjolein 't Hart, and Herman van der Wee, eds., *Urban Achievement in Early Modern Europe*, 81–96. Cambridge: Cambridge University Press.

East, W. Gordon. 1965. *The Geography Behind History*. New York: W. W. Norton.

Easterlin, Richard A. 1961. "Regional Income Trends, 1840–1850." In Seymour Harris, ed., *American Economic History*, 525–47. New York: McGraw-Hill.

Edler de Roover, Florence. 1945. "Early Examples of Marine Insurance." *The Journal of Economic History* 5:172–200.

Ehrenberg, Richard. [1928] 1985. *Capital and Finance in the Age of the Renaissance: A Study of the Fuggers and Their Connections*. Fairfield, NJ: Augustus M. Kelley.

Eisenstein, Elizabeth L. 1979. *The Printing Press as an Agent of Change*. Cambridge: Cambridge University Press.

Elliot, J. H. 1966. *Imperial Spain 1469–1716*. New York: Mentor Books.

Engerman, Stanley L., and Kenneth L. Sokoloff. 1997. "Factor Endowments, Institutions, and Differential Paths of Growth Among the New World Economies." In Stephen Haber, ed., *How Latin America Fell Behind*, 260–304. Stanford: Stanford University Press.

Epstein, Steven A. 1996. *Genoa and the Genoese, 958–1528*. Chapel Hill: University of North Carolina Press.

Ertman, Thomas. 1997. *Birth of the Leviathan: Building States and Regimes in Medieval and Early Modern Europe*. Cambridge: Cambridge University Press.

Esposito, John I., ed. 1980. *Islam and Development: Religion and Sociopolitical Change*. Syracuse: Syracuse University Press.

Fanfani, Amintore. [1934] 2003. *Catholicism, Protestantism, and Capitalism*. Norfolk, VA: HIS Press.

Farah, Caesar E. 1994. *Islam: Beliefs and Observances*. 5th ed. Hauppauge, NY: Barron's.

Fei, Hsiao-tung and Chih-i Chang. 1945. *Earthbound China*. Chicago: University of Chicago Press.

Finke, Roger, and Rodney Stark. 1992. *The Churching of America, 1776–1990*. New Brunswick: Rutgers University Press. 2005: 2nd ed., *The Churching of America, 1776–2000*.

Finlay, Robert. 1992. "Portuguese and Chinese Maritime Imperialism: Camoes's Lusiads and Luo Maodeng's Voyage of the San Bao Eunuch." *Comparative Studies in Society and History* 34:225–41.

Finley, M. I. 1981. *Economy and Society in Ancient Greece*. New York: Viking Press.

———. 1980. *Ancient Slavery and Modern Ideology*. New York: Viking Press.

———. 1973. *The Ancient Economy*. Berkeley: University of California Press.

———. 1970. "Aristotle and Economic Analysis." *Past and Present,* issue 47, 3–25.

———. 1965. "Technical Innovation and Economic Progress in the Ancient World." *The Economic History Review* 18:29–45.

———. 1959. "Technology in the Ancient World." *The Economic History Review* 12:120–25.

Firebaugh, Glenn, and Frank D. Beck. 1994. "Does Economic Growth Benefit the Masses? Growth, Dependence, and Welfare in the Third World." *American Sociological Review* 59:631–53.

Fletcher, Richard. 1997. *The Barbarian Conversion: From Paganism to Christianity*. New York: Henry Holt.

Fogel, Robert William. 1989. *Without Consent or Contract: The Rise and Fall of American Slavery*. New York: W. W. Norton.

Fogel, Robert William, and Stanley L. Engerman. 1974. *Time on the Cross: The Economics of American Negro Slavery*. 2 vols. Boston: Little, Brown.

Forbes, Robert J. 1955. *Studies in Ancient Technology*. Leiden: Brill.

Frank, Andre Gunder. 1972. *Lumpenbourgeoisie, Lumpendevelopment: Dependence, Class, and Politics in Latin America*. New York: New York University Press.

———. 1967. *Capitalism and Underdevelopment in Latin America: Historical Studies of Chile and Brazil*. New York: Monthly Review Press.

Frank, Tenney. 1940. *An Economic Survey of Ancient Rome*. Vol. 6. Baltimore: Johns Hopkins University Press.

Fryde, E. B. 1963. "Chapter VII: Public Credit, with Special Reference to North-Western Europe." In *The Cambridge Economic History of Europe,* vol. 3, *Economic Organization and Policies in the Middle Ages,* 430–553. Cambridge: Cambridge University Press.

Gardner, Helen, and Sumner McK. Crosby. 1959. *Helen Gardner's Art Through the Ages*. New York: Harcourt, Brace, & World.

Gerschenkron, Alexander. 1970. *Europe in the Russian Mirror: Four Lectures in Economic History*. Cambridge: Cambridge University Press.

Gibbon, Edward. [1776–88] 1994. *Decline and Fall of the Roman Empire*. New York: Modern Library.

Gies, Frances, and Joseph Gies. 1994. *Cathedral, Forge, and Waterwheel: Technology and Invention in the Middle Ages*. New York: HarperCollins.

Gies, Joseph, and Frances Gies. 1969. *Leonard of Pisa and the New Mathematics of the Middle Ages*. New York: Crowell.

Gilchrist, John. 1969. *The Church and Economic Activity in the Middle Ages*. New York: St. Martin's Press.

Gill, Anthony. 2005. "The Political Origins of Religious Liberty: A Theoretical Outline." *Interdisciplinary Journal of Research on Religion* 1 (in press).

———. 2004. "Weber in Latin America: Is Protestant Growth Enabling the Consolidation of Democratic Capitalism?" *Democratization*, vol. 2, no. 4, 1–25.

———. 1999. "The Struggle to Be Soul Provider: Catholic Responses to Protestant Growth in Latin America." In *Latin American Religion in Motion*, Christian Smith and Joshua Prokopy, eds., 14–42. New York: Routledge.

———. 1998. *Rendering unto Caesar: The Catholic Church and the State in Latin America*. Chicago: University of Chicago Press.

Gimpel, Jean. 1976. *The Medieval Machine: The Industrial Revolution of the Middle Ages*. New York: Penguin Books.

———. 1961. *The Cathedral Builders*. New York: Grove Press.

Gingerich, Owen. 1975. " 'Crisis' Versus Aesthetic in the Copernican Revolution." *Vistas in Astronomy* 17:85–93.

Glotz, Gustave. [1925] 1965. *Ancient Greece at Work*. New York: Barnes & Noble.

Goldthwaite, Richard A. 1987. "The Medici Bank and the World of Florentine Capitalism." *Past and Present* 113:3–31.

Gooren, Henri. 2002. "Catholic and Non-Catholic Theologies of Liberation: Poverty, Self-Improvement, and Ethics Among Small-Scale Entrepreneurs in Guatemala City." *Journal for the Scientific Study of Religion* 41:29–45.

Gordon, Mary L. 1924. "The Nationality of Slaves Under the Early Roman Empire." *Journal of Roman Studies* 14:93–111.

Gordon, Murray. 1989. *Slavery in the Arab World*. New York: New Amsterdam Books.

Goubert, Pierre. 1997. *The Ancien Régime: French Society, 1600–1750*. London: Phoenix Giant.

Grant, Edward. 1996. *The Foundations of Modern Science in the Middle Ages: Their Religious, Institutional, and Intellectual Contexts*. Cambridge: Cambridge University Press.

———. 1994. *Planets, Stars, and Orbs: The Medieval Cosmos, 1200–1687*. Cambridge: Cambridge University Press.

Grant, Michael. 1978. *A History of Rome*. London: Faber & Faber.

Gray, H. L. 1924. "The Production and Exportation of English Woollens in the Fourteenth Century." *The English Historical Review* 39:13–35.

Greif, Avner. 1994. "On the Political Foundations of the Late Medieval Commercial Revolution: Genoa During the Twelfth and Thirteenth Centuries." *The Journal of Economic History* 54:271–87.

Grossman, Gregory. 1963. "Notes for a Theory of the Command Economy." *Soviet Studies* 15:101–23.

Grundmann, Herbert. [1961] 1995. *Religious Movements in the Middle Ages*. 2nd ed. Notre Dame, IN: University of Notre Dame Press.

Guilmartin, John F., Jr. 1974. *Gunpowder and Galleys: Changing Technology and Mediterranean Warfare at Sea in the Sixteenth Century*. Cambridge: Cambridge University Press.

Gurevich, Aaron. 1995. *The Origins of European Individualism*. Oxford: Blackwell.

Habakkuk, H. J. 1967. *American and British Technology in the Nineteenth Century*. Cambridge: Cambridge University Press.

Hage, Jerald, Maurice Garnier, and Bruce Fuller. 1988. "The Active State, Investment in Human Capital, and Economic Growth." *American Sociological Review* 53:824–37.

Hale, J. R. 1977. *Florence and the Medici*. London: Thames & Hudson.

Hall, John A. 1986. *Powers and Liberties: The Causes and Consequences of the Rise of the West*. Berkeley: University of California Press.

Hamilton, Richard F. 1996. *The Social Misconstruction of Reality*. New Haven: Yale University Press.

Hammond, Mason. 1946. "Economic Stagnation in the Early Roman Empire." *The Journal of Economic History* 6 (supplement):63–90.

Hanson, Victor Davis. 2001. *Carnage and Culture: Landmark Battles in the Rise of Western Power*. New York: Doubleday.

Hartwell, Robert. 1971. "Historical Analogism, Public Policy, and Social Science in Eleventh- and Twelfth-Century China." *The American Historical Review* 76:690–727.

———. 1966. "Markets, Technology, and the Structure of Enterprise in the Development of the Eleventh-Century Chinese Iron and Steel Industry." *The Journal of Economic History* 26:29–58.

Hayek, F. A. 1988. *The Fatal Conceit: The Errors of Socialism*. Chicago: University of Chicago Press.

Hayes, Carlton, J. H. 1917. *Political and Social History of Modern Europe*. 2 vols. New York: Macmillan.

Henry, Margaret Y. 1927. "Cicero's Treatment of the Free Will Problem." *Transactions and Proceedings of the American Philological Association* 58:32–42.

Herlihy, David. 1957. "Church Property on the European Continent, 701–1200." *Speculum* 18:89–113.

Herre, Franz. 1985. *The Age of the Fuggers*. Augsburg: Augsburg Historical Books.

Hibbert, Christopher. [1974] 2003. *The House of Medici: Its Rise and Fall*. New York: HarperCollins.

Hickey, Anne Ewing. 1987. *Women of the Roman Aristocracy as Christian Monastics*. Ann Arbor, MI: UMI Research Press.

Hilton, R. H. 1952. "Capitalism—What's in a Name?" *Past and Present,* issue 1, 32–43.

Hilton, Walter. 1985. *Toward a Perfect Love*. Translated by David L. Jeffrey. Portland, OR: Multnomah Press.

Hime, Henry W. L. 1915. *Origin of Artillery*. London: Longmans, Green.

Historical Statistics of the United States, Colonial Times to 1970. 2 vols. Washington, DC: U.S. Department of Commerce.

Hitchins, H. L., and William E. May. 1951. *From Lodestone to Gyro-Compass*. London: Hutchinson's Scientific and Technical Publications.

Hodges, Richard. 1998. "The Not-So-Dark Ages." *Archaeology* 51 (Sept./Oct.): 61–78.

Hodgson, Marshall G. S. 1974. *The Venture of Islam*. 3 vols. Chicago: University of Chicago Press.

Holmes, G. A. 1960. "Florentine Merchants in England, 1346–1436." *The Economic History Review,* new series, 13:193–208.

Howard, Rhoda E., and Jack Donnelly. 1986. "Human Dignity, Human Rights, and Political Regimes." *The American Political Science Review* 80:801–17.

Howarth, David. 1974. *Sovereign of the Seas: The Story of Britain and the Sea*. New York: Atheneum.

Huff, Toby. 1993. *The Rise of Early Modern Science: Islam, China, and the West*. Cambridge: Cambridge University Press.

Huffman, Joseph P. 1998. *Family, Commerce, and Religion in London and Cologne: Anglo-German Emigrants, c. 1000–c. 1300*. Cambridge: Cambridge University Press.

Hunt, Edwin S. 1994. *The Medieval Super-Companies: A Study of the Peruzzi Company of Florence*. Cambridge: Cambridge University Press.

Hunt, Edwin S., and James M. Murray. 1999. *A History of Business in Medieval Europe, 1200–1550*. Cambridge: Cambridge University Press.

Hutchinson, Lincoln. 1902. "Oriental Trade and the Rise of the Lombard Communes." *The Quarterly Journal of Economics* 16:413–32.

Hyland, Ann. 1994. *The Medieval Warhorse: From Byzantium to the Crusades*. London: Grange Books.

Innes, Matthew. 2000. *State and Society in the Early Middle Ages: The Middle Rhine Valley, 400–1000*. Cambridge: Cambridge University Press.

Ireland, Rowan. 1993. "The *Crentes* of Campo Alegre and the Religious Construction of Brazilian Politics." In Virginia Garrard-Burnett and David Stoll, *Rethinking Protestantism in Latin America*, 45–65. Philadelphia: Temple University Press.

Israel, Jonathan L. 1998. *The Dutch Republic: Its Rise, Greatness, and Fall, 1477–1806*. Corrected paperback ed. Oxford: Clarendon Press.

Jaki, Stanley L. 2000. *The Savior of Science*. Grand Rapids, MI: W. B. Eerdmans.

———. 1986. *Science and Creation*. Edinburgh: Scottish Academic Press.

Jeffrey, David Lyle. 1996. *People of the Book: Christian Identity and Literary Culture*. Grand Rapids, MI: W. B. Eerdmans.

———. 1979. *By Things Seen: Reference and Recognition in Medieval Thought*. Ottawa: University of Ottawa Press.

Jenkins, Philip. 2002. *The Next Christendom: The Coming of Global Christianity*. Oxford: Oxford University Press.

Johnson, Paul. 2003. *Art: A New History*. New York: HarperCollins.

Jones, A. H. M. 1964. *The Later Roman Empire, 284–602*. 3 vols. Oxford: Oxford University Press.

———. 1959. "Over-Taxation and the Decline of the Roman Empire." *Antiquity* 33:39–43.

———. 1956. "Slavery in the Ancient World." *The Economic History Review* (2nd ser.) 9:185–99.

Jones, E. L. 1987. *The European Miracle: Environments, Economies, and Geopolitics in the History of Europe and Asia*. 2nd ed. Cambridge: Cambridge University Press.

Kaelber, Lutz. 1998. *Schools of Asceticism: Ideology and Organization in Medieval Religious Communities*. University Park: Pennsylvania State University Press.

Kaeuper, Richard W. 1979. "The *Societas Riccardorum* and Economic Change." In David Lyle Jeffrey, ed., *By Things Seen: Reference and Recognition in Medieval Thought*, 161–72. Ottawa: University of Ottawa Press.

———. 1973. *Bankers to the Crown: The Riccardi of Lucca and Edward I*. Princeton: Princeton University Press.

Kamen, Henry. 2002. *Spain's Road to Empire: The Making of a World Power, 1492–1763*. London: Allen Kane.

———. 1978. "The Decline of Spain: A Historial Myth." *Past and Present*, vol. 81:24–50.

Kehr, Marguerite Witmer. 1916. "The Doctrine of the Self in St. Augustine and in Descartes." *The Philosophical Review* 25:587–615.

Killerby, Catherine Kovesi. 2002. *Sumptuary Law in Italy, 1200–1500*. Oxford: Oxford University Press.

King, Peter. 1999. *Western Monasticism: A History of the Monastic Movement in the Latin Church*. Kalamazoo, MI: Cistercian Publications.

Kinser, Samuel. 1971. "Ideas of Temporal Change and Cultural Process in France, 1470–1535." In A. Molho and J. Tedeschi, eds., *Renaissance: Studies in Honor of Hans Baron*, 703–57. DeKalb, IL: Northern Illinois State University Press.

Klein, Julius. 1920. *The Mesta*. Cambridge: Harvard University Press.

Kreutz, Barbara M. 1991. *Before the Normans: Southern Italy in the Ninth and Tenth Centuries*. Philadelphia: University of Pennsylvania Press.

Kuhn, Thomas S. 1962. *The Structure of Scientific Revolutions*. Chicago: University of Chicago Press.

Kwass, Michael. 1998. "A Kingdom of Taxpayers: State Formation, Privilege, and Political Culture in Eighteenth Century France." *The Journal of Modern History* 70:295-339.

Lambert, Malcolm. 1992. *Medieval Heresy*. Oxford: Basil Blackwell.

Landes, David S. 1998. *The Wealth and Poverty of Nations*. New York: W. W. Norton.

———. 1994. "What Room for Accident in History? Explaining Big Changes by Small Events." *The Economic History Review* (new series) 47:637-56.

Lane, Frederic Chapin. [1934] 1992. *Venetian Ships and Shipbuilders of the Renaissance*. Baltimore: Johns Hopkins University Press.

———. 1973. *Venice: A Maritime Republic*. Baltimore: Johns Hopkins University Press.

———. 1963. "Venetian Merchant Galleys, 1300-1334, Private and Communal Operation." *Speculum* 38:179-204.

Lang, Graeme. 1997. "State Systems and the Origins of Modern Science: A Comparison of Europe and China." *East-West Dialogue* 2:16-31.

Lapidus, Ira M. 1967. *Muslim Cities in the Later Middle Ages*. Cambridge: Harvard University Press.

League of Nations. 1945. *Industrialization and Foreign Trade*. Geneva: League of Nations.

Leighton, Albert C. 1972. *Transport and Communication in Early Medieval Europe, A.D. 500-1100*. Newton Abbot (UK): David & Charles.

Lenski, Gerhard, Patrick Nolan, and Jean Lenski. 1995. *Human Societies: An Introduction to Macrosociology*. 7th ed. New York: McGraw-Hill.

Lewis, Bernard. 2002. *What Went Wrong?* Oxford: Oxford University Press.

———. 1990. *Race and Slavery in the Middle East*. Oxford: Oxford University Press.

Limberger, Michael. 2001. " 'No Town in the World Provides More Advantages': Economies of Agglomeration and the Golden Age of Antwerp." In *Urban Achievement in Early Modern Europe,* Patrick O'Brien, Derek Keene, Marjolein 't Hart, and Herman van der Wee, eds., 39-80. Cambridge: Cambridge University Press.

Lindberg, David C. 1992. *The Beginnings of Western Science*. Chicago: University of Chicago Press.

———. 1986. "Science and the Early Church." In David C. Lindberg and Ronald L. Numbers, eds., *God and Nature: Historical Essays on the Encounter Between Christianity and Science,* 19-48. Berkeley: University of California Press.

———. 1978. *Science in the Middle Ages*. Chicago: University of Chicago Press.

Lindberg, David C., and Ronald L. Numbers, eds. 1986. *God and Nature: Historical Essays on the Encounter Between Christianity and Science*. Berkeley: University of California Press.

Lipson, E. 1937. *Economic History of England*. London: A. and C. Black.

Little, Lester K. 1978. *Religious Poverty and the Profit Economy in Medieval Europe*. Ithaca: Cornell University Press.

Lloyd, T. H. 1982. *Alien Merchants in England in the High Middle Ages*. New York: St. Martin's Press.

Lopez, Robert S. 1979. "The Practical Transmission of Medieval Culture." In David Lyle Jeffrey, ed., *By Things Seen: Reference and Recognition in Medieval Thought,* 125-42. Ottawa: University of Ottawa Press.

——. 1976. *The Commercial Revolution of the Middle Ages, 950–1350*. Cambridge: Cambridge University Press.

——. 1967. *The Birth of Europe*. New York: M. Evans and Company.

——. 1964. "Market Expansion: The Case of Genoa." *The Journal of Economic History* 24:445–64.

——. 1956. "Back to Gold, 1252." *The Economic History Review* (new series) 9:219–40.

——. 1952. "The Trade of Medieval Europe: The South." In *The Cambridge Economic History of Europe*, vol. 2, *Trade and Industry in the Middle Ages*, 257–354. Cambridge: Cambridge University Press.

——. 1937. "Aux origines du capitalisme genois." *Annales* 9:429–54.

Love, John. 1986. "Max Weber and the Theory of Ancient Capitalism." *History and Theory* 25:152–72.

Lovejoy, Paul E. [1983] 2000. *Transformations in Slavery: A History of Slavery in Africa*. Cambridge: Cambridge University Press.

Luzzato, Gino. 1961. *An Economic History of Italy: From the Fall of the Roman Empire to the Beginning of the Sixteenth Century*. London: Routledge & Kegan Paul.

Macfarlane, Alan. 1978. *The Origins of English Individualism*. Oxford: Blackwell.

Macfarlane, Alan, and Gerry Martin. 2002. *Glass: A World History*. Chicago: University of Chicago Press.

Machiavelli, Niccolo. [1525] 1988. *Florentine Histories*. Princeton: Princeton University Press.

MacMullen, Ramsay. 1988. *Corruption and the Decline of Rome*. New Haven: Yale University Press.

Macmurray, John. 1938. *The Clue to History*. London: Student Christian Movement Press.

Malinowski, Bronislaw. [1922] 1961. *Argonauts of the Western Pacific*. New York: E. P. Dutton.

Manucy, Albert C. 1949. *Artillery Through the Ages*. Washington, DC: U.S. Government Printing Office.

Marcus, G. J. 1961. *A Naval History of England I: The Formative Centuries*. Boston: Little, Brown.

Mariscal, Elisa, and Kenneth L. Sokoloff. 2000. "Schooling, Suffrage, and the Persistence of Inequality in the Americas, 1800–1945." In Stephen Haber, ed., *Political Institutions and Economic Growth in Latin America*, 159–217. Stanford, CA: Hoover Institution Press.

Martin, David. 2002. *Pentecostalism: The World Their Parish*. Oxford: Blackwell.

——. 1990. *Tongues of Fire: The Explosion of Protestantism in Latin America*. Oxford: Blackwell.

Martin, John. 1997. "Inventing Sincerity, Refashioning Prudence: The Discovery of the Individual in Renaissance Europe." *The American Historical Review* 102:1309–42.

Martin, John Frederick. 1991. *Profits in the Wilderness: Entrepreneurship and the Founding of New England Towns in the Seventeenth Century*. Chapel Hill: University of North Carolina Press.

Mason, Stephen F. 1962. *A History of the Sciences*. Rev. ed. New York: Macmillan.

Matthew, Donald. 1992. *The Norman Kingdom of Sicily*. Cambridge: Cambridge University Press.

Matthew, K. S. 1997. *Indo-Portuguese Trade and the Fuggers of Germany*. New Delhi: Manohar.

Matthews, George T., ed. 1959. *News and Rumor in Renaissance Europe (The Fugger Newsletters)*. New York: Capricorn Books.

Mattingly, Garrett. 1962. *The Armada*. Boston: Houghton Mifflin.

May, William E., and John L. Howard. 1981. "Compass." *Encyclopaedia Britannica*. 15th ed.

Mayr-Harting, Henry. 1993. "The West: The Age of Conversion (700–1050)." In John McManners, ed., *The Oxford History of Christianity*, 101–29. Oxford: Oxford University Press.

Mazzaoui, Maureen Fennell. 1972. "The Cotton Industry of Northern Italy in the Late Middle Ages: 1150–1450." *The Journal of Economic History* 32:262–86.

McAdam, Doug. 1988. *Freedom Summer*. New York: Oxford University Press.

McGrath, Alister E. 1999. *Science and Religion*. Oxford: Blackwell.

McNeill, William H. 1982. *The Pursuit of Power: Technology, Armed Force, and Society Since A.D. 1000*. Chicago: University of Chicago Press.

———. 1974. *Venice: The Hinge of Europe, 1081–1797*. Chicago: University of Chicago Press.

———. 1963. *The Rise of the West*. Chicago: University of Chicago Press.

Mecham, J. Lloyd. [1934] 1966. *Church and State in Latin America*. Chapel Hill: University of North Carolina Press.

Meltzer, Milton. 1993. *Slavery: A World History*. New York: Da Capo Press.

Meyer, Hans. 1944. *The Philosophy of St. Thomas Aquinas*. St. Louis: B. Herder.

Miller, Edward. 1965. "The Fortunes of the English Textile Industry During the Thirteenth Century." *The Economic History Review* 18:64–82.

———. 1963. "The Economic Policies of Governments: France and England," in *The Cambridge Economic History of Europe*, vol. 3, 290–339. Cambridge: Cambridge University Press.

Mills, Paul S., and John R. Presley. 1999. *Islamic Finance: Theory and Practice*. London: Macmillan.

Miskimin, Harry A. 1984. *Money and Power in Fifteenth Century France*. New Haven: Yale University Press.

Moeller, Bernd. 1972. *Imperial Cities and the Reformation: Three Essays*. Philadelphia: Fortress Press.

Mommsen, Theodor E. 1951. "St. Augustine and the Christian Idea of Progress: The Background of the City of God." *Journal of the History of Ideas* 12:346–74.

Monroe, Arthur Eli. 1975. *Early Economic Thought: Selections from Economic Literature Prior to Adam Smith*. New York: Gordon Press.

Montgomery, Field-Marshal Viscount (Bernard). 1968. *A History of Warfare*. New York: World.

Moore, R. I. 1994. *The Origins of European Dissent*. Toronto: University of Toronto Press.

Moorman, John. 1968. *The Franciscan Order from Its Origins to 1517*. Oxford: Clarendon Press.

Morris, Colin. [1972] 2000. *The Discovery of the Individual, 1050–1200*. Toronto: University of Toronto Press.

Mumford, Lewis. 1967. *The Myth of the Machine*. Vol. I. New York: Harcourt Brace Jovanovich.

———. 1939. *Technics and Civilization*. New York: Harcourt Brace.

Murray, John J. 1970. *Antwerp in the Age of Plantin and Brueghel*. Norman: University of Oklahoma Press.

Myers, A. R. 1975. *Parliaments and Estates in Europe, to 1789*. London: Thames & Hudson.

Nasr, Seyyed Hossein. 1993. *An Introduction to Islamic Cosmological Doctrines*. Albany: State University of New York Press.

Needham, Joseph. 1980. "The Guns of Khaifengfu." *Times Literary Supplement*, Jan. 11.

———. 1954–84. *Science and Civilization in China*. 6 vols. Cambridge: Cambridge University Press.

Nef, John U. 1952. "Chapter VII: Mining and Metallurgy in Medieval Civilization." In *The Cambridge Economic History of Europe*, vol. 2, *Trade and Industry in the Middle Ages*, 429–92. Cambridge: Cambridge University Press.

———. 1943. "The Industrial Revolution Reconsidered." *The Journal of Economic History* 3:1–31.

———. 1936. "A Comparison of Industrial Growth in France and England from 1540 to 1640: III" *The Journal of Political Economy* 44:643–66.

———. 1934. "The Progress of Technology and the Growth of Large-Scale Industry in Great Britain, 1540–1640." *Economic History Review* 5.

Nelson, Benjamin. 1969. *The Idea of Usury: From Tribal Brotherhood to Universal Otherhood*. 2nd ed. Chicago: University of Chicago Press.

Neugebauer, O. 1975. *A History of Ancient Mathematical Astronomy*. 3 vols. New York: Springer-Verlag.

Neuhaus, Richard John. 1999. "The Idea of Moral Progress." *First Things* (Aug./Sept.) 95:21–27.

Nicholas, David. 1997. *The Growth of the Medieval City: From Late Antiquity to the Early Fourteenth Century*. London: Longman.

———. 1991. "Of Poverty and Primacy: Demand, Liquidity, and the Flemish Economic Miracle, 1050–1200." *The American Historical Review* 96:17–41.

———. 1988. *The van Arteveldes of Ghent: The Varieties of Vendetta and the Hero in History*. Ithaca: Cornell University Press.

———. 1987. *The Metamorphosis of a Medieval City: Ghent in the Age of the Artevelds, 1302–1390*. Lincoln: University of Nebraska Press.

Nicol, Donald M. 1988. *Byzantium and Venice: A Study in Diplomatic and Cultural Relations*. Cambridge: Cambridge University Press.

Niebuhr, Reinhold. 1949. *Faith and History*. New York: Charles Scribner's Sons.

Nisbet, Robert. 1980. *History of the Idea of Progress*. New York: Basic Books.

———. 1973. "The Myth of the Renaissance." *Comparative Studies in History of Society* 15:473–92.

North, Douglass C. 1966. *The Economic Growth of the United States, 1790–1860*. New York: W. W. Norton.

North, Douglass C., and Robert Paul Thomas. 1973. *The Rise of the Western World: A New Economic History*. Cambridge: Cambridge University Press.

O'Brien, Patrick. 2001. "Reflection and Meditations on Antwerp, Amsterdam and London in Their Golden Ages." In *Urban Achievement in Early Modern Europe*, Patrick O'Brien, Derek Keene, Marjolein 't Hart, and Herman van der Wee, eds., 3–35. Cambridge: Cambridge University Press.

O'Callaghan, E. B., ed. 1855. *Documents Relative to the Colonial History of New York*. Vol. 5. Albany, NY: Weed, Parsons.

O'Connor, Mary. 1979. "Two Kinds of Religious Movements Among the Maya Indians of Sonora, Mexico." *Journal for the Scientific Study of Religion* 18:260–68.

O'Donovan, Oliver, and Joan Lockwood O'Donovan, eds. 1999. *A Sourcebook in Christian Political Thought*. Grand Rapids, MI: W. B. Eerdmans.

Olsen, Glenn. 1969. "Italian Merchants and the Performance of Papal Banking Functions in the Early Thirteenth Century." In David Herlihy, Robert S. Lopez, and Vsevold Slessarev, eds., *Economy, Society, and Government in Medieval Italy: Essays in Memory of Robert L. Reynolds*. Kent: Kent State University Press.

Ostrogorsky, George. 1957. *The History of the Byzantine State*. New Brunswick: Rutgers University Press.

Ozment, Steven. 1980. *The Age of Reform, 1250–1550: An Intellectual and Religious History of Late Medieval and Reformation Europe*. New Haven: Yale University Press.

——. 1975. *The Reformation in the Cities*. New Haven: Yale University Press.

Pagden, Anthony. 1990. *Spanish Imperialism and the Political Imagination*. New Haven: Yale University Press.

Palmer, Alan. 1992. *The Decline and Fall of the Ottoman Empire*. New York: Barnes & Noble.

Panzer, Joel S. 1996. *The Popes and Slavery*. New York: Alba House.

Parker, Geoffrey. 1970. "Spain, Her Enemies and the Revolt of the Netherlands, 1559–1648." *Past and Present* 49:72–95.

Parsons, Talcott. 1937. *The Structure of Social Action*. New York: McGraw-Hill.

Partington, J. R. [1960] 1999. *A History of Greek Fire and Gunpowder*. Baltimore: Johns Hopkins University Press.

Paullin, Charles O. 1932. *Atlas of Historical Geography of the United States*. Washington, D.C.: Carnegie Institution.

Pennock, J. Roland. 1944. "Reason, Value Theory, and the Theory of Democracy." *The American Political Science Review* 38:855–75.

Peragallo, Edward. 1938. *Origin and Evolution of Double Entry Bookkeeping*. New York: American Institute.

Pike, Ruth. 1962. "The Genoese in Seville and the Opening of the New World." *The Journal of Economic History* 22:348–78.

Pirenne, Henri. [1936] 1958. *A History of Europe from the End of the Roman World in the West to the Beginnings of the Western States*. New York: Doubleday Anchor.

——. [1922] 1955. *Mohammed and Charlemagne*. New York: Barnes & Noble.

——. 1925. *Medieval Cities*. Princeton: Princeton University Press.

——. 1914. "The Stages in the Social History of Capitalism." *The American Historical Review* 19:494–515.

Poggi, Gianfranco. 1978. *The Development of the Modern State*. Stanford, CA: Stanford University Press.

Pollman, Judith. 1999. *Religious Choice in the Dutch Republic*. Manchester: Manchester University Press.

Postan, Michael. 1952. "Chapter IV: The Trade of Medieval Europe: The North." In *The Cambridge Economic History of Europe*, vol. 2, *Trade and Industry in the Middle Ages*, 119–256. Cambridge: Cambridge University Press.

Pounds, N. J. G. 1974. *An Economic History of Medieval Europe*. London: Longman.

Powell, Milton B., ed. 1967. *The Voluntary Church: Religious Life, 1740–1860, Seen Through the Eyes of European Visitors*. New York: Macmillan.

Raftus, J. A. 1958. "The Concept of Just Price: Theory and Economic Policy: Discussion." *The Journal of Economic History* 18:435–37.

Rahner, Karl. 1975. *Encyclopedia of Theology*. New York: Seabury Press.

Rapp, Richard T. 1975. "The Unmaking of the Mediterranean Trade Hegemony: International Trade Rivalry and the Commercial Revolution." *The Journal of Economic History* 35:499–525.

Ratliff, William. 2003. *Doing It Wrong and Doing It Right: Education in Latin America and Asia*. Stanford, CA: Hoover Institution Press.

Read, Conyers. 1933. "Queen Elizabeth's Seizure of the Duke of Alva's Pay-Ships." *The Journal of Modern History* 5:443–64.

Read, Piers Paul. 1999. *The Templars*. New York: St. Martin's Press.

Reade, Winwood. 1925. *The Martyrdom of Man*. London: Watts.

Reynolds, Terry S. 1983. *Stronger Than a Hundred Men: A History of the Vertical Water Wheel*. Baltimore: Johns Hopkins University Press.

Robertson, H. M. 1933. *Aspects of the Rise of Economic Individualism: A Criticism of Max Weber and His School*. Cambridge: Cambridge University Press.

Robinson, Charles Henry. 1923. *History of Christian Missions*. New York: Charles Scribner's Sons.

Rodinson, Maxime. 1978. *Islam and Capitalism*. Austin: University of Texas Press.

Root, Hilton L. 1994. *The Fountain of Privilege: Political Foundations of Markets in Old Regime France and England*. Berkeley: University of California Press.

Rörig, Fritz. 1967. *The Medieval Town*. Berkeley: University of California Press.

Rosen, Edward. 1971. *Three Copernican Treatises*. 3rd ed. New York: Octagon Books.

Rosenberg, Nathan, and L. E. Birdzell Jr. 1986. *How the West Grew Rich: The Economic Transformation of the Industrial World*. New York: Basic Books.

Rostovtzeff, M. 1957. *The Social and Economic History of the Roman Empire*. 2nd ed. 2 vols. Oxford: Clarendon Press.

———. 1941. *The Social and Economic History of the Hellenistic World*. 3 vols. Oxford: Clarendon Press.

Runciman, Steven. 1958. *The Sicilian Vespers: A History of the Mediterranean World in the Later Thirteenth Century*. Cambridge: Cambridge University Press.

———. 1933. *Byzantine Civilisation*. New York: Longmans, Green & Co.

Russell, Bertrand. 1922. *The Problem of China*. London: George Allen & Unwin.

Russell, Josiah Cox. 1972. *Medieval Regions and Their Cities*. Newton Abbot (UK): David & Charles

———. 1958. *Late Ancient and Medieval Population*. Transactions of the American Philosophical Society 48:3:3–152.

Saeed, Abdullah. 1996. *Islamic Banking and Interest*. Leiden: E. J. Brill.

Salzman, L. F. 1923. *English Industries in the Middle Ages*. Oxford: Oxford University Press.

Samuelsson, Kurt. [1961] 1993. *Religion and Economic Action: The Protestant Ethic, the Rise of Capitalism, and the Abuses of Scholarship*. Toronto: University of Toronto Press.

Sapori, Armando. 1970. *The Italian Merchant in the Middle Ages*. New York: W. W. Norton.

———. [1937] 1953. "The Culture of the Medieval Italian Merchant." In Frederic C. Lane and Jelle C. Riemersma, eds., *Enterprise and Secular Change: Readings in Economic History*, 53–65. Homewood, IL: Richard D. Irwin.

Sayer, Derek. 1991. *Capitalism and Modernity: An Excursus on Marx and Weber*. London: Routledge.

Schaff, Philip. [1855] 1961. *America: A Sketch of Its Political, Social, and Religious Character*. Cambridge, MA: Belknap Press.

Schlaifer, Robert. 1936. "Greek Theories of Slavery from Homer to Aristotle." *Harvard Studies in Classical Philology* 47:165–204.

Schluchter, Wolfgang. 1981. *The Rise of Western Rationalism*. Berkeley: University of California Press.

Shedd, Thomas Clark. 1981. "Railroads and Locomotives." *Encyclopaedia Britannica*. Chicago: University of Chicago Press.

Shepard, Max A. 1933. "William of Occam and the Higher Law, II." *The American Political Science Review* 27:24–38.

Sherkat, Darren E., and T. Jean Blocker. 1994. "The Political Development of Sixties Activists: Identifying the Influence of Class, Gender, and Socialization on Protest Participation." *Social Forces* 72:821–42.

Smelser, Neil. 1994. *Sociology*. Cambridge, MA: Blackwell-UNESCO.

Smith, Adam. [1776] 1981. *An Inquiry into the Nature and Causes of the Wealth of Nations*. 2 vols. Indianapolis: Liberty Fund.

Smith, Christian. 2002. "*Las Casas* as Theological Counteroffensive: An Interpretation of Gustavo Gutiérrez's *Las Casas: In Search of the Poor for Jesus Christ.*" *Journal for the Scientific Study of Religion* 41:69–73.

Smith, Preserved. [1923] 1962. *Erasmus: A Study of His Life, Ideals and Place in History.* New York: Ungar.

Sokoloff, Kenneth L. 2002. "The Evolution of Suffrage Institutions in the New World: A Preliminary Look." In Stephen Haber, ed., *Crony Capitalism in Economic Growth in Latin America,* 75–107. Stanford, CA: Hoover Institution Press.

Sombart, Werner. [1909] 1962. *The Jews and Modern Capitalism.* New York: Collier Books.

———. [1916] 1953. "Medieval and Modern Commercial Enterprise." In Frederic C. Lane and Jelle C. Riemersma, eds., *Enterprise and Secular Change: Readings in Economic History,* 25–40. Homewood, IL: Richard D. Irwin.

———. 1915. *Quintessence of Capitalism.* London: TF Unwin, Ltd.

———. 1902. *Der moderne Kapitalismus.* Leipzig: Duncker & Humblot.

Southern, R. W. 1970a. *Medieval Humanism and Other Studies.* New York: Harper Torchbooks.

———. 1970b. *Western Society and the Church in the Middle Ages.* London: Penguin Books.

———. 1953. *The Making of the Middle Ages.* New Haven: Yale University Press.

Spufford, Peter. 2002. *Power and Profit: The Merchant in Medieval Europe.* New York: Thames & Hudson.

Stark, Rodney. 2003a. *For the Glory of God: How Monotheism Led to Reformations, Science, Witch-Hunts, and the End of Slavery.* Princeton: Princeton University Press.

———. 2003b. "Upperclass Asceticism: Social Origins of Ascetic Movements and Medieval Saints." *Review of Religious Research* 45:5–19.

———. 2003c. *Sociology.* 9th ed. Belmont, CA: Wadsworth.

———. 2001. *One True God: Historical Consequences of Monotheism.* Princeton: Princeton University Press.

———. 1985. "From Church-Sect to Religious Economies." In Phillip E. Hammond, ed., *The Sacred in a Post-Secular Age,* 139–49. Berkeley: University of California Press.

———. 1983. "Religious Economies: A New Perspective." Paper delivered at a Conference on New Directions in Religious Research, University of Lethbridge.

———, and Roger Finke. 2000. *Acts of Faith: Explaining the Human Side of Religion.* Berkeley and Los Angeles: University of California Press.

Stoll, David. 1990. *Is Latin America Turning Protestant?* Berkeley and Los Angeles: University of California Press.

Strait, Paul. 1974. *Cologne in the Twelfth Century.* Gainesville: Florida State University Press.

Strieder, Jacob. 1931. *Jacob Fugger the Rich: Merchant and Banker of Augsburg, 1459–1525.* New York: Adelphi.

Supple, Barry. 1959. *Commercial Crisis and Change in England, 1600–1642.* Cambridge: Cambridge University Press.

Swetz, Frank J. 1987. *Capitalism and Arithmetic: The New Math of the 15th Century.* LaSalle, IL: Open Court.

Tawney, R. H. [1926] 1962. *Religion and the Rise of Capitalism: A Historical Study.* New York: Harcourt, Brace & World.

Taylor, George V. 1967. "Noncapitalist Wealth and the Origins of the French Revolution." *The American Historical Review* 72:469–96.

———. 1964. "Types of Capitalism in Eighteenth-Century France." *The English Historical Review* 79:478–97.

TeBrake, William H. 1993. *A Plague of Insurrection: Popular Politics and Peasant Revolt in Flanders, 1323–1328*. Philadelphia: University of Pennsylvania Press.

Thrupp, Sylvia A. 1965. "Chapter V. The Guilds." In M. M. Postan, E. E. Rich, and Edward Miller, eds., *The Cambridge Economic History of Europe,* vol. 3; *Economic Organization and Policies in the Middle Ages,* 230–80. Cambridge: Cambridge University Press.

Tobin, Stephen. 1996. *The Cistercians: Monks and Monasteries of Europe*. Woodstock, NY: Overlook Press.

Tocqueville, Alexis de. [1835–39] 1956. *Democracy in America.* 2 vols. New York: Vintage Books.

Trevor-Roper, H. R. [1969] 2001. *The Crisis of the Seventeenth Century: Religion, the Reformation, and Social Change*. Indianapolis: Liberty Fund.

Trinkaus, Charles. 1976. "Humanism, Religion, Society: Concepts and Motivations of Some Recent Studies." *Renaissance Quarterly* 29:676–713.

———. 1949. "The Problem of Free Will in the Renaissance and the Reformation." *Journal of the History of Ideas* 10:51–62.

Troeltsch, Ernst. 1991. *Religion in History*. Minneapolis: Fortress Press.

Turner, Bryan S. 1974. *Weber and Islam: A Critical Study*. London: Routledge & Kegan Paul.

Turner, Paul R. 1979. "Religious Conversion and Community Development." *Journal for the Scientific Study of Religion* 18:252–60.

Udovitch, Abraham L. 1970. *Partnership and Profit in Medieval Islam*. Princeton: Princeton University Press.

Ullman, Walter. 1966. *The Individual and Society in the Middle Ages*. Baltimore: Johns Hopkins University Press.

Usher, Abbott Payson. 1966. *A History of Mechanical Inventions*. Cambridge: Harvard University Press.

———. [1934] 1953. "The Origins of Banking: The Primitive Bank of Deposit." In Frederic C. Lane and Jelle C. Riemersma, eds., *Enterprise and Secular Change: Readings in Economic History,* 262–91. Homewood, IL: Richard D. Irwin.

Van Houtte, J. A. 1966. "The Rise and Decline of the Market and Bruges." *The Economic History Review* 19:29–47.

van Roey, Jan L. R. 1981. "Antwerp." *Encyclopaedia Britannica*. Chicago: University of Chicago Press.

van Werveke, H. 1963. "Chapter I: The Rise of the Towns." In *The Cambridge Economic History of Europe,* vol. 2, *Economic Organization and Policies in the Middle Ages,* 3–41. Cambridge: Cambridge University Press.

Verhulst, Adriaan. 1991. "The Decline of Slavery and the Economic Expansion of the Early Middle Ages." *Past and Present,* issue 133, 195–203.

Vogt, Joseph. 1974. *Ancient Slavery and the Ideal of Man*. Oxford: Oxford University Press.

Wagar, W. Warren. 1967. "Modern Views of the Origins of the Idea of Progress." *Journal of the History of Ideas* 28:55–70.

Walbank, Frank William. 1952. "Trade and Industry Under the Later Roman Empire in the West." In *The Cambridge Economic History of Europe,* vol. 2, *Trade and Industry in the Middle Ages,* 33–85. Cambridge: Cambridge University Press.

Waldron, Jeremy. 2002. *God, Locke, and Equality*. Cambridge: Cambridge University Press.

Waley, Daniel. 1988. *The Italian City-Republics*. 3rd ed. London: Longman.

Walker, P. C. Gordon. 1937. "Capitalism and the Reformation." *The Economic History Review* 8:1–19.

Waterbolk, H. T. 1968. "Food Production in Prehistoric Europe." *Science* 162: 1093–1102.

Watt, W. Montgomery. 1965. *Muhammad at Medina*. London: Oxford University Press.

——. 1961. *Muhammad: Prophet and Statesman*. London: Oxford University Press.

Weber, Max. [1924] 1976. *The Agrarian Sociology of Ancient Civilizations*. London: NLB.

——. [1919–20] 1966. *General Economic History*. New York: Collier.

——. [1916–17] 1958. *The Religion of India: The Sociology of Hinduism and Buddhism*. Glencoe, IL: Free Press.

——. [1904–5] 1958. *The Protestant Ethic and the Spirit of Capitalism*. New York: Charles Scribner's Sons.

——. [1917–19] 1952. *Ancient Judaism*. Glencoe, IL: Free Press.

——. [1921] 1951. *The Religion of China: Confucianism and Taoism*. Glencoe, IL: Free Press.

Webster, Richard A. 1981. "Colonialism." *Encyclopedia Britannica*. Chicago: University of Chicago Press.

Wedgewood, C. V. 1961. *The Thirty Years War*. New York: Doubleday.

Wegg, Jervis. 1924. *The Decline of Antwerp Under Philip of Spain*. London: Methuen.

Wesson, Robert G. 1978. *State Systems: International Pluralism, Politics, and Culture*. New York: Free Press.

White, Lynn, Jr. 1967. "The Historical Roots of Our Ecologic Crisis." *Science* 155:1203–7

——. 1962. *Medieval Technology and Social Change*. Oxford: Oxford University Press.

——. 1954. "The Spared Wolves." *Saturday Review of Literature* 37 (Nov. 13).

——. 1940. "Technology and Invention in the Middle Ages." *Speculum* 15:141–56.

Whitehead, Alfred North. [1925] 1967. *Science and the Modern World*. New York: Free Press.

Wickham, Chris. 1989. *Early Medieval Italy: Central Power and Local Society, 400–1000*. Ann Arbor: University of Michigan Press.

——. 1984. "The Other Transition: From the Ancient World to Feudalism." *Past and Present,* issue 103, 3–36.

Witt, Ronald G. 1971. "The Landlord and the Economic Revival of the Middle Ages in Northern Europe, 1000–1250." *The American Historical Review* 76:965–88.

Wittfogel, Karl A. [1957] 1981. *Oriental Despotism: A Comparative Study of Total Power*. New York: Vintage Books.

Yang, L. S. 1952. *Money and Credit in China*. Cambridge, MA: Harvard University Press.

Yearbook of American Churches, 1962. New York: National Council of Churches of Christ in the U.S.A.

Ziegler, Philip. 1971. *The Black Death*. New York: Harper Torchbooks.

Index

PHOTO © LYNNE ROBERTS

RODNEY STARK is University Professor of the Social Sciences, Baylor University. Before earning his Ph.D. at the University of California, Berkeley, he was a staff writer for several major publications. Among his many books are the influential studies *The Rise of Christianity* and *One True God: Historical Consequences of Monotheism.*

ABOUT THE TYPE

The text of this book was set in Legacy, a typeface
family designed by Ronald Arnholm and issued in
digital form by ITC in 1992. Both its serifed and
unserifed versions are based on an original type
created by the French punchcutter Nicholas Jenson
in the late fifteenth century. While Legacy tends to
differ from Jenson's original in its proportions,
it maintains much of the latter's characteristic
modulations in stroke.